A Companion to
Homer's *Odyssey*

James Morrison

GREENWOOD PRESS
Westport, Connecticut • London

Library of Congress Cataloging-in-Publication Data

Morrison, James V., 1956–
  A companion to Homer's *Odyssey* / James Morrison.
    p. cm.
  Includes bibliographical references (p.) and index.
  ISBN 0–313–31854–9 (alk. paper)
  1. Homer. Odyssey—Handbooks, manuals, etc. 2. Odysseus (Greek mythology) in
  literature—Handbooks, manuals, etc. 3. Epic poetry, Greek—History and
  criticism—Handbooks, manuals, etc. I. Title.

PA4167.M75 2003
883′.01—dc21   2002075311

British Library Cataloguing in Publication Data is available.

Library of Congress Catalog Card Number: 2002075311
ISBN: 0–313–31854–9

First published in 2003

Greenwood Press, 88 Post Road West, Westport, CT 06881
An imprint of Greenwood Publishing Group, Inc.
www.greenwood.com

Printed in the United States of America

The paper used in this book complies with the
Permanent Paper Standard issued by the National
Information Standards Organization (Z39.48–1984).

10 9 8 7 6 5 4 3 2 1

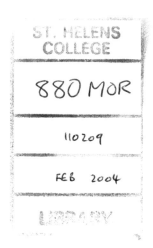
Copyright Acknowledgments

The author and publisher gratefully acknowledge permission for the use of the following
material:

Excerpt from *Omeros* by Derek Walcott. Copyright © 1990 by Derek Walcott.
Reprinted by permission of Farrar, Straus and Giroux, LLC.

Excerpt from *Inferno* by Dante. Trans. A. Mandelbaum (New York: Bantam, 1980).
Reprinted by permission of Bantam Books, a division of Random House, Inc.

Excerpt from "Ulysses" by Alfred Lord Tennyson in *The Poems of Tennyson,*
vol. I. Ed. C. Ricks (Berkeley: University of California Press, 1987). Reprinted by
permission of the University of California Press.

To my parents, who quoted Vergil—one of Homer's descendants—
on suitable occasions:
Forsan et haec olim meminisse iuvabit.
("Perhaps someday we will remember even these trials with pleasure.")

"Ulysses [the Latin name for Odysseus] is son to Laertes, but he is father to Telemachus, husband to Penelope, lover of Calypso, companion in arms of the Greek warriors around Troy, and King of Ithaca. He is subjected to many trials, but with wisdom and courage came through them all. . . . He was the first gentleman in Europe." *(James Joyce, commenting as to whether any writer has ever presented a complete all-round character in literature.)*
—Frank Budgen, *James Joyce and the Making of Ulysses*

CONTENTS

Contents

Maps appear on pp. x, 30, and 50.

INTRODUCTION

The goal for this "companion" is to help the first-time reader appreciate Homer's marvelous story from almost 3,000 years ago. I discuss the *Odyssey* itself in detail and introduce background material necessary to situate Homer's work in its historical context. No prior knowledge of Greek mythology or the ancient world is expected.

CONTENTS

Three introductory chapters provide the necessary information regarding mythological background and cultural context. "The *Odyssey* as Literature" offers a synopsis of the Trojan War story, analyzes the overall design of the epic (aided by charts), and explores the features of oral poetry found in Homer's work. "Homeric Values" examines heroism, moral issues facing travelers, and the relationship between humans and the gods. "Homer and History" briefly discusses Homer's own historical times and those earlier eras that are—to varying degrees—reflected in his poetry.

The main body of this companion discusses each of the twenty-four books (or chapters) of the *Odyssey* with respect to plot, characterization, and other literary features. I argue that Homer uses three themes (homecoming, hospitality, and identity) to unify his story of Odysseus' adventures after Troy and his return to Ithaca. Odysseus is presented as both heroic and profoundly human—a crea-

Map 1. *Odysseus' Journeys.* Locales in the Aegean and eastern Mediterranean were familiar to Homer's audience. Later Greeks identified locales in the west as the sites of Odysseus' amazing encounters. By permission of the Ancient World Mapping Center.

ture destined to suffer. Of particular interest are the techniques—speech, action, and implied or explicit comparison—by which Homer constructs each figure's identity. Basic literary devices such as divided plot, patterns of threes, simile, flashback, and foreshadowing are employed to shape the audience's experience of this sophisticated tale. This analysis should facilitate discussion and appreciation of Homer's epic in terms of plot, structure, and thematic connections. This very old work is still relevant to young people's lives—it's hard not to identify with qualities found in Telemachus or Nausicaa.

I should perhaps mention that throughout the introductory and central chapters, sidebars introduce features of ancient Greek society, Homer's influence on later literature, and etymological anecdotes for the reader who wishes to pursue such paths. Three maps depict the familiar and fabulous locales visited by Odysseus and his son around the Mediterranean Sea—and beyond! Illustrations supply views of the still-standing walls of Troy and portrayals of Odysseus' exploits by ancient Greek and later artists.

There are several appendices to aid the student and teacher. The first supplies a list of the main characters with a pronunciation guide. Second, a synopsis of Homer's influence on later art, literature, and the movies is presented. A third appendix explores various ways for the teacher to engage students, including a student judiciary, storytelling, and art projects. Finally, there are suggestions for further reading, viewing of movies, and on-line resources.

USING THIS COMPANION

As readers of this companion, I have in mind those who are encountering Homer for the first time. Homer's works can be enjoyed by first-time readers; they can also be read and reread with ever-increasing fascination and wonder. There were certainly Greeks who heard Homer for the first time, but I suspect that he may have had a following—I call them Homer-heads (à la the Deadheads and those who have "Gone Phishing")—who heard Homer sing his songs many times. These connoisseurs would be more sensitive to nuance and detail, and be better able to anticipate the significance of the "Agamemnon" story and the roles of surrogate wives and fathers.

Like Homer, I am also thinking in terms of multiple audiences. This companion may also be valuable for those who have read the *Odyssey* more than once, such as high-school and college teachers, who are not experts in antiquity or the Greek world, but find themselves confronting questions about mythology, history, and Homer's techniques of storytelling. This work seeks to offer at least a few answers to such readers. I have a prefatory note regarding which translation a teacher may choose to adopt. The appendices offer suggestions for different projects for high-school and college classes, including reading Homer aloud in order to approximate the experience of Homer's original performance.

Finally, I have in mind the general reader—someone not in a class in school—who is reading for enjoyment, for what Harold Bloom calls "the reader's sublime," that thrill you experience while sitting in a chair, imagining another world.

HOW TO BEGIN

Using this book as a companion should make the reading of a truly remarkable work a richer experience. Begin with Homer: read the first book of the *Odyssey* before looking at "Book One" in this companion; only after you have drunk from the fountain of Homer should you read these remarks that discuss the epic itself. The introductory chapters may be read at any time—as preparation to your initial voyage or when a particular issue becomes especially urgent. Appendices should be consulted as needed: for the modern pronunciation of character's names or connecting Homer to his literary—and cinematic—descendants.

I would like to think that this volume differs from other books about Homer's *Odyssey* in several ways. My intention has been to present in accessible, jargon-free prose an interdisciplinary approach to one of the greatest works ever composed. I have introduced topics ranging from mythology, history, and women's position in ancient Greek society to Greek ideas about beauty, the circumstances of an oral poet's performance, and why the recent Mars probe is called "2001 Mars Odyssey." Illustrations, maps, and sidebars serve to demonstrate the richness and breadth of Homer's world.

For those who read Homer and wish to understand more, this is the best advice: go to Greece. See the world Homer and his characters knew. Smell the food, breathe the air, swim in Poseidon's sea. This book runs at best a very distant second, but I hope to have re-created to some degree the world and culture of Homer, and explored the artistry of this wonderful work of literature.

THANKS

This book has resulted from my reading of Homer's *Odyssey* (both silent and aloud), many discussions with teachers, students, and friends, research over the past twenty years, and several trips to Greece (and one to Turkey). I would especially like to thank Cathy Callaway, Don Cameron, Joan Morrison, Robert Morrison, Leah Rissman, and Ruth Scodel. I very much appreciate Elizabeth Morrison's work illustrating so many scenes. This manuscript was written while I held the NEH Chair of Humanities at Centre College. I am most grateful to Lynn Malloy of Greenwood Press: this book began as an idea of hers.

A NOTE ON TRANSLATIONS

While Homer composed the *Odyssey* in Greek, this companion—not linked to any particular translation—is designed for those reading an English translation. Every translation, while losing something of the original, seeks to capture one or more features: meter, poetic language, repeated phrases (formulae), accessibility, etc. When I quote a passage, the translation will be my own very literal, line-by-line translation, which makes no attempt to imitate Homer's noble language or swift metrical patterns. The only virtues are that each line of Greek poetry is translated into one line of English translation and that the formulaic language is preserved.

Though no translation is perfect, there are several very good ones. The most popular translations of Homer's *Odyssey* today are by Lattimore, Fitzgerald, and Fagles. Lattimore's version offers a line-by-line translation with a six-beat line—which somewhat approximates Homer's hexameter. (Cook's translation—also quite good—does the same.) Fitzgerald is a great poet and his translation in blank verse (iambic meter) is very beautiful, but he fails to match each line of Homeric verse with one in English. Fagles' translation is quite colloquial—and perhaps strays the furthest from Homer's original. I should also mention the recent translation by Lombardo, which is also accessible and results from public performance, so that reading it aloud works extremely well.

There are other options. Merrill's translation brilliantly recaptures Homer's own meter: dactylic hexameter. Mandelbaum's version is very good, while Rieu offers a prose translation, which unfortunately leads many readers to think of the *Odyssey* as a novel.

There's a long history of translating Homer into the English language—Alexander Pope rendered the *Iliad* into rhymed couplets in 1720. Anyone interested in this topic should take a look at *Homer in English*, a volume that covers over 600 years of English adaptation and reflection of Homer's epics, including excerpts from Chapman's translation made famous in Keats' poem "On First Looking into Chapman's Homer" (also included in *Homer in English*). For the difficulties of translating Homer, you may wish to read Matthew Arnold's nineteenth-century essay "On Translating Homer." Arnold finds Homer's essential qualities to be rapidity, plainness and directness in expression, plainness and directness in ideas, and nobility. Good advice, but difficult to achieve in practice.

A wholly different avenue of approaching Homer in English is to *listen* to his works. Fagles' translation of the *Odyssey* now exists in audiocassette, read by the English actor Ian McKellen.

The reader may confront some difficulty in finding the same section discussed in this companion in his or her translation. My translations and references follow the Greek text of Homer with the result that those using translations by Fagles or Fitzgerald, for instance—which often employ more than one line of English to render each Greek line—will have to approximate which section I'm rendering. (Both of these texts indicate the numbering of Greek lines at the top of the page.) Regarding transliteration of names, see my note in the appendix "Who's Who?"

Editions referred to (all in paperback):
Homer. *The Odyssey*. Tr. Albert Cook. New York: W.W. Norton & Co., 1974.
Homer. *The Odyssey*. Tr. Robert Fagles. New York: Penguin, 1996.
Homer. *The Odyssey*. Tr. Robert Fagles. Audiocassette, narrated by Ian McKellen. New York: Penguin, 1996.
Homer. *The Odyssey*. Tr. Robert Fitzgerald. New York: Vintage, 1990.
The Odyssey of Homer. Tr. Richmond Lattimore. New York: Harper & Row, 1965.
Homer. *Odyssey*. Tr. Stanley Lombardo. Indianapolis: Hackett, 2000.
The Odyssey of Homer. Tr. Allen Mandelbaum. Berkeley: University of California Press, 1990.
Homer. *The Odyssey*. Tr. Rodney Merrill. Ann Arbor: University of Michigan Press, 2002.
Homer. *The Odyssey*. Tr. E.V. Rieu. London: Penguin, 1946.
Homer in English. Ed. George Steiner. London: Penguin, 1996.

THE *ODYSSEY* AS LITERATURE

A Classic is a book which with each rereading offers as much of a sense of discovery as the first reading.

—Italo Calvino, *Why Read the Classics?*

THE STORY OF THE *ODYSSEY*

The *Odyssey* tells the story of a man trying to get home to his wife and family. In many ways, he is extraordinary. While the goddess Athena advises him, the sea god Poseidon makes his life miserable; he confronts monsters and magic; he is offered immortality; he travels to the underworld and lives to tell about it; he is a hero and a king. He is especially distinguished by his ingenuity and a capacity to endure many troubles and not give up. And yet—for all these remarkable qualities—he is in many profound ways like us. He is a husband, father, and son; he weeps when he loses his comrades; and after twenty years away his fondest desire is to see his homeland again. Homer shows us these two sides of Odysseus: the hero of Troy and King of Ithaca, and a soldier who after a long absence does everything in his power to be reunited with his family.

Homer tells the story of Odysseus' journeys and sufferings in a remarkably sophisticated way, yet a five-year-old child finds many of the fantastic episodes wonderfully accessible: the blinding of the Cyclops or Circe turning men into pigs, for example. The whole of the *Odyssey*, however, displays interwoven stories of father and son, past, present, and future, mortals and immortals; it is a work of art unified by the themes of hospitality, homecoming, and identity; and for much of European literature it provides a model for what becomes known as the comic plot—not for its humor (though there are jokes, Odysseus himself does not smile until book 22), but because it ends happily. It shares with many familiar fairy tales some sense of "happily ever after."

One particular challenge is that modern readers differ from Homer's original audience—and I do mean a *listening* audience—in several significant ways. First, the *Odyssey* would have been sung to a live audience. The members of that audience *heard* the *Odyssey*, they didn't *read* it. A great deal of insight may be gained if someone reads aloud a book—or even twenty lines—of Homer's poem: this offers some understanding of what that original performance may have been like. As we shall see, reading words aloud off a written page—even memorizing and reading—sharply contrasts with the spontaneous, improvisational performance of a singer in Homer's day (see "Oral Poetry and Written Literature").

In addition, Homer was not the first poet to tell the story of Odysseus. Over a number of days—or more likely nights—the singer/composer of the *Odyssey* would present the story of Odysseus to an audience who already knew the story of the judgment of Paris, the siege of Troy, the deaths of Achilles and Agamemnon, the Trojan horse, and Odysseus' journeys. To put you somewhat in the same position, I include a brief background to what Homer's original audience may have known about the basic storyline (see "The Epic Tradition: Trojan War Stories").

In fact, Homer takes advantage of his audience's previous familiarity with the epic tradition to shape his story in a subtle way. Because of his audience's prior knowledge, Homer is under no obligation to retell the story of Odysseus' life or the sack of Troy or even to remind his audience who Zeus or Agamemnon or Penelope is. Instead, as Aristotle says in the *Poetics*, Homer constructs his story around a single event: the return of Odysseus, long after Troy is sacked. Yet Homer is ambitious. He adds a broader temporal dimension to his story by the use of flashback and prophecy. Indeed, in four books of the epic (out of twenty-four books) Odysseus himself becomes the storyteller and recounts many of his most memorable adventures. Elsewhere we learn of Odysseus' childhood and his death—but this is always subordinate to the main event: getting Odysseus home.

What this boils down to is that almost everyone enjoys the *Odyssey* of Homer. There's something for everyone: romance, magic, treachery, blood and guts, the majesty (and sometimes less than admirable behavior) of the Olympian gods, and the noble (and not so noble) action of heroes. The goal in this "Companion" is to make clear the marvelous design and artful complexity found in the *Odyssey*.

THE EPIC TRADITION: TROJAN WAR STORIES

As I have said, Homer was not the first to sing about Achilles, Odysseus, the Olympian gods, and the Trojan War. He was working in an oral poetic tradition hundreds of years old. The audience must have been familiar with that tradition, too. When Homer sang the *Odyssey*, members of the audience would have been previously acquainted with many of the characters and episodes associated with what will be referred to here as "the epic tradition." Everyone—poet and audience—would have taken it for granted that Zeus is Poseidon's brother and Athena's father, that Agamemnon and Menelaus are brothers, and that Troy was defeated not by military attack but by the strategem of the wooden horse.

The goal of this section is to make your experience of reading Homer's *Odyssey* more like the experience of Homer's original audience. In order to do that, several gaps in the background to Odysseus' story must be fleshed out, episodes that Homer either ignores or only briefly alludes to. It's a great story and well worth knowing.

The larger tradition may be broken down into eight episodes.

• Wedding of Peleus and Thetis.
• Judgment of Paris.
• Abduction of Helen.
• Gathering of the Greeks at the Bay of Aulis.
• Ten-Year Siege of Troy.
• Deaths of Hector and Achilles.
• The Wooden Horse and the Sack of Troy.
• Homecoming of the Greeks.

Wedding of Peleus and Thetis

A good place to begin is during that time long ago when mortals and immortals frequently encountered one another. In fact, it was possible for people to marry divinities—in this case, a mortal man, Peleus, marries a sea goddess, Thetis. The wedding was to be a grand affair. All the gods and goddesses would be there—only one goddess failed to receive an invitation, the goddess Eris (her name means "strife" or "rivalry"). The last thing anyone wanted was for her to appear and stir up trouble, as the goddess of strife is likely to do.

But Eris learned of the wedding and decided to go anyway. She crashed the party and got her revenge. When Eris arrived, she rolled a glittering golden apple among the gathered guests. Upon it was inscribed: "To the fairest." All the goddesses started quarreling, each claiming that the apple must be hers for she was the most beautiful of all the goddesses. Pandemonium reigned. Finally, Zeus put a halt to the arguing and insisted that the apple could only properly belong to one of three goddesses: either his wife, Hera, or his daughter, Athena, or his other daughter, Aphrodite.

But that was as far as Zeus was willing to go. The last thing he wanted was to have to decide between these three deities—a loser's game if ever there was one. So he quickly came up with a plan. "I know," Zeus announced, "we'll let someone else decide!" This leads us to our next installment, but it should be mentioned that the wedding of Peleus and Thetis did go on as planned, and a child—half-god and half-mortal (that is, a hero)—was born: Achilles, the central character of the *Iliad*, who also makes two cameo appearances in the *Odyssey* (alas, in the underworld).

Judgment of Paris

Zeus chooses a mortal man to decide which of the three goddesses was the most beautiful—a divine beauty contest nowhere near Atlantic City! The man he chose was Paris, who surprisingly was both a prince of Troy and a shepherd, herding his flocks on the slopes of Mount Ida near Troy (in Asia Minor, modern-day Turkey). So the god Hermes (a messenger and escort god) brought the three goddesses to parade in front of Paris on a lonely hillside. Paris was to decide which was the most beautiful, but first Hermes asked whether the goddesses should be judged with their clothes on or off, and—after profound reflection—Paris replied that he could probably do a better job if they took their clothes off. Artists have been grateful ever since.

It is sad to say that the goddesses did not compete fairly—each of them offered a bribe to Paris. Hera, the wife of Zeus, offered great political power to Paris if he chose her. Athena, Zeus' daughter, offered great glory in battle. And Aphrodite, the goddess of love and beauty, offered him the most beautiful woman on earth—but only if she were to win the contest.

The Competitive Greeks

Everybody likes to win, but for the Greeks it was a way of life—not only for the goddesses lining up before Paris. The competitive athletic games, the Olympics, were invented by the Greeks, perhaps during Homer's own lifetime. We may not find stripping naked and competing for honor all that unusual—although we prefer to wear gym shorts, T-shirts, and Nikes—but for much of human history such physical toil was reserved for slaves and serfs. Not so for the Greeks: they strove for victory and glory on the athletic field and beyond. Writers of tragedy and comedy, poets, and public speakers, all competed for prizes to determine who was the best. It has even been argued that the great length of Homer's epics is a result of this competitive spirit: longer is better, so Homer outdid his peers with the *Iliad* and the *Odyssey*. Greek science and philosophy—and the idea of responding to criticism—may well have resulted from practices found in Greek deliberative assemblies and courtrooms, where each speaker sought to defeat his rival by making the most persuasive argument.

Hera and Athena didn't have a chance. Paris chose Aphrodite as the most beautiful goddess (the apple was hers), but the "judgment" of Paris led to two problems. First of all, Paris became hated by the poor losers, Hera and Athene—as was all Troy, since he was a Trojan. These two goddesses would continually champion the cause of the Greeks in the upcoming war and do everything in their power to bring suffering to the Trojans. The second problem was that the most beautiful woman on earth was already married.

Abduction of Helen

Paris traveled from Troy to Sparta in southern Greece (the Peloponnesus). He was welcomed into the home of the Spartan king, Menelaus, and there he met Menelaus' wife, Helen, the fairest woman alive (she's also a daughter of Zeus, by the way). Menelaus did what any good host does: inviting Paris into his home, he offered him food and drink and a place to sleep. Each day Menelaus would take his guest hunting with him, but one time Paris declined. While the unwitting husband was away, Paris ran off with his host's wife, Helen.

There are two versions of what happened between Paris and Helen—both were current in antiquity. In the first, Paris abducted Helen, forcing her to come with him to Troy. In this scenario, Helen was an unwilling victim. But the second version holds that Helen fell under the sway of Aphrodite, fell in love with Paris, and abandoned home and family of her own accord to sail away with this tall, dark, handsome stranger. So we call this episode "The Abduction of Helen" but many poets prefer the idea of "The Seduction of Helen." Such is the power of Aphrodite.

Gathering of the Greeks at the Bay of Aulis

Helen's journey with Paris is another action with serious consequences. In addition to Paris violating the code of hospitality—you are not supposed to run off with your host's silverware or his wife—Menelaus was a powerful king with an even more powerful brother, Agamemnon, king of Mycenae (also in the Peloponnesus). The upshot was that Agamemnon gathered all the Greeks on the west side of the Aegean Sea at the Bay of Aulis. The fleet was so large that later it was said that Helen's was "the face that launched a thousand ships."

The Amazing Greek Language: A Greek by Any Other Name

Notice that Homer calls the Greeks either Argives, Achaeans, or Danaans. In Homer's poetic tradition, these terms were used interchangeably to mean "the Greeks," depending on metrical considerations (see "Oral Poetry and Written Literature"). Your translator may simply call them "Greeks." In fact, the ancient and modern Greek word for "Greek" is "Hellene"; Greece is called "Hellas." "Greek" originally referred to a tribe in Western Greece, a term the Italians then applied to all Greeks—it's often foreigners who name a people. "Welsh" is what the invading Anglo-Saxons called those "foreigners"—really native Britons—living in what we now call England.

But this sea voyage came at great cost, a tragic episode that Homer never mentions. It is said that the winds wouldn't blow and the fleet couldn't sail because Artemis was angry at Agamemnon for killing her sacred deer. Agamemnon was forced to sacrifice his eldest daughter, Iphigenia, so that the ships could make their way to Troy and avenge the dishonor Paris had brought upon all Greece. Homer chooses to suppress this "detail" and never mentions the sacrifice of Agamemnon's daughter—or how Clytemnestra, his wife, might have felt about it. In the *Odyssey*, Clytemnestra is simply an unfaithful wife.

Ten-Year Siege of Troy

This brings us finally to Troy. The Greek fleet landed at Troy and put the city under siege. Many sons of the King and Queen of Troy, Priam and Hecuba, died defending their homeland, but the mighty fortress held out for more than nine years.

Deaths of Hector and Achilles

In the tenth year of the war, the best warriors—Hector on the Trojan side and Achilles for the Greeks—were killed in battle. Homer's *Iliad*, set in that final year of the war, culminates with the death and burial of Hector—and the prophesied death of Achilles. With Hector's death, however, the fate of Troy is sealed. Yet the city is taken not by force, but by stealth.

The Wooden Horse and the Sack of Troy

After ten years of fighting—and the death of Achilles—the Greeks devise a trick to make their way into Troy. They pretend to have given up by sailing out of sight and leaving behind a towering wooden statue of a horse. The Trojans foolishly bring it into their city—believing it will protect them—but in fact, the structure is filled with armed Greek men who emerge from the statue at night, kill the guards, and open the gates of Troy to the entire Greek army, now returned to Troy.

The city is looted and burned. King Priam is killed; many of the Trojan women become concubines or slaves for the Greek warriors. After ten long years the Greeks have avenged Paris' "theft" of Helen, and the Greeks now plan their return home.

Literature after Homer

In Appendix 2, you will find a more complete list of works in later European literature that concern Odysseus and the Trojan War, but I must mention a few favorites. Aeschylus produced a trilogy (three plays), entitled *The Oresteia*, which explores the homecoming of Agamemnon with the sacrifice of Iphigenia as a central feature. It is instructive to compare the three plays, *Agamemnon, Libation Bearers,* and *The Eumenides,* with how Homer recounts the "Agamemnon" story in the *Odyssey*. Aeschylus emphasizes Clytemnestra's motivation for Agamemnon's murder—the sacrifice of their daughter. For the

---

sack of Troy, two especially notable treatments are Euripides' tragedy *The Trojan Women*, which takes place just after the city is sacked, and the second book of Vergil's *Aeneid*, which vividly describes the actual destruction of the city, interestingly told in retrospect by Aeneas, a Trojan survivor at the court of the Carthaginian queen, Dido.

Homecoming of the Greeks

The Greeks who survived the war looked homeward, but we must remember that many lay buried in Troy, including Achilles, Antilochus (one of Nestor's sons, referred to in *Odyssey* book 3), and Ajax—who was killed not in battle but by suicide. It turns out that when Achilles died, there was another contest—this time to determine which warrior would inherit Achilles' arms (his battle gear). The finalists were Odysseus and Ajax; Odysseus won (again cheating and bribery are alleged); and out of shame or madness Ajax slew himself. (For more, read Sophocles' tragedy *Ajax*.) This information will help explain Ajax's cameo appearance in *Odyssey* book 11.

Many Greeks, however, did reach home. Nestor returned to Pylos. After seven long years, Menelaus and Helen made it to Sparta. Even Agamemnon returned to his unfaithful wife, Clytemnestra, and her lover. All of these events from the wedding of Achilles' parents down to the homecoming of other Greek heroes provide the backdrop for Homer's story of the adventures of Odysseus (on Greek mythology in general, see Morford and Lenardon in "Further Reading" and the Internet Classics Archive in "Homer On-Line").

THE STRUCTURE OF THE *ODYSSEY*

Homer's epic design is complex. I will suggest two ways to think about how the poet organizes events, shifts the focus between Telemachus and Odysseus, and manipulates the difference between narrative time (the sequence of story-telling) and chronological time (the actual sequence of events).

Two Halves: Books 1–12 and 13–24

The epic now consists of 24 books, although the book division itself dates long after Homer's lifetime. Nevertheless, many of the book divisions and larger groups of books fit patterns of symmetry and balance. The simplest way to divide up the epic is into two halves: books 1–12 tell of Odysseus' journeys; books 13–24 recount his adventures once he arrives back in Ithaca. There is an alternation between travel and stability, between settings abroad and at home. This is not a bad place to begin, but among other weaknesses it fails to account for Telemachus, Odysseus' son, as a major figure.

One feature in this "Two-Halves Model" that leaps out at the reader is that the second half of the epic introduces a series of recognition scenes. When writing his work of literary criticism the *Poetics*, Aristotle argues that scenes of recognition and reversal are the poet's chief means of "engaging" his audience (he uses a fancier word—*psychagogeo*—which means "leads—or enchants—the soul"). The poet uses such scenes to produce great emotional impact upon the audience. Reversal scenes are those in which a character goes from good to bad fortune or vice versa. An example of reversal is Oedipus, who at the beginning of Sophocles' play *Oedipus the King* is an honored king with a loving wife and much power and wealth. Yet his fortune "reverses" or drastically shifts, so that by the end of the play, he is powerless, blind, stripped of his kingdom, and driven into exile. Such events stir the audience's emotions.

Recognition scenes occur when a character learns something he or she didn't know before. (Sophocles' Oedipus experiences both reversal of fortune and recognition—Aristotle praises this highly—when he learns that the man he has killed is his father and the woman he has married is his own mother.) In the *Odyssey* one of the major themes is identity. This theme not only concerns who the characters are, but also refers to their skill in determining when to reveal their identity and when to conceal it. Much of the second half of the *Odyssey* consists of Odysseus slowly revealing his identity to various characters. Telemachus learns his father has returned in book 16, but it's not until book 22 that the suitors—his rivals in love and power—discover that the beggar is Odysseus; Penelope finds out only in book 23 that her husband is finally home. In the following chart, I have indicated the sequence of recognition scenes in the second half of the *Odyssey*, indicating Odysseus' relationship with the character to whom he is revealed.

Recognition Scenes in Books 13–24

Book	Who Recognizes Odysseus	Odysseus' Relationship
13	Athena	dutiful mortal
16	Telemachus	father
17	Argos, the dog	master
19	Eurycleia, a servant	master
21	Eumaeus, Philoetius	master
22	Suitors	rival
23	Penelope	husband
24	Laertes	son

The Divided Plot: The "Telemachy" and the "Odyssey"

A second way of thinking about the *Odyssey*'s plot is to follow the main characters. Telemachus is the central figure in books 1–4, Odysseus in books 5–8. That is, Homer first tells a "Telemachy"—a story about Telemachus—then he tells an "Odyssey," or story about Odysseus. Books 9–12 also concern Odysseus, but consist of flashbacks in which Odysseus becomes the storyteller and recounts his own adventures after the sack of Troy until he reaches Calypso's island.

Then books 13–14 return to "real" time—at least, it's not exclusively flash-backs—again with Odysseus as protagonist arriving in Ithaca. Book 15 picks up with Telemachus where book 4 left off, at the palace of Menelaus in Sparta. For the first fifteen books then, Homer has pursued a divided plot—focusing on one major character at a time, and shifting back and forth. Finally, in book 16 father and son are reunited, as the parallel plots are fused leading to the end of the epic. In books 16–24 Odysseus and Telemachus plot against and defeat the suitors. This idea is represented graphically as follows:

Divided Plot: "Telemachy" and "Odyssey"

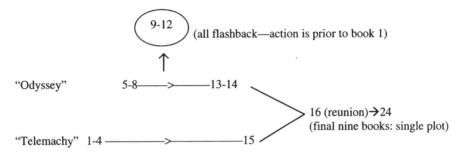

The neat patterning of four books, four books, four books in the first half is partly illusory, since the book divisions are not Homer's own. In fact, whoever made the book divisions appears to have followed the sort of divided plot design described here. Still Homer doesn't shy away from a sophisticated narrative. Instead he offers his solution for how to tell two stories at once: begin with one, leave it in suspense and start the other, and alternate until the two stories become one. Only then can the entire story be brought to some sort of satisfactory closure.

Structure of Odysseus' Flashback Adventures (Books 9–12)

There are two other patterns used to organize the narrative. The first is the recurrence of three episodes in Odysseus' set of tales told at the court of the Phaeacians in books 9–12. Book 9, 10, and 12 each consists of basically three stories. Homer tells two short ones and then elaborates on the third. This is both a way for the poet to keep a simple pattern in mind and allows the audience to tell which are the more important episodes: the third is longer and therefore has a greater claim on our attention.

Thus the pattern for three of the four books is represented in the following chart:

Odysseus' Flashback Adventures in Books 9–12

9	*10*	*11*	*12*
Cicones	Aeolus	"underworld"	Sirens
Lotus-Eaters	Laestrygonians		Scylla and Charybdis
Cyclops	Circe		Cattle of the Sun

Note that the third episodes are the richest and most significant: Cyclops, Circe, and Odysseus' men eating the cattle of the Sun.

And what about Odysseus' tales of the "underworld" in book 11? Here, too, without forcing things too much, we find a similar pattern of threes. Odysseus meets three characters after sacrificing: Elpenor, Teiresias, and his mother Anticleia. When Alcinous insists that the story not end, Odysseus tells of three Trojan heroes: Agamemnon, Achilles, and the silent Ajax. Finally, Odysseus views three notorious criminals who suffer eternal punishment: Tityus, Tantalus, and Sisyphus.

Underworld Tales (book 11)

After the sacrifice:	Elpenor/Teiresias/Anticleia
Trojan War heroes:	Agamemnon/Achilles/Ajax
Punishments:	Tityus/Tantalus/Sisyphus

I have sketched out these schemes in order to highlight certain aspects of the narrative; there are, of course, some important plot developments that these schemes fail to incorporate. In book 12 Odysseus returns to the straits between Scylla and Charybdis after his ship is destroyed (this follows the episode on Helius' island); indeed, he returns to Circe's island after the "underworld" journey at the beginning of book 12. And Odysseus meets other figures in the "underworld," including the so-called "catalog of women" and a phantom of Heracles. Not every figure or episode is accounted for by the patterns suggested here. Still, from the oral poet's perspective, these basic patterns are a deliberate aid to the composition process; for the audience, these structures keep the long poem from degenerating into one darn story after another, by offering texture and rhythm. Balance and symmetry would have been understood by even an illiterate, listening audience. In fact, such an audience may have been quite skilled in appreciating the artistry of such long narratives.

ORAL POETRY AND WRITTEN LITERATURE

Homer's *Iliad* and *Odyssey* mark the beginning of Greek literature. But Homer didn't see it that way. He didn't ask, "How shall I begin Western civilization?" In fact, Homer looked *back* to an oral tradition that extended over many previous generations—perhaps as much as 500 years!

Homer's relationship with that tradition goes under the general heading of "The Homeric Question." It's not just one question but several, concerning composition, date, authorship, the epic tradition, and the unity of these epics. How were the epics composed—orally or in written form? If Homer was illiterate and performed these songs live before a listening audience, how did these two epics reach us in written form? And who was Homer? How did he differ from the singers before him? What did he owe to them? Did Homer compose all of the *Iliad* or just part of it (and all or just part of the *Odyssey*)? Did the same singer who composed the *Iliad* compose the *Odyssey* or could these works be by

Illustration 1. *Harp-Player from Keros.* Miniature marble statue of a seated musician playing a harp. Dates from 2800–2300 B.C.E. By permission of the Ministry of Culture of Greece (National Archaeological Museum of Greece, Athens, Greece).

different singers? (We'll worry about dates in the chapter on history.) And then there's the clincher: Is it possible for oral poetry to be of as high quality as written literature? These are the puzzles contained in the Homeric Question.

While these issues will never be definitively resolved, I would like to offer evidence for what I consider the most probable answers. Homer was a singer who performed his epic songs live and aloud to a listening audience; he probably never read or wrote (and could, as legend tells us, have been blind); he owed a great deal to previous generations of singers but showed his individual brilliance; and by looking at Homer's historical context, we can come up with a plausible reconstruction of how—and why—the epics were first recorded in written form. For Homer and his audience, the *Iliad* and the *Odyssey* were performances to be heard, not books to be read. While the rest of this companion will treat the *Odyssey* as a work of literature, I would now like to explore its oral dimension.

Let's focus on the *Odyssey*. It's a long work, its design is intricate, the characters are richly developed, and there are sophisticated patterns—for the entire work and within sections. Its quality has seldom been matched by later works. The evidence that this was originally an oral composition comes from three areas: scenes within the *Odyssey*, analysis of Homer's style, and comparative studies of twentieth-century oral poets. Let's examine these in turn.

In the poem, Homer suggests a model for his own performance of the *Odyssey* with two singers who perform before audiences. In the first book, Phemius performs for the suitors at Odysseus' house; later at the court of the Phaeacians, the blind singer Demodocus sings three songs for Alcinous and his guests. We might also mention the fact that Odysseus is often telling stories (and being compared to a singer)—one-sixth of the entire *Odyssey* consists of him telling his adventures after leaving Troy. In each case, we note that the performer does not work from a written text—in fact, there are virtually no references to writing in the epics.

Both Phemius and Demodocus accompany their singing with a stringed instrument, a type of four-stringed lyre (in Greek, it's called a *phorminx*—see illustration). Of course, all that survives for us are words on the page, but these performances must have included melody and gesture, and perhaps the mimicking of voices. Imagine reading only the words of Bob Dylan in contrast to hearing him perform.

In the *Odyssey* singers perform in social settings: at a party, festival, or competitive games. The songs were to some extent extemporaneous. A member of the audience may request a song on a particular topic: for example, Demodocus' third song comes in response to Odysseus' desire to hear a Trojan horse song. Also there's a fascinating performer-audience interaction. Several times an audience member cuts off a singer in midflow: Penelope tells Phemius to stop singing the sad song about the Greeks' painful return from Troy; twice Alcinous interrupts Demodocus when Odysseus weeps in response to Trojan War songs.

Singers may be praised and showered with gifts. Odysseus rewards Demodocus for his artistry with a choice cut of the roast. In book 11 when Odysseus says it's late and time for bed (right in the middle of his own "underworld" story), Alcinous and Arete lavishly praise his storytelling skills and promise many valuable goods as a kind of payment for his songs. From internal evidence then, singing and listening to songs is part of Homeric society with a recognized set of rules for request, singing, and response. This picture may be idealized, yet other types of evidence support the idea that Homer was a singer much like Phemius or Demodocus.

The second type of evidence that Homer's poems were sung is stylistic, the most technical aspect of our exploration and difficult to appreciate in translation. An obvious feature in Homer's poetry is repetition. This is most evident when mortals, immortals, or places are introduced. Odysseus is frequently called "crafty Odysseus"—not two or three times, but dozens of times. Zeus is "cloud-gatherer Zeus," Athena is "gray-eyed Athena," Ithaca is "conspicuous Ithaca," and Troy is "steep Ilium." Each of these phrases—a noun plus a descriptive adjective (or *epithet*)—is called a *formula* and offers the singer a half-line of verse. In fact, formulae (noun-epithet phrases) may not correspond to context: heaven may be referred to as "starry heaven" even in the middle of the day when no stars are visible; "swifted-footed Achilles" may be sitting down. One of the singer's objectives is to compose poetry rapidly before an audience, so whenever he needs to refer to Odysseus, he'll use a formula, such as "crafty Odysseus" and he's already composed half the line.

The effect of this method of composition is that much of the *Odyssey* consists of repetition—and not only lines and half-lines. Whole scenes, such as arming, bathing, or sacrifice scenes, are recounted in the same—or much the same—way each time they are introduced. In arming scenes, for example, the hero always puts on his greaves (shin guards) first, then his breastplate, sword, shield, and helmet, before finally picking up a spear. For oral singers composing before a live audience—without the aid of writing—there is no stigma against repetition.

Ancient and Modern Poetry

The unit of Homeric poetry is a line of verse, containing between twelve and seventeen syllables. Each line is metrical, but does not rhyme. The meter—called dactylic hexameter—is *quantitative*, which means that it is made up of long and short syllables. In contrast, much of English poetry follows a *stress* accent (rather than long and short syllables) and rhymes at the ends of lines. A professor at Berkeley has now written a translation of Homer that captures this metrical pattern (using stress accents—see Merrill in "Further Reading"). Read the following aloud:

Tell' me, Muse', of the man' versatile' and resource'ful, who wan'dered
Man'y a sea'-mile, af'ter he ran'sacked Troy's' holy cit'y.
Man'y the men' whose towns' he observed,' whose minds' he discov'ered,
Man'y the pains' in his heart' he suf'fered travers'ing the sea'way,
Fight'ing for his' own life' and a way' back home' for his com'rades.

The English version of this meter consists of a set of six "feet" or units; within each unit there is a stressed (or accented) syllable followed by two (sometimes one) unstressed (or unaccented) syllables. In musical notation, the pattern for one line of verse would look like this:

Among other things, the meter helps the singer and the audience to remember the words in a line of verse—just as it is easier to remember words to a song when the tune is in your head. People in antiquity are always quoting Homer.

Before going further, we must pay homage to two men who have analyzed Homeric verse in such terms: Milman Parry and Albert Lord. In the 1920s Parry argued that Homeric style was traditional. By traditional, he meant that an extraordinary amount of the epics derived from an oral tradition that was created not by a single poet, but by many generations of singers. Phrases such as "cloud-gatherer Zeus" and "swift-footed Achilles" were built up over time, forming a repertoire each new poet drew upon as he sang. Homer was not the first to sing of "swift-footed Achilles." Rather he inherited that phrase from the oral tradition. Such formulae were aids to composing long epic songs. That is, Homer inherited the way in which he told the story—the *style* is not unique to any one poet. Homer's verse contains many formulae that are repeated throughout the epic and had been for centuries. Repetition is not bad; originality in diction (word choice and expression) is not always the singer's goal.

We might add that, in addition to lines, half-lines, and typical scenes, the subject and the characters were not original either. Other singers sang of the Trojan War and the Greeks' return, of Achilles and Odysseus, of Zeus and Hera and Athena. None of this was original—in our sense—with Homer. He inherited these stories and characters.

Before looking at what may be distinctive in Homer, we turn to the third type of evidence. In addition to internal and stylistic material, there is the comparative evidence provided by oral singers from the twentieth century. Soon after Parry published his papers arguing that Homeric style was traditional, he and his student (and successor) Albert Lord conducted field studies on the Balkan peninsula in Europe. Beginning in the 1930s, Parry and Lord interviewed and recorded South Slavic (or Serbo-Croatian) oral singers who performed songs live before a listening audience. Like Phemius and Demodocus, these South Slavic singers did not work from a written text—many were illiterate. The subject of the South Slavic songs—and the style in which they were sung—was also inherited, a legacy of generations of singers who preceded them. In the past seventy years, studies of oral singers from many other parts of the globe—Egypt, India, Turkey, Mongolia, etc.—have supplemented the insights Parry and Lord obtained from their studies.

The greatest insight was the idea of "composition-in-performance." Composition-in-performance means that when a singer appears before a live audience, the performance of his songs is improvisational. Each performance would be a bit different. In fact, the concept of a "verbatim" song—sung word for word—has no meaning to these illiterate singers. The best comparison here is to jazz, which is also improvised at each performance, yet also consists of preexisting units (not formulae, but scales, melodies, and riffs). In jazz, improvisation does not mean anyone can "make it up" as he goes along; great skill is involved in preparing for each performance, yet each performance is unique.

Like jazz performers, oral singers would adapt songs to the occasion and to the behavior and response of the audience. If someone in the audience fell asleep, the singer might introduce a character in his song who falls asleep and is ridiculed by his friends and relatives. If a member of the audience was rude and not paying attention, the singer might bring his song to an abrupt end—or could introduce an episode about a rude character in order to shame the disruptive listener into silence. Alternatively, if the audience was particularly engaged—entranced by the magic of the song—a singer could expand and elaborate by making the battle scenes longer or introducing passionate speeches and extended similes to heighten the spell of his storytelling.

From the *Odyssey* itself then, we have a model for an oral performer; from Homer's style we can deduce an oral tradition; from contemporary singers' performances, we find situations analogous to Homer's. Yet these arguments have worried many readers of Homer—for several reasons. If the general story, characters, and even the words, phrases, and episodes (once sung and now on the page) were part of a tradition, then what did Homer contribute? How was he original? In what ways can we legitimately say Homer composed the *Iliad* and the *Odyssey*? Also, while almost everyone acknowledges that Homer owes a debt to preceding generations of singers, many still resist the idea that marvelous works, such as the *Iliad* and the *Odyssey*, could have been composed by an "illiterate" singer, without the technology of writing. For works as great as these, so the argument goes, writing must have been necessary.

While truly in the realm of speculation, we must confront these problems head-on. In many ways, the *Iliad* and the *Odyssey* are like other works of literature (they may be read and analyzed in terms of theme, plot, character, and so on), yet in an important sense, we need a different kind of aesthetic (or principle to judge art) in order to understand oral literature—or at least to understand some of its features.

Here we must distinguish between aspects of the *Odyssey* that are peculiar to oral poetry and aspects that all stories—written or not—hold in common. At one level, that of the individual line, the noun-epithet pair, and the typical scene, we must contemplate a different set of aesthetic values. These oral songs must not be judged by the same standards as written literature, such as novels, where the skill of the writer (and here we *do* mean a writer who writes for a reading public) consists in part in the invention of episode and language. For oral poets, repetition is not necessarily a bad thing; a poet should not be criticized for repeated phrases and scenes that he may have inherited from earlier singers; he didn't strive to express something with different words every time he sang; originality in this sense is not the highest goal. Homer wasn't seeking to create brand-new characters nor was his purpose to invent a completely new story.

The more important goal is that the singer produce living verse before a live audience. In fact, we might say that the singer is forced by the performative situation to use a particular method of composition, namely using inherited phrases and typical scenes. If Odysseus is about to speak, Homer prefaces that speech with the words "And so spoke godlike Odysseus." Homer uses this expression every time, without fear that his audience would become bored or desire a variation on this basic way of introducing a speech. In fact, the traditional style—the storehouse of lines, half-lines, and typical scenes—enables the singer to improvise and compose as he goes along. If the singer had to invent a new way of saying things every time he opened his mouth, he wouldn't be able to produce line after line on the spot before an audience.

But in other respects, Homeric epic is like other written literature. Character development and plot structure are two examples of similarities oral song shares with written literature. In fact, Homer in many ways set the standard that later written literature has tried to match. Western literature has looked back to Homer for inspiration, so it is not surprising to find similarities.

Consider Homer's characters. Some figure named Odysseus existed long before Homer—formulae such as "crafty Odysseus and "godlike Odysseus" must have been used for generations. Yet Homer's construction of Odysseus' character as we have it in the *Odyssey*—his skills, speeches, relationships, and so on—is admired for many of the reasons we admire the characters of Charles Dickens. There is a difference between the existence of characters (who appeared in earlier songs) and how those characters are represented in a particular singer's performance. (The depiction of the characters of Odysseus, Penelope, and Telemachus will be explored at length in the discussion of books 1–24.)

Homeric Characterization

Homer's presentation of character will be examined at length in the discussion of books 1–24, yet it may be valuable at this point to anticipate his method. The poet uses a variety of techniques to present his characters, including: (1) the character's words; (2) the character's actions; (3) observations by other characters; (4) the poet's own remarks and explicit comparisons (including similes); and (5) suggested or implied comparisons.

Let me offer a few examples of each. First, we will examine using a figure's own words to indicate character. Consider the youths Telemachus and Nausicaa. When in book 1 Telemachus tells Penelope that she should go upstairs, because he's the man of the house, we recognize a young man who is attempting to assert his independence from his parents. In book 6, Nausicaa tells her companions that she could imagine someone like Odysseus as her husband, yet she is more subtle when speaking directly to Odysseus. In his presence, she imagines that one of the dockworkers in town might see them together and say he is her fiancé. This reveals an adolescent, concerned about her future and her reputation, yet fascinated by this eloquent stranger. For all her youth, Nausicaa reveals considerable tact in masking her inner feelings. Homer is an expert at using what a character says to reveal the soul within.

Regarding action, hospitality is central: one's actions as a guest or host determine a great deal. In book 1, Telemachus invites Athena (in disguise) into his house and offers her food and drink. Nausicaa is the only female at the beach who does not run from Odysseus; in fact, she insists upon helping this stranger in distress. She offers him clothes, food, and drink, and leads him into town. These actions establish Telemachus and Nausicaa as intelligent hosts who know the rules of hospitality.

Of course, Homer often employs a combination of words and deeds to reveal character. The Cyclops Polyphemus reveals his character both by words—the gods, he says, will receive no respect from him—and by action: he eats his guests. The suitors prove to be unwelcome guests who virtually occupy Odysseus' home—they never leave. These are further instances of the importance of hospitality for judging a character's worth.

Most major characters are also defined by what other characters say about them. While remarkably Odysseus does not appear until book 5 of the epic, we hear a great deal about him—all of it positive—from Athena, the townsmen of Ithaca, Nestor, Menelaus, and Helen. Late in the epic, Odysseus is criticized for killing the suitors and losing all the men he led to Troy—what sort of king is this?—yet the singer Phemius mentions the presence of a god helping Odysseus during battle. Divine assistance indicates divine favor—no small thing!

In book 6, Odysseus describes Nausicaa in flattering terms, asking whether she is a goddess. While we may be forgiven for questioning his sincerity—after all, he's desperately seeking help—this is an instance where a character's description is supported by the more authoritative description of the poet himself. Homer has already compared Nausicaa to the goddess Artemis. Of course, we need to distinguish between (a) what other characters say and (b) what the poet says. Here, too, it's a combination of methods—a character's comments reinforced by what Homer says—that helps to construct the figures of the epic.

The poet's own remarks are of considerable interest, yet Homer is famous for saying little directly in his own voice. While describing actions, the poet often omits the physical description of characters, such as height, weight, or hair color. It's impossible to tell what Helen looked like. More significantly the poet never says flat out, "Antinous was a bad man" or "Alcinous was a good host." Homer narrates but does not explicitly judge, preferring indirect description, such as similes. These, however, are no less effective. At various times, Odysseus is compared to a hungry lion, a weeping woman who has lost her husband in battle, a shipwright drilling a plank, and a singer. Each of these comparisons highlights a particular aspect, experience, or skill of Odysseus.

Often Homer's comparisons are not explicitly stated but only implied. Odysseus may be implicitly contrasted with Agamemnon (whose wife is unfaithful), Menelaus (who will live forever in the Elysium fields), and Achilles and his own crew (who fail to make it home). Penelope is compared explicitly to Clytemnestra, the unfaithful wife of Agamemnon, yet Homer also suggests that we compare her to those competitors for Odysseus' love: Calypso,

Circe, and Nausicaa. And let's not ignore the gods. Athena is also character-ized by her words and actions, leading us to the realization that she and Odysseus are in many ways alike—they share an affinity for deception and disguise (see especially 13.291–310). That is, many of the major figures of the epic are defined not only by their words and deeds (or what is said about them by others); we also learn about them by their similarities with and dif-ferences from other characters. We might call this "characterization-by-comparison."

Given Homer's preference for similes and implied comparisons, we should note the effect. The reader (or listener) is not passive, but actively engaged, probing those comparisons when encountering these figures. Homer's reti-cence in judging forces us to take on this role. At one level, we view these fig-ures as fictional, yet we find ourselves speaking about their motivations, psychology, memories, and desires as though they were real people. This is due to Homer's success at making his characters come alive—a truly mar-velous feat!

Let's turn to plot. While the general background story of the Trojan War was not invented by Homer, the specific tales he chooses to tell were in some sense original. In the *Iliad*, Homer decided to tell not the entire story of the Trojan War but rather only the story of Achilles' anger, withdrawal from battle, and return. Homer has no need to retell the story of the entire war—the audience knows it anyway. As far as the *Odyssey* is concerned, surely other poets sang about the homecoming of the Greeks—perhaps of Agamemnon and Odysseus—but Homer may well have been the first, while focusing on Odysseus, to introduce the parallel story of Agamemnon, Clytemnestra, Aegisthus, and Orestes as counter-point to his main tale set in Ithaca.

In both oral and written literature, the composer decides when it's the right moment to elaborate and expand by introducing speeches and similes. Indeed, using speech to reveal character is an area where many feel Homer is preemi-nent (see sidebar "Homeric Characterization"). Also the language of epic simi-les (extended comparisons) may well be peculiar to each poet; adapting similes to a particular episode is recognized as a mark of Homer's greatness.

Finally, any storyteller has the job of unifying his work, and without ques-tion, one of Homer's goals is to produce a unitary work—a song that tells the story *only* of Achilles' anger or Odysseus' return. Homer unifies the *Iliad* by fo-cusing on the wrath of Achilles and using the motif of supplication to bring co-herence to the work. We will explore how in the *Odyssey*, Homer uses the themes of homecoming, hospitality, and identity to tell the story of Odysseus. Yet Homer aspires to even greater ambition. While apparently limiting himself to a narrow sliver of the heroic world, by means of comparisons, flashbacks, and foreshadowing, Homer considers the beginnings of the war, the sack of Troy, and even the end of Odysseus' life. Yet these are always kept subordinate to the poet's main goal: telling how Odysseus returned and regained his kingdom.

Homer is a traditional poet and yet he is original in significant ways. While we can't tell with precision which particular episodes, similes, characters, or lines may have first been sung by Homer, the unity, design, and coherence of both epics are surely something Homer created. Homer was an oral poet who composed before a live audience, drawing upon a well-established oral tradition, and yes! it is possible for oral poetry to be as sophisticated and of the same high quality as written literature. Homer is a genius, not at the level of line and typical scene, but—on the larger scale—in characterization, plot design, creating thematic unity, and introducing similes and speeches. And let's not neglect length itself. To have achieved all this on such an immense scale is nothing short of astonishing.

Now we need to ponder the question of how and why these oral epics were recorded in writing, for Homer's genius is supported by another fact: his epics were recorded in writing (though fragments of some later singers' works also survive). To have gone to all the trouble of writing down over 27,000 lines of verse indicates that some of Homer's own listeners must have considered him superior. In regard to the mechanics of preserving song in written form, the best explanation is that, although Homer was an oral poet, he could have dictated his song to a scribe who wrote down each line as he sang. In fact, some have speculated that there may have been six or more scribes: when Homer sang the first line, one scribe would write that down, a second scribe would record the second line, and so on—this method would allow for the normal rapidity of composition-in-performance.

But why were these epics recorded? Who would have undertaken such an enterprise? To answer these questions, we must examine the historical context. The Greek alphabet was invented sometime in the eighth century B.C.E. (before the common era), which is when Homer appears to have lived. Yet even with the new technology of writing, the project of writing two long epics would have been tremendously expensive and time-consuming. In the period preceding Homer, there were many smaller estates (kingdoms? fiefdoms?) run by the local lords—let's call them kings. Yet significant political and social change took place in the eighth century: a shift from pastoral herding to fixed agriculture, a population explosion, military innovations, all which led an emerging aristocratic elite to challenge these kings' power. Royal authority was under attack.

A petty king could well have seen the Homeric poems as endorsing his status. The Homeric epics are many things, but they are not socially revolutionary. They generally reinforce the idea of monarchy (note that all the good guys, even Eumaeus and Eurycleia, are the children of kings). This is the best explanation I have heard for preserving Homer's poems: that an eighth-century king, challenged by a rising cadre of aristocrats, was looking to justify his rule. In fact, such kings would have had the resources to fund such a recording project—and the motive! (This hypothesis comes from Richard Janko, who has built on Lord's work.) If this hypothesis is correct, we might imagine Homer singing of the heroic age, as an age when men were stronger and braver and performed great deeds. It was also a time when kings were in charge. On this view, the *Iliad* and the *Odyssey* ratify the idea of kingship against a more aristocratic form of government. Admittedly, this is speculative, but given what we know of Homer's time, it makes some sense and would help to explain undertaking the monumental task of preserving these long poems in writing.

So where does this leave us? For readers today, the *Odyssey* is a book. We read it silently as we do novels, such as *A Tale of Two Cities* or *The Catcher in the Rye*. The *Odyssey* can certainly be appreciated like any other book, but also provides us with an opportunity. We can attempt to recreate those original performances of Homer. I am thinking not only of books-on-tape, though this is one way to go. (The *Odyssey* is now available on audiocassette, narrated by Ian McKellen.)

Another option is that we ourselves take on the role of singers. Over the last ten years or so, many colleges have had day-long public readings of the whole or parts of the *Iliad* and the *Odyssey*. In many ways, this is not a re-creation of the original Homeric performance. There's no improvisation by a singer who responds to an audience's reactions, since these modern recitations are aided by the text. We do, however, gain insight into what it is like to hear a story, to have the words ringing in our heads rather than lying silent on the page. Hearing takes longer than reading—approximately four times as long. Yet my personal experience has been that hearing the *Odyssey* is more vivid than reading it. You appreciate details in ways that are impossible when you're reading alone and silently. I can only recommend that you gather a group to read, say, the four books of adventures told by Odysseus (books 9–12), taking turns around a circle (or in a theater) to appreciate anew the genius of Homer. His words were meant to be heard (begin with Lord; then see Beissinger, J.M. Foley, Havelock, Janko, Nagy, Ong, and Parry in "Further Reading").

HOMERIC VALUES

For it is honorable and glorious for a man to fight
for his country and children and wedded wife
against the enemy. And death will come whenever
the Fates decree. But let him march forward
holding his spear high and keeping his brave heart
behind his shield, first to mingle in war.
For there is no way for a man to escape death
which is ordained, not even if his race is descended from the gods.
—Callinus, seventh-century Greek poet

HEROISM AND SHAME CULTURE

Heroism was essential to the ancient Greeks, for heroes and heroines offered models for living one's life. Think of the role Jesus plays for many today who wear bracelets with the letters WWJD (What Would Jesus Do?). Yet Greek heroes did not always act in accordance with what we consider moral values; rather, they demonstrated their heroism by action and success.

Let's begin with a definition of the hero (or female heroine). The word "hero" is a Greek word with three meanings, linked to lineage, era, and behavior. First, in a narrow sense, a hero is a mortal with one human and one divine parent. Achilles' father is a man, Peleus, but his mother, Thetis, is a sea goddess. Achilles is a hero in this technical sense; other examples include Aeneas (whose mother is Aphrodite) and Heracles ("Hercules" in Latin—Zeus is his father).

Second, the label of hero may have to do with a particular time period. The Greeks refer to the time when heroes lived as the "heroic age." In a looser sense, anyone who lived in the heroic age was a hero. Both Odysseus' mother and father were human, not divine, yet he is considered a hero by virtue of the fact that he lived in the age of heroes.

Third, someone may be heroic by his or her actions, consisting of great deeds, personal sacrifice, or a transcendent vision. This is a sense familiar to us today. We still speak of heroes in war, politics, and—with amazing frequency—sports and music.

For the Greeks, heroes were stronger and greater than men in later times (that is, in Homer's own day). As Homer puts it:

> Tydeus' son, Diomedes, took up a stone in his hand,
> a great accomplishment, a stone which two men, such as exist today,
> could not carry. (*Iliad* 5.302–304)

Heroes were also physically handsome, in part because—even without a divine parent—they were descended from the gods. Nausicaa's great-great-grandfather was the god Poseidon; Agamemnon's great-great-grandfather was Zeus. All this contributes to what is called "epic distance," the realization that heroes lived in a different time and were distinctively more impressive than Homer's contemporaries. Still, the essence of heroism is action: heroes need to accomplish something.

The deeds performed by heroes are varied. Journeying to the "underworld"—and returning—is considered heroic; it symbolizes a triumph over death (once Heracles literally defeats Death in a wrestling match). Jason went off to the ends of the world to retrieve the golden fleece. Many of Homer's heroes demonstrate their heroism in battle. We may speak of "the heroic code," a set of rules by which warriors become famous and demonstrate their heroism. In the *Iliad*, Hector, leader of the Trojans, articulates the heroic code:

> "I've learned to be brave
> always, and to fight in the front ranks of the Trojans,
> winning my father great glory and glory for myself." (*Iliad* 6.444–446)

The essence of heroic action is risking one's life. Hector has learned to fight in front where it is most dangerous. Yet that's also where one wins great glory (see also the speech of Sarpedon, Zeus' son, at *Iliad* 12.310–328). The premise of heroism then is mortality—even with one divine parent, heroes and heroines will die. Risking one's life in battle is a defining feature of heroism. (There are exceptions such as Heracles, Aeneas, and in the *Odyssey*, apparently Menelaus and Helen, who will live forever as gods.)

So we have a definition of the hero and a code of conduct. In addition, there are rewards and what might be called "enforcement" of the heroic code. The rewards in part are tangible: many material goods are given to those who risk their lives in battle (tripods, gold, captive women, and more). In addition, heroes are honored by their people and may even achieve what Homer calls "imperishable glory," the distinction of having singers recall great feats of heroes long after their deaths.

The heroic code is enforced by public pressure. Indeed, an essential part of warrior society is public esteem or, alternatively, public disgrace. Those who risk their lives are honored in society; those who are cowards and run away from battle are disgraced in the eyes of society. Hector speaks of this:

> "But I would be terribly ashamed
> before the men of Troy and the Trojan women trailing their long robes
> if I would skulk away from battle like a coward." (*Iliad* 6.441–443)

This sort of society where public pressure plays such a dominant role often goes under the name of "shame culture." While no people on earth operate wholly under a shame culture (or wholly under its contrast, a "guilt culture"), this concept offers insight into the motivation of heroes.

The central idea that distinguishes shame culture from guilt culture is that in a guilt culture, if you do something wrong—even if nobody knows—you would feel bad or "guilty." Your conscience would trouble you. In a shame culture, what matters is the public perception. If you do well in battle—a public display of valor—you are honored and rewarded. If you are about to avoid danger, you feel public pressure to conform to society's ideals.

The distinction between shame and guilt culture may be demonstrated by contrasting the Old and New Testaments of the Bible. People have often connected the Ten Commandments ("Thou shalt not kill," etc.) with shame culture, because these prohibitions concern public acts that are condemned by society. The Sermon on the Mount, by contrast, speaks of what you may feel in your heart: "I say that he who looks at another woman with a desire to commit adultery has already committed adultery in his heart" (Matt. 5.28). Note that the person "who looks at another woman with a desire to commit adultery" has *done* nothing; no public action has taken place. And no one could know about these private desires. Still Jesus condemns such feelings in one's heart. It's truly a revolutionary moment when inner feelings and convictions became as significant as public actions. In the *Iliad* and the *Odyssey*, however, public actions weigh more heavily than inner feelings. It's not how you feel, it's what you do.

So much for the conventions of society. If Homer were your everyday poet, that might be as far as it goes. But Homer perceives the limitations and contradictions in such a world. He is fascinated by "violations" of the heroic code. In fact, both the *Iliad* and the *Odyssey* present majors figures, Achilles and Odysseus, who are not typical heroes submitting to the rules of society. In the *Iliad*, there is no greater hero than Achilles—he's the best fighter at Troy. Yet Homer tells the story of Achilles "dropping out." The valiant warrior leaves battle, threatens to go home, and watches as the Greeks—his own allies—begin to lose in battle. When the desperate Greeks come to his camp and beg for his help by offering gifts, Achilles asserts that no gifts are equal to the value of his life. He will no longer risk his life for reward and honor. He sees two choices:

"If I remain here and fight around the Trojans' city,
my journey home is gone, but there will be undying glory.
If I go back home to my dear fatherland,
my noble glory is gone, but there'll be a long life
for me, and the stroke of death will not find me quickly." (*Iliad* 9.412–416)

Although later changing his mind, at this point Achilles appears inclined to go home, see his father once again, marry, and settle down to a relatively obscure life. Yet how can the greatest hero leave what he does best? Is Achilles still a hero if he abandons his allies and the goal of sacking Troy? Well, yes—in a technical sense—he's the son of a goddess, so he's a hero. Yet clearly what matters more is how Achilles acts and whether he proves himself to be heroic. As the heroic code fails to answer life's problems, Achilles pursues a personal quest for meaning. Homer's brilliant masterpiece explores Achilles' doubt, withdrawal, and return.

Odysseus is also a puzzle. He, too, is a warrior; he fights and wins many riches. In the *Odyssey*, however, he learns that to succeed—for success is also a heroic goal—he must at times be cautious and even endure insults in his own home. While proving his valor by fighting, Odysseus proves his superiority and genius by a different mode of operation. Some have seen the early adventures—such as the sacking of the Cicones and his insistence on shouting out his name to the blinded Polyphemus in book 9—as "Iliadic" heroism, the sort of behavior that works on the plain of battle, but not in the strange world Odysseus journeys through on his way home. To survive in the wild and woolly world of Circe, Calypso, Scylla and Charybdis, and the Sirens, Odysseus must adopt a new attitude. Charging bravely ahead with a battle cry is not the way to go (see *Odyssey* 12.116–119). Odysseus must discover a new way of dealing with the unusual challenges facing him. We note that even the Trojan War is won not by Achilles' prowess in battle, but by a trick (thought up by Athena and Odysseus): the deception of the large wooden horse that the Trojans mistakenly assume will protect their city. And trickery—not always associated with heroism—is one of Odysseus' great strengths.

Odysseus therefore may be seen as a different kind of hero. While he's no coward, has a healthy appreciation for material goods, and wants the respect of his peers, Odysseus achieves glory in part by underhandedness, by stealth, and by deception. Here, too, Homer offers his audience something of a paradox: a tricky hero.

The cliché even in antiquity was that the *Iliad* was for men, while the *Odyssey* was for women. I certainly reject this—it suggests that women are unlikely to appreciate the *Iliad*—yet there *is* a truly wonderful set of female characters in the *Odyssey*: Nausicaa, Circe, Calypso, Athena, and Penelope. One reason so many wonderful female characters appear in the *Odyssey*, I think, is that in Homer's patriarchal, macho world, women can more easily mirror the "tricky" heroism Odysseus demonstrates than the military heroism of the *Iliad* (in general, women do not fight in battle, though again there's an exception: the Amazons)—and Homer loves to explore similarities between characters. Penelope in particular shows how endurance and craftiness lead to success—she is no less heroic than her husband (see Dodds and Williams in "Further Reading" and Diotima in "Homer On-Line").

MORALITY, HOSPITALITY, AND THE GODS

In addition to the heroic code, there was a code of hospitality (or guest-friendship) that has its own set of rules. Hospitality may better reflect a society at peace, while the heroic code stipulates rules for wartime. In addition, hospitality provides an intersection between etiquette, morality, and the gods.

Hospitality is a reciprocal relationship: a host is expected to welcome a traveler (even a stranger!) into his home, offer a bath, food, and drink, and—only then—ask who this person might be. It's fascinating that one of the questions is: "Are you a pirate?" The guest is expected to treat his host courteously and with respect (unlike Paris, who stole Helen, his host's wife!). Of course, not everyone is a good host or guest, but it becomes clear that everyone pretty much knows the rules—even the Cyclops Polyphemus. It's important for us to learn the obligations on both sides of the equation, for in the *Odyssey* Homer uses hospitality as a means of revealing character—and helping us to judge people.

The first scene at Ithaca shows a goddess in disguise arriving at Odysseus' home. There was a proverb that travelers may be the gods in disguise (*Odyssey* 17.485–487)—Athena plays this role several times. The suitors ignore her, but Telemachus rushes up and invites her into his home. This is the first instance where Homer asks us to apply the code of hospitality to the various characters in the epic in order to distinguish good from bad. Homer never comments on someone's hospitable behavior—he expects his readers to recognize appropriate behavior in accordance with the code of hospitality.

The Amazing Greek Language

Interestingly, the Greeks have just one word for both "host" and "guest"—*xenos*. When Odysseus asks the Cyclops for a guest gift, a derivative of this word is used: *xenion,* or "gift-that-a-host-gives-a-guest." In Greek, *xenos* can comprise a wide range of meanings: "host," "guest," "traveler" (that is, potential guest), and "stranger," for out-of-town travelers are generally unknown. There is the town of Xenia, Ohio, but the most common appearance of this word in English is xenophobia. Literally this means "fear of strangers or fear of foreigners," yet it generally contains a sense of hostility rather than fear—and it doesn't mean "fear of Xena, the warrior princess."

Given the code of hospitality, we need to examine the issues of right and wrong and human relations with the gods. There was no set of commandments or laws that governed all Greeks in Homer's time, but moral principles certainly existed. We see this most easily by considering Zeus' roles. Zeus, the chief god associated with the sky and weather (he wields a thunderbolt), is described as Zeus Xenios, Zeus Horkios, and Zeus Hikesios: Zeus who watches over hospitality (*xenios*), over oaths (*horkios*), and over suppliants (*hikesios*). While all Greeks are expected to abide by the code of hospitality, if violations occur, kings or those in power would be expected to punish such violators. If no such enforcement takes place at the human level, Zeus would bring retribution upon bad guests and hosts. In similar fashion, Zeus is the final judge on those who break their oaths and those who show no mercy to suppliants (those who beg for help).

In the *Odyssey*, Homer tells the story of Odysseus' journey home. Odysseus' goal is blocked by the hostility of Poseidon, yet he is helped by the goddess Athena. True, it's hard to say that Odysseus deserves Poseidon's enmity or Athena's concern. Odysseus is not always a saintly guy, but Homeric morality is quite distinct from the ideals of Christianity: humility is no virtue and Odysseus' adulteries are not explicitly condemned (the old double standard?). As mentioned above, success is the goal of Greek heroes—not virtue or goodness. Heroes sack cities and are honored with tripods and captive women for doing so. These aren't Boy Scouts!

All moral questions in the *Odyssey* are complicated for several reasons. Part of the problem derives from the fact that in Homeric epics there is only an implicit morality—Homer does not praise or condemn in his own voice. This leaves the audience (and readers) to play the role of judge. Also, particular actions are not always condemned. The suitors lie and plot against the lives of their foes, but so does Odysseus (and he's unfaithful to his wife). Why should we consider Odysseus the good guy and the suitors the bad guys? Or—to put it another way—how does Homer influence our reactions in such a way that we root for Odysseus and against the suitors? Is it simply that the suitors are bad guests and that Athena is Odysseus' ally (and that we sympathize with Penelope and Telemachus)? Is it because the story is told to a great extent from Odysseus' perspective?

Homer's epics are open-ended to this extent. During the fifth century, tragedians treated Odysseus as an amoral opportunist who would do or say anything to get what he wanted. Often he was cowardly as well. We might say that's a later version of the figure of Odysseus, but all Odysseus' traits in tragedy are found one way or another in the *Odyssey*. Not only is he tricky, but he lies to and manipulates even those who care about him. His goal is success, not virtue. And yet Homer is delighted with these skills, which are mirrored in Athena—a formidable goddess who also uses deception yet certainly is deserving of respect.

There are moral lessons in the *Odyssey* against excessive behavior (the suitors) and against disobedience to divine prohibitions (Odysseus' crew). A Christian, Jew, or Muslim may say it's wrong to disobey god; in Homer, it's not so much immoral as stupid. Odysseus' men swore not to eat the cattle of the Sun; the suitors should wise up and not abuse Penelope's hospitality. The toughest nut to crack concerns vengeance. Poseidon persecutes Odysseus for the blinding of his son, Polyphemus; Odysseus slays the suitors for their actions. There's a sort of justice in vengeance, but without divine resolution, where does it end? Violence begets violence. Homer explores this problem and provides a solution only in the final scene of the epic.

HOMER AND HISTORY

When Schliemann started digging into the ruins in 1870 he discovered that the mound at Hissarlik was a layer cake, consisting of nine Troys built one on top of another.

—R. Hooper, *Representative Chapters in Ancient History*

HISTORICAL LAYERS IN HOMER'S POEMS

We now turn to the topic of Homer and history. Questions abound. How historical is Homer? Do his epics accurately reflect how people lived? And did the Trojan War actually take place? These issues are extremely complicated—there are no easy answers. Let's begin with our modern perspective on ancient history and then see how Homer relates to that.

Historians distinguish three important periods:

Mycenaean Period (part of the Bronze Age)	1600–1100 B.C.E.
Dark Ages	1100–800 B.C.E.
Archaic Period	800–480 B.C.E.

In the *Mycenaean Period* in Greece (1600–1100 B.C.E.), well-fortified palaces dominated the countryside around them (the period is named for Agamem-

Illustration 2. *The Walls of Troy.* Defensive walls on the east side of Troy, approximately 1200 B.C.E. By permission of Joyce Kuschke.

non's home, Mycenae). Kings operated with the support of an elaborate bureaucracy for collecting taxes, storing supplies, and keeping records (they had a writing system called Linear B). Evidently the Mycenaeans (who were Bronze Age Greeks) were a warrior society, which traded around the Aegean Sea and at one point controlled the island of Crete.

The Amazingly Early Greek Language

The Mycenaeans had a syllabic writing system, Linear B. This script was deciphered in 1952 by an English architect, Michael Ventris, who proved that it was used to record Greek on the mainland—in Mycenae, Thebes, and Pylos (Nestor's home)—and on the island of Crete. Preserved on fire-burnt clay tablets, Linear B preserves no literature; rather, it was used to record palace inventories. Still, it shows us the Greek language that was used in the Bronze Age, long before the Greek alphabet was used to record Homer's poems.

Located by the Hellespont in Asia Minor, Troy was a wealthy, strategically located Bronze Age city, involved in large-scale trade (see Map 2). From archaeological evidence, we know that there were various cities at the site of Troy stretching back to 3000 B.C.E.—each built upon the remains of the one below it. Of the various cities at Troy, the ones labeled Troy VI and Troy VIIA (counting

Illustration 3. *Detail of "Ship Fresco" from Thera.* Detail from a fresco found in Thera (modern Santorini) in the central Aegean, approximately seventeenth century B.C.E. The frescoes that run around four walls of a room depict an overseas voyage in which the fleet visits harbors and towns (perhaps representing a military venture?). By permission of the Ministry of Culture of Greece (New Prehistoric Museum of Thera).

from the bottom where the oldest city was), from the period 1280–1180 B.C.E., have been considered the likeliest candidates to be "Homer's Troy." Yet no archaeological evidence demonstrates that Mycenaean Greeks were involved in the destruction of these cities. It's possible—the Mycenaean Greeks were powerful at this time and Troy was a tempting target—but not proven.

Following the height of the Mycenaean period, we confront a period of instability and disruption, which ushered in the *Dark Ages* (1100–800 B.C.E.). The story the Greeks told in antiquity was that invaders came down from the north. This is also possible, but—whoever it was—much of Mycenaean civilization was devastated. Palaces and towns were abandoned, population levels dropped, trading was disrupted, and writing vanished. It's also in this period that someone introduced the technology of iron (which was tougher than bronze). As far as we can tell—and this is in many respects a "dark" age—in the wake of these invasions, local chieftains ruled their primarily pastoral estates.

In the eighth century, we find another shift, the beginning of the *Archaic Period* (800–480 B.C.E.). Indeed, the eighth century has been called a Greek "Renaissance" due to its many profound changes. A world of city-states now emerged (*polis* is the Greek term for city-state, from which we get the term "politics"). City-states were independent territories comprising an urban center and the surrounding countryside. Other eighth-century changes included a shift from herding to fixed agriculture; in warfare, the use of hoplite (or full-body) armor; a rise in population and subsequent colonization; and the emergence of various Panhellenic (or "all-Greek") religious locales, in particular, Olympia honoring Zeus and Delphi (famous for its oracle) honoring Apollo. When Greeks gathered at these Panhellenic celebrations, poems such as Homer's may have been performed. At the beginning of this period, the Greek alphabet was also invented (derived from a Phoenician script).

This completes our quick historical survey. Now obviously Homer was not thinking in terms of Mycenaean, Dark, and Archaic Ages (B.C.E. alone would have

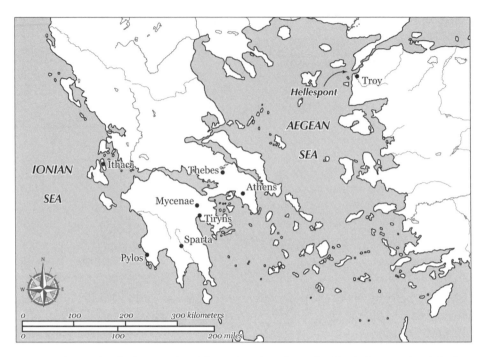

Map 2. *Greece in the Bronze Age.* The major sites from the Greek Bronze Age. The irregular peninsula of southern Greece with the sites of Mycenae, Pylos, and Sparta is called the Peloponnesus. By permission of the Ancient World Mapping Center.

mystified him!). Yet he did look from his own period back to an earlier age. He and his contemporaries called it the "heroic age." For the sake of argument, let's label the subject of Homer's poem the Mycenaean Age, which we would date to at least 400 years before Homer (Homer lived somewhere in the mid-eighth century B.C.E.—say 750 or so—while the sack of Troy occurred close to 1200).

How historical is Homer? Does he accurately reflect the Mycenaean Bronze Age? All the intricacies of this topic cannot be pursued here, but in general the answer is no. While Homer self-consciously looked back to an earlier time, to a large extent his poems reflect his own period of Archaic Greece. Travel and trading by sea; athletic contests; full body armor; and cremation for burial: all these are found in Homer's poems—*and* in the eighth century. We see this also with diet and politics. Homer's heroes eat an awful lot of meat and this may have been true in the Dark Ages (when people subsisted on their herds). Yet Homer reflects his own times in similes that refer to harvesting grain and fishing—the more usual Archaic Age diet. In the *Iliad* and the *Odyssey* the many kings who control relatively small territories may be based on Dark Age kings whose authority came under attack in Homer's day. But in general, Homer's work reflects his own time period, not that of an earlier era.

Homeric poetry incorporates two fascinating features from the eighth century: colonization and competitive games. In the eighth century B.C.E., the Greek population grew explosively—in some areas by perhaps as much as 800 percent (which itself is related to the switch from herding to fixed agriculture). Various cities in Greece sent off some of their people to found colonies in the Western Mediterranean (Sicily, southern Italy) and in the Black Sea area (each colony was politically independent of its "mother-city"—or *metropolis*). Odysseus' tales of one-eyed monsters, witches, and huge whirlpools echo to some extent the stories of colonists who journeyed outside the familiar world of the Aegean and eastern Mediterranean and returned to tell such sailor yarns.

Also sometime in the eighth century, the Olympic games began (according to legend, in 776 B.C.E.). The Greeks were unique in the ancient world, since they gloried in the toil and excitement of running faster and throwing javelins farther than their competitors. Every four years Greeks would gather at Olympia to honor Zeus by competing in these games. Such athletic competitions also appear in Homer's works. In book 23 of the *Iliad*, competitions in running, chariot racing, archery, wrestling, and boxing are held in honor of the death of Achilles' friend, Patroclus. In book 8 of the *Odyssey*, Odysseus reluctantly joins in a discus-throwing contest, far surpassing his Phaeacian rivals. And speaking of Panhellenic activity, the Trojan War was itself a Panhellenic venture—Greeks from different polities joining together in the common quest of sacking a city. So both the athletic competition and the Trojan War itself appear to mirror the Panhellenic gatherings and celebrations of Homer's day. In each case—travel, athletic competition, Panhellenic events—we find Homer taking practices from his own time and projecting them into an earlier heroic age.

It's not quite so simple though. Just as at the site of Troy there are archaeological layers of cities from different eras, so Homer's epics may also be thought of as containing different layers deriving from diverse historical periods—and from his own invention. In a few ways Homer does recall the earlier Bronze Age. The most powerful cities in Homer's poems—Mycenae, Pylos, Troy—*were* powerful in the Bronze Age. Homer also describes bronze weaponry and chariots, which *were* used in that earlier period (historians find it humorous that in the *Iliad* heroes use chariots somewhat like taxis—merely to get to battle—for historically Bronze Age warriors fought *from* chariots). In book 10 of the *Iliad*, Homer describes a boar-tusk helmet, which was not used in Homer's day. Archaeologists have, however, uncovered boar-tusk helmets from the Bronze Age. Apparently, these various implements of military technology were kept alive for Homer in the oral tradition reaching back many generations. Still, Homer fails to record the Mycenaeans' elaborate palace bureaucracy, writing system, or burial practice of inhumation (that is, burial in the ground rather than cremation).

In many ways then, Homer's poems are an amalgam of past, contemporary, and fictional elements. The topic of Homer and History is complex. Regarding the Bronze Age, Homer recalls bronze weapons, yet he is wrong on many counts: burial, writing, military tactics, and so forth. To some extent, there's a layer of Dark Age society: the kings (who may still exist in the Archaic period) and a meat-based diet, for example. To a very large extent, however, what Homer has done is to project his own time into the heroic world, so that the epics contain eighth-century features such as small-time kings; a diet (in similes) of fish and grain; extensive sea travel; and athletic competition.

Are we any closer to answering the question: Did the Trojan War take place? Until the mid-nineteenth century (C.E.), many believed the Trojan War to have been fiction, invented by Homer. That view was upset by a German businessman, Heinrich Schliemann (1822–1890), who in the 1870s went to excavate in Asia Minor and found the city (or rather cities) of Troy. Schliemann also dug at Mycenae in Greece, proving Mycenae to be (as Homer said) "rich-in-gold." Excavations continue to this day in Greece and around the area of Troy. While several of the cities of Troy were destroyed—by earthquake, fire, and probably attack—it is impossible to identify the invader. As already mentioned, it could have been the Mycenaean Greeks, but this is merely one of several possibilities.

More importantly, to say that Homer's works tell the story of an actual event from 400 years before—in say, 1200 B.C.E.—is to misunderstand what oral poetry is capable of. Actual historical events could certainly provide the subject of a song—but each singer will modify and adapt that story to reflect his own time period. While the Mycenaean Greeks may have attacked and even sacked Troy in the Bronze Age, Homer does not describe the major episodes of that war in his poems in a historically accurate manner. The best we can say is that Homer may loosely recall the military deeds of Mycenaean Greeks, but it's really more like the game "telephone" in which people sit in a circle and one whispers something to his or her neighbor, and that person whispers to his or her neighbor, and so on. What you end up with differs radically from the first message. The historical value of Homer's epic for the Bronze Age is extremely limited, for the figures and society he describes—their values, politics, and culture—are predominantly refracted through an eighth-century lens (see Raaflaub and Thomas in "Further Reading").

REAL AND FANTASTIC GEOGRAPHY

The key distinction in Homeric geography is between familiar places—those spots known to sailors, traders, and other contemporaries of Homer—and what we might call "imaginative" or "fantastic" geographical locales, such as the Cyclops' cave or the land of the dead at the ends of the earth—places that are not normally found on a trader's route. That is, it's probably best to think about locales in Homer's *Odyssey* by attempting to see them through eighth-century B.C.E. eyes.

As we have seen, much of the *Odyssey* reflects Homer's own time: it's rooted in the eighth century. The Aegean Sea, the eastern Mediterranean, Asia Minor (where Troy lies), mainland Greece (Mycenae, Pylos, Sparta), and Egypt were familiar to Homer's audience. When Menelaus tells how he got stuck on the island of Pharos off the Egyptian coast, this would have clicked with Homer's audience (4.354–359, although Proteus was not part of the usual Egyptian experience). The island of Ithaca lies at the western edge of this world, close to the Adriatic, Southern Italy, and Sicily—places where colonization took place in the eighth century and later.

The Greeks used the sky and stars to orient themselves. Odysseus naturally uses east and west—the rising and setting of the sun—to describe his journeys. When he leaves Calypso's island, Odysseus keeps what we call the Big Dipper in the north on his left (*Odyssey* 5.269–280)—her island must be far to the west of Greece.

After his Trojan adventures, the signal that Odysseus is entering a realm of fantasy is the storm he recounts in book 9.

> "But a wave, the current, and the North Wind forced me
> away as I was doubling Cape Malea, and drove me past Cythera." (9.80–81)

Cape Malea and the island of Cythera were familiar terrain at the southern region of the Peloponnesus (see Map 1: "Odysseus' Journeys"). To be driven south and west of this point for nine days was to enter a world that in historical terms was just beginning to be explored in Homer's day. As I suggested above, Odysseus' tales of monsters, Sirens, and whirlpools to some extent imitates the sorts of tales traders and colonists would have told their Greek compatriots in the Aegean area. Note where Odysseus ends up after the storm: the land of the Lotus-Eaters, the island of the Cyclopes, Aeolus' island (which never stays rooted in one spot—10.1–3); he meets the Lastrygonians and Circe; he visits the land of the dead and sails past the Sirens, Scylla, and Charybdis, landing on Thrinacia, where the Sun's cattle grazed (there are also the islands of Calypso and the Phaeacians). These constitute Homer's fantastic geography.

We don't want to describes these places as "hard to find on a map," because there weren't any maps in Homer's day. It's worth mentioning that *later* Greeks attempted to locate these spots; still today when you visit southern Italy and nearby areas, tour guides will point out Circe's island or the whirlpool of Charybdis in the Straits of Messina. So—just for fun—I've indicated on Map 1 where the ancients located the various locales visited by Odysseus. Many spots are in the area of Greek colonization. Greeks after Homer located the Phaeacians—last stop before Ithaca—just up the coast from Ithaca on the island of Corcyra (modern Corfu). I repeat that such a map is an anachronism—Homer's audience would not have thought in terms of a map. More likely their ideas would have been along the lines of: "Oh, that was far to the east," or "I heard of such places in the far north," or "That's near where the sun sets," and so on.

I should mention how Homer's contemporaries conceived of the world itself. It seems that they didn't think of earth as a sphere, but rather as more of a round disk—sort of a frisbee. Above the frisbee-earth was the vault of heaven, below was Tartarus where the Titans, who tried to overthrow Zeus, were punished (see the description of Homer's contemporary, Hesiod, in *Theogony* 717–743). A symbolic representation of the world in Homer's day appears in book 18 of the *Iliad*. The god Hephaestus makes a shield for the hero Achilles, yet Homer's description of that shield is quite elaborate. It could be thought of as a divine vision of the universe, including the sun, moon, stars, cities, fields, and so on. The overall design is that of a round disk with the river Ocean running around the rim (see *Iliad* 18.478–608, especially 18.607–608). This helps us in thinking about Odysseus' journey to the land of the dead. It's not a journey down (like Aeneas' or Dante's), but *out* to the edge of the earth. Odysseus has to cross the river Ocean to reach the realm of the dead (*Odyssey* 11.13–22). It gives you a headache trying to conceptualize it—it's beyond the edge of the flat earth—something like imagining what's beyond the edge of the universe—Yikes! So once again, Homer suggests a place far off the beaten path that is not part of any sailor's itinerary.

Greek Science Arises in the "New" World

When many people today think of ancient Greece, Athens comes to mind—in large part due to those famous Athenians: the playwrights Aeschylus, Sophocles, Euripides, and Aristophanes, the historian Thucydides, the philosophers Socrates and Plato, and the orator Demosthenes. These are Greeks who lived in the city-state of Athens where the Parthenon still stands. Yet they lived in a later period—the classical world of the fifth and fourth centuries B.C.E.—centuries after Homer. Many of the famous and influential Greeks from the Archaic period—the age of Homer and the next couple of centuries—came from what we might call the "New World," Sicily and southern Italy, which was colonized by Greeks in Homer's lifetime and soon after. Among the early philosophers and scientists who lived in this area are Pythagoras the mathematician (remember the Pythagorean theorem?) and Empedocles, who came up with the idea that everything was composed of earth, air, fire, and water (Aristotle later borrowed Empedocles' idea). Others, such as Thales, who is said to have predicted a solar eclipse—and perhaps Homer himself—lived in what is no longer Greece today, but along the west coast of Turkey in Asia Minor. Athens became a magnet for ideas and art and democracy in the fifth century, but in the Archaic period many new ideas arose at the edge of the Greek world, not in the center of it (see Cromer in "Further Reading").

HOMER'S *ODYSSEY*

BOOK ONE

We can never recommend enough a first-hand reading of the text itself. . . . No book which discusses another book can ever say more than the original book under discussion.

—Italo Calvino, *Why Read the Classics?*

Book 1 has three main sections: the proem (or introductory section) that contains an invocation to the Muse, an assembly of the gods, and Athena's encounter with Telemachus on the island of Ithaca. Yet this bare summary does little justice to Homer's intentions. While beginning his story, the poet also establishes certain thematic connections that will prove central to the entire work. Let us look at each section, noting how Homer prepares us for the tale to follow.

PROEM: INVOCATION OF THE MUSE (1.1–21)

The epic begins with the singer invoking (or calling upon) the Muse to sing the story of a man who has journeyed much. The ancient Greek idea was that the singer needed inspiration from one of the gods to be able to sing at all. In fact, the singer might almost be thought of as a vehicle—a "medium"—through which the divinity sings. At least that is what the opening suggests. (The *Iliad* begins the same way: "Sing, goddess, of the wrath of Peleus' son Achilles.") In the *Odyssey*, the poet calls specifically upon one of the Muses to sing, or at the very least to aid him in the creation of this song.

Patrons of the Arts

The Muses are the daughters of Zeus (the chief Greek god) and the goddess Mnemosyne, which means "memory." Elsewhere we hear of nine Muses, but Homer isn't picky—he needs only one of them to help.

These opening lines contain several extraordinary features, most startling of which is the fact that the hero, Odysseus, is not named until line 21. The subject of this story, the man who suffers much and journeys all over the earth, remains anonymous for the first twenty lines! Now you might think that's no big deal—after all, the front of the book clearly states "The Odyssey"—we know the story's about Odysseus (which is all the word *Odyssey* means: "the story of Odysseus"). But in imagining the performance of the singer before a live audience, I suspect that such an audience would expect the singer to state flat out what his subject was. The contrast with the *Iliad* is instructive. The very first line of that epic states the subject ("wrath") and the hero's name complete with patronymic: "Achilles, son of Peleus" or "Peleus'-son" much like our Johnson, "son of John," or my favorite, Morrison, "son of Morris."

My point is that the poet's decision *not* to name Odysseus in the first twenty lines introduces one of the three major themes of the Odyssey: *identity*. (I will focus on three themes—the poem contains countless themes we could pursue.) As Homer's audience (and readers) come to learn, the theme of identity is approached from several directions, but for now let us think of it as a binary operation with two options: *either you reveal who you are or you don't*. As we see in book 1, Athena herself refrains from revealing who she is when she meets Telemachus: she lies, calling herself Mentes, son of Anchialus. Athena's disguise is simply one example of the theme of identity—in this case she conceals who she is. For the epic as a whole, we find that if Odysseus wishes to survive, get home, and reclaim his kingdom, he needs to learn when it is appropriate to say, "I am Odysseus, son of Laertes, King of Ithaca" and when he should lie, or pretend he didn't hear the question, or come up with a trick name: "I am Nobody—Mr. Nobody to you!"

A second theme is that of *homecoming*. The opening lines tell us that the man who wandered much and saw many cities "fought for his own life and for the homecoming of his companions" (1.5). For all his efforts, Odysseus (as yet unnamed) failed to bring his companions home, but it was their fault, for they ate the cattle of the Sun (another god). A few lines later, Homer sets the context of his story by telling us that when all those heroes who had escaped death were at home, there remained one man alone "missing his wife and his homecoming," kept by the goddess Calypso.

It is helpful to think of the theme of homecoming as similar to the theme of identity, as a polarity consisting of two extremes: *either you achieve your home-*

coming or you don't. Odysseus' men do not, Achilles does not—he dies and is buried on the windy plains of Troy. The point for Homer's audience is to recognize these two possibilities. This is what's at stake for Odysseus: either he will make it home or he will fail, like his companions. Homer neatly doubles the suspense (will Odysseus make it?) by having Odysseus' son Telemachus go on his own journey. Like his father, Telemachus must also strive to accomplish his own homecoming (as we shall see, against an ambush of many men).

The Amazing Greek Language

The Greeks had a word for homecoming, *nostos*, which translators render "journey home," "return," or "homecoming." The first song-within-a-song in the epic is a story of homecoming: Phemius, the Ithacan bard, sings of the "mournful homecoming of the Greeks" (1.326–327), which makes Penelope weep. In modern English, we get our word "nostalgia," from *nostos*: "nostalgia" literally means "homecoming pain" or the pain (*algos*) from being away from home—something many first-year college students experience. You might also think of Dorothy in *The Wizard of Oz*: "There's no place like home." The situation is desperate for Odysseus, who after twenty years away wants to die (1.57–59). The *Oxford English Dictionary* defines nostalgia as "extreme homesickness" and interestingly cites an early use of "nostalgia" from another ocean voyager: Captain Cook in 1770, who sailed around the world.

As the proem ends, we learn that Poseidon, the sea god, was angry at this hero, who finally is named: "godlike Odysseus." It's unlikely that Homer's audience had no inkling that Homer was about to sing about Odysseus (perhaps some town crier advertised the upcoming epic song: "Tonight: The Journeys of Odysseus!"). What is clear is that the entire work is unified by the themes of *identity* and *homecoming* and the poet has planted the seeds for both ideas in the opening lines of this epic of over 12,000 lines.

ASSEMBLY OF THE GODS (1.22–95)

The first episode takes place on Mount Olympus, the tallest mountain in Greece, home of the "Olympian" gods. This scene leads to Athena's intervention in Telemachus' life, but again something remarkable happens. When getting up to speak before all the gods (except Poseidon, Odysseus' nemesis, who conveniently is out of town), Zeus says *nothing* about Odysseus! He does, however, raise an important issue—are men and women responsible for their own suffering, or is it the gods' fault?

"It's amazing that mortals now blame the gods,
for they say that trouble comes from us. But they themselves
have pain beyond measure from their own recklessness." (1.32–34)

This is an utterly profound question to which I personally would like an answer. The debate over the cause of evil—personal responsibility or divine infliction?—recurs throughout the epic. Not every passage in Homer's work supports Zeus' claim that the gods are free from blame.

Second, the most bizarre thing is that Zeus focuses not on Odysseus but on the household of another Greek king, Agamemnon, who led the Greeks to Troy. Zeus begins with the story of Aegisthus, who seduced Agamemnon's wife while Agamemnon was away fighting the Trojan War. Aegisthus did this in spite of the gods' warning him not to woo another's man wife, with the threat that vengeance would come from Agamemnon's son, Orestes.

What is Homer up to? Is his mind wandering? Is he having second thoughts about telling a really big epic about Odysseus? In fact, our poet knows exactly what he's doing, though without a doubt this is challenging for his audience, which may be thinking: "What's going on? Why am I hearing about Agamemnon's marital troubles?" The answer is that Homer is setting up a *foil*, or contrasting story, to the main story of Odysseus and his family. That is, even before dealing with the homecoming of Odysseus, Homer sets up a parallel situation. This allows us to compare and contrast the key figures in the main story with those in the "Agamemnon" story.

We might call this *characterization-by-comparison*. It works like this. The key figures in the *Odyssey* are king Odysseus, wife Penelope, son Telemachus—oh, and the suitors who are trying to marry Penelope and (soon) kill Telemachus! Each of these figures has a counterpart in the Agamemnon story: king Agamemnon, wife Clytemnestra, son Orestes—and the successful seducer, Aegisthus. We can represent these similarities in the following chart.

Odysseus' and Agamemnon's Families

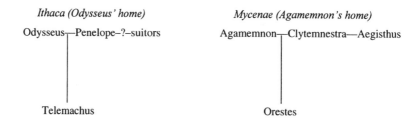

Homer's strategy is that every time we hear about Agamemnon, we are meant to compare and contrast his situation with Odysseus' situation. Every time we hear the name of Clytemnestra and her infidelity, we must ask of Penelope—will she remain faithful or will she, like Clytemnestra, take a lover (one of the suitors) in her husband's absence? Notice that Zeus mentions Agamemnon's son, Orestes, and indeed it is not long before Athena retells the "Agamemnon" story to Telemachus with an emphasis on the way in which Orestes avenged his father's death and won great fame for himself.

"Haven't you heard of the fame divine Orestes won
among all men, when he killed his father's murderer,
devious Aegisthus who killed his famous father?" (1.298–300)

That is, we might think of the figures in the Agamemnon story as role models—both positive and negative—for the major figures in this epic. Will Penelope prove herself better than Clytemnestra? Will Telemachus act as nobly as Orestes?

Homer takes a tremendous risk here. He is complicating his story about Odysseus by bringing in a completely different tale about Agamemnon in the hope that the gains in complexity will outweigh any momentary confusion.

Mythological Highlighting and Suppression

All storytellers emphasize certain episodes and downplay others. It is interesting to note that Homer has simplified the Agamemnon story by wholly omitting the figure of Iphigenia, daughter of Agamemnon, who in many versions of this story (e.g., Aeschylus' tragedy *Agamemnon*) is said to have been sacrificed by her father so that the Greek fleet could sail to Troy. But she has no counterpart on the Ithacan side of things—Telemachus has no sisters—so Homer has airbrushed her out of the picture. This is one example of what we might call mythological "suppression."

Meanwhile, back at the divine assembly, Athena, daughter of Zeus, brings up the sad case of Odysseus, again reminding us that Atlas' daughter, Calypso, still holds Odysseus captive. Zeus speaks highly of Odysseus, blames the problem on his brother Poseidon, and endorses the idea of helping Odysseus get home (that is, achieve his *homecoming*—theme #1). Part of Athena's claim to fame is as the goddess of wisdom and she has clearly thought this out ahead of time: Hermes, the messenger god, will go to Calypso's island to announce that the Olympians have decreed it is time to release Odysseus; she will go to Ithaca to see Telemachus and "put courage in his heart" (1.89). Homer presents Athena's actions and their consequences over the next four books; it is not until book 5 that we witness Hermes on his errand to release Odysseus.

Homer the Gambler

Homer takes many risks—and the stakes are high. He chooses to begin his story with Telemachus in Ithaca and does not present Odysseus until book 5. The poet gains suspense and offers a very unusual perspective on Odysseus (see discussion in book 5), but the risk is that his audience will get up and leave (or close the book?), frustrated by the failure of Odysseus to appear. Homer runs similar risks in the *Iliad*. He gambles by letting Achilles—the main man in that work—drop out of sight for seven books (books 2–8) and *never* does he present the sack of Troy.

ATHENA IN ITHACA (1.96–444)

The third part of book 1 takes place in Ithaca. Homer introduces several main characters: Telemachus and Penelope, son and wife of the absent Odysseus, and the unruly suitors, who order steak every night from Odysseus' kitchen.

Let's begin with Telemachus. We learn three important things about Telemachus. First, he misses his father and daydreams that one day Odysseus will stride into the house and clear out the suitors. Second, we learn that Telemachus is a good host. When Athena arrives (in disguise) at the front door, Telemachus is angry that this guest is left standing there. He immediately invites her in, offers food and drink, and only then asks who she is and where she comes from. Later he offers a guest-gift (1.310–313). (See "Morality, Hospitality, and the Gods.") This side of Telemachus' character allows Homer to present a third theme: *hospitality*. As with the other themes, there are two sides to hospitality: *either you are a good host (or guest) or a bad one*. By his very first actions, Telemachus immediately proves to be the perfect host. By contrast, the suitors demonstrate that they are the worst of all possible guests: they never leave! Homer emphasizes the code of hospitality, which, as we shall see, serves as a touchstone by which we may judge the moral worth of almost every figure in the epic.

Third, we learn that Telemachus has not yet grown up—he's on the threshold of adulthood, but he hasn't crossed into maturity yet. Athena says this explicitly: "You can't keep clinging to boyhood, since you're not a kid anymore!" (1.296–297) Athena's job is to help Telemachus get his act together. She starts issuing orders: drive out the suitors, marry off Penelope if that's what she wants, and get a ship and find out what's happened to your father.

The effect is immediate. Telemachus starts to mature right before our eyes, as he rebukes his mother (a bit harshly perhaps) and orders the suitors out. Homer indicates the change in Telemachus not only by what he says, but also by the reactions of his mother and the suitors, who clearly have never seen Telemachus stand up for himself before. When Penelope complains about Phemius' song and requests a different subject, Telemachus insists he is in charge.

> "But you, go to the women's quarters and see to your tasks,
> the loom and spindle, and command your attendants
> to do their work. Discussion will be the concern
> of all the men, and especially of me, for the control of the house is mine!"
> She went back in the house, amazed at Telemachus. (1.356–360)

In fact, what we have here is a second plot of the *Odyssey*: "The Maturation of Telemachus," to which Homer devotes the first four books. The main plot, "The Return of Odysseus," really begins in book 5. It's not until book 16—two-thirds of the way through the epic—that Homer unites father and son, moving from a divided plot to a single story line.

Athena is a fascinating character. Her arrival in Ithaca offers another instance of the identity theme: she disguises herself and refrains from revealing her identity to Telemachus. But she also plays the role of what I like to call the *surrogate*, in this case, a surrogate father. On this point, Homer is quite explicit. Telemachus has never known his father—he's about twenty and Odysseus left when he was an infant. When Athena lays out plans for his future, Telemachus says,

> "Stranger, you have offered excellent advice to me,
> like a father to a son." (1.307–308)

(Notice that she also puts her spear in Odysseus' spear rack, thus filling the place of the absent father—1.127–129.)

The *Odyssey* is a work of fiction, yet it often reveals profound insights into real-life problems. In this case, the problem is one that is much discussed today: the importance of an adult male role model for developing boys. In the epic Telemachus finally meets an older "father-figure" who doesn't pamper him but tells him to grow up. We will meet other surrogates shortly, especially the surrogate wives of Odysseus.

Allow me to examine one other great exchange, which concerns the identity theme—this time with respect to Telemachus. Athena remarks upon the similarity between Telemachus and Odysseus—he's got his father's eyes—and asks him "if you are truly the son of Odysseus himself" (1.207). In part this raises the question of whether Telemachus will prove himself worthy of his remarkable father, but another aspect of this question is crucial to the entire epic. Telemachus' answer is revealing:

> "My mother says I am Odysseus' son, but I myself
> don't know, for no man really knows his father." (1.215–216)

This is a very delicate way of introducing the whole issue of Penelope's fidelity to her husband. If she is faithful (both before and after Odysseus leaves), then Telemachus indeed is Odysseus' son; if she has taken a lover—like Agamemnon's wife Clytemnestra—then all bets are off and Telemachus' paternity would remain in doubt. (All I would say at this point is, keep alert for clues concerning Penelope's fidelity.)

There are many fascinating figures in this first book. I promise to return to Penelope, the suitors, the singer Phemius, and the servant Eurycleia. Readers often worry that there will be too many characters to keep track of, but Homer is on *your* side. While there are dozens of suitors, he introduces only two early on by name: Antinous (four syllables: see Appendix 1) and the more subtle Eurymachus. Homer has no desire to overwhelm his audience with a phone book full of characters. By the end of this book, however, he has accomplished a great deal. The major family figures are established: husband, wife, and son. The dangers are clear: Calypso and Poseidon threaten Odysseus' homecoming, and the suitors are courting Penelope and making life miserable for Telemachus. The thematic connections of the epic have also been established: identity, homecoming, and hospitality. Let us now see how Homer builds upon this foundation.

BOOK TWO

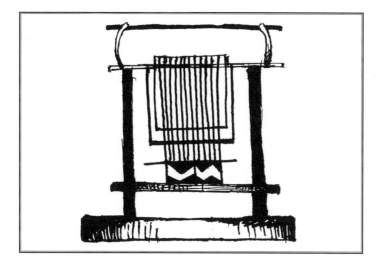

The central episode in book 2 is the assembly of the people of Ithaca called by Telemachus. Yet he fails to achieve his purpose: no one will help him drive the suitors out. It could be said that the events of book 2 do not advance the plot at all—in the end Telemachus still takes the trip Athena planned for him in book 1. Why has Homer included this scene? The poet teaches us at least three important aspects of the story: Telemachus continues his process of maturation; the people of Ithaca are shown to be intimidated by the suitors; and Homer reveals a fascinating side of Penelope. This book—like so many in the first half of the epic—has a retrospective feel: the characters are constantly looking back, and telling stories about what they remember. In fact, the ability to listen critically to other people's stories is another skill of great importance that Telemachus, among others, must learn—think of how Athena mixes truth and falsehood in her story in book 1!

Telemachus is the central figure in book 2. He now establishes himself publicly by calling an assembly, denouncing the suitors, and announcing plans for his journey. We also get a glimpse of his previous relationship with the suitors when Antinous says, "Come, eat and drink with me, as we did before" (2.305). Yet now Telemachus effectively makes his case and stands up to the suitors when challenged. Once again Athena helps the young man with encouragement (disguised as Mentor, an Ithacan—not Mentes—this time), arranging a boat and crew for the trip (disguised for a bit as Telemachus!—2.383–392), and even sending a favorable west wind once they're underway. In book 1, Telemachus sent his mother to her room and rebuked the suitors; here, in a more public space—outside the household—he proves himself as a capable public speaker, one of the many skills he apparently inherits from his father. Not only is Telemachus growing up right before our eyes; he is also beginning to answer Athena's question—are you really Odysseus' son?

We also encounter the townspeople of Ithaca for the first time. The most important thing we learn in book 2 is that, for all their fondness of Odysseus and sympathy for Telemachus, they will not intervene in the dispute between Odysseus' family and the suitors. As one of the leading suitors, Eurymachus, says,

> "I think that the sons of the Achaeans will not stop their courting—
> for all its pain—since we fear no one,
> not even Telemachus, though he may speak well." (2.198–200)

Mentor, an old family friend, gets angry at the crowd's silence, but the assembly breaks up without any action taken. These islanders were out of touch with what was going on in Odysseus' house and Homer plans to leave them that way until the final book of the epic.

While not much happens in book 2 to advance the plot, it is significant that various possibilities are eliminated. The suitors are clearly in the wrong regarding the code of hospitality. They are condemned by Athena who tells Telemachus:

> "Now then, ignore the reckless suitors' plots and schemes,
> for they are senseless and unjust.
> They know nothing of death and black fate
> which are close and in a single day will destroy them all." (2.281–284)

In the end it will be up to Odysseus and his family (and faithful servants)—and *not* the people of Ithaca—to seek justice from the suitors. (Another possibility is eliminated: Telemachus will not force Penelope to choose a husband or send her away—he fears public shame and retribution from the Furies, those spirits of vengeance—2.130–137.)

Third, we turn to a great favorite among Homer's listeners and readers—Penelope's trick with the loom. It is from the suitor Antinous (again Homer focuses our attention on the same two leaders, Antinous and Eurymachus) that we hear of Penelope's strategem. For more than three years Penelope had promised to marry one of the suitors, but only after she finished weaving a funeral shroud for her father-in-law, Laertes (whom we do not meet until book 24). Each day she sits at the loom weaving, but each night she secretly unweaves what she has woven during the day. This doesn't say much for the mental quickness of the suitors—you'd think they'd catch on sooner or later—but after an unfaithful servant informs them of the trick, the suitors catch Penelope in the act and insist that she resolve upon picking a new husband.

From Antinous' account, we discover that Penelope is as crafty as her famous husband, a good match for wily Odysseus. When discussing heroism in ancient

Greece it is easy to focus on the brave deeds in battle, facing the Cyclops, sailing through the storms of Poseidon—but this is an almost exclusively male heroism. Penelope offers us a glimpse of how a woman may use her wits to combat the enemies at—and inside—her door. In fact, when telling the story of her guile, Antinous attributes great fame to her:

> "Great is the glory she wins
> for herself." (2.125–126)

Penelope, too, can be heroic and live on in the songs of poets. When we first met Penelope in book 1, she was weeping, apparently helpless (much like Odysseus' first appearance in book 5). Yet she is not powerless. This second perspective informs us that, like her husband, Penelope is crafty and—like Odysseus—she may be capable of enduring great suffering (see Cohen and Winkler in "Further Reading.").

Homer introduces other nice features in book 2. Dogs—there are two who accompany their master Telemachus to the assembly—take on greater significance later in the epic. Dogs are faithful and in this work come to symbolize a true homecoming. The poet also includes a dramatic omen. When Telemachus calls upon the gods—Zeus in particular—to visit punishment upon the suitors, Zeus responds by sending an especially violent bird omen: twin eagles tearing at each other just above the crowd. This triggers a recollection by the seer Halitherses, who made a prediction when Odysseus left for Troy:

> "I said that he would suffer many evils, lose all his companions,
> and, in the twentieth year, unknown to all,
> return home. And now all this is coming to pass." (2.174–176)

I hope this doesn't sound too much like a horoscope: "No one appreciates you. Change in residence, marital status possible." Yet this omen is rejected by the suitors. As Eurymachus says,

> "Many birds fly under the rays of the sun,
> but not all of them are portents." (2.181–182)

This is merely one instance of foreshadowing used to punctuate the stages of Odysseus' return.

Still the result of the events in book 2 is the unfolding of Telemachus' "Excellent Adventure." His first independent ocean voyage is aided not only by Athena, but also by the servant Eurycleia. Telemachus succeeds in becoming his own man, in part by breaking away from Penelope—he makes Eurycleia swear she won't tell Penelope of his journey for a dozen days (2.373–376). This servant's fidelity is noteworthy, for it is clear that Odysseus cannot expect help from the townspeople of Ithaca. The next question is: Whom can Odysseus trust in his own home? As we depart from the scene in Ithaca with Telemachus, we know of one disloyal servant who has betrayed Penelope's weaving trick, yet this is balanced by the devotion of Telemachus' confidante Eurycleia.

BOOK THREE

In book 3 Telemachus continues to grow up, as he arrives in Pylos, meets Nestor, hears several stories, gains a companion, and continues on to Sparta by horse and chariot. We learn a bit more about Odysseus and his role in the Trojan War, but in fact Nestor's knowledge is limited.

The events and characters in book three are significant with regard to the major themes of the epic. Nestor proves himself to be a good host (Telemachus plays the respectful guest). Nestor has achieved what Odysseus has not—a homecoming—and thus we may contrast his success with Odysseus' ongoing toils. What is most striking in Pylos, however, is that we find a household obviously in fine order, sharply contrasting with Ithaca—there are no unwanted guests lounging around, ordering pizza, and charging it to Nestor's account. Telemachus is given a glimpse of how a household—and a kingdom—should be run. While Nestor might not be a father figure, he does present himself to Telemachus as a ruler in control of his own affairs.

Book 3 may be divided into three sections: Arrival, Sacrifice, and Feast; the Stories of Nestor; and Sacrifice and Telemachus' Journey to Sparta.

ARRIVAL, SACRIFICE, AND FEAST (3.1–3.101)

When Telemachus arrives, Nestor and his people are making a sacrifice. Telemachus is initially hesitant toward approaching Nestor, but Athena instructs him well:

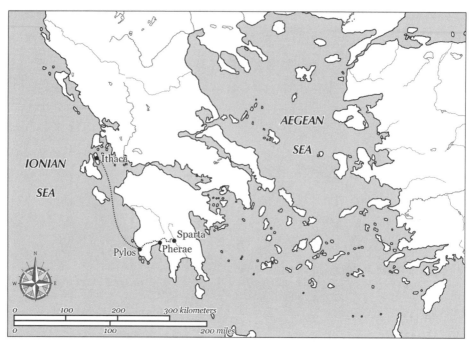

Map 3. *Telemachus' Journeys.* Telemachus' sea voyage to Pylos and the land journey to Sparta was familiar terrain to Homer's audience. By permission of the Ancient World Mapping Center.

> "Go right up now to horse-taming Nestor.
> We will learn the knowledge he hides in his heart.
> Beseech him yourself to speak truthfully.
> He won't lie, for he is too wise." (3.17–20)

It is significant that Nestor's sacrifice honors Poseidon, god of the sea; at the end of book 3, the people of Pylos sacrifice to Athena. Nestor is certainly reverent to all the gods, yet Homer highlights the two most significant gods in this epic: Poseidon, Odysseus' divine antagonist, and Athena, who aids both father and son.

It would be wrong to think of Poseidon as an enemy. The sea is Poseidon's realm and anyone venturing there needs to acknowledge his great power. Only by seeking his favor do travelers have a chance for successful voyages. After the sack of Troy, Nestor describes his return journey:

> "We offered many thighs of bulls
> to Poseidon, as we crossed the great sea." (3.178–179)

Evidently, Nestor makes it home by gaining Poseidon's indulgence with repeated sacrifice. As we shall see, there will never be closure in the *Odyssey*—or peace in Odysseus' life—until Odysseus can somehow propitiate the powerful god of the sea.

Nestor and his son, Pisistratus, prove themselves to be good hosts: they welcome the travelers to the sacrifice and feast; only after the meal do they ask the identity of Telemachus. (Hospitality also includes spending the night and evidently having the host's daughter bathe his guest—see 3.464–468.) In fact, Nestor states one rule of the good host:

"Now it is better to investigate and ask
our guests who they are, after they've enjoyed their meal." (3.69–70)

Nestor even wonders whether they might be pirates. There is nothing clever in Telemachus's reply: he is from Ithaca, the son of Odysseus. It is at this point that Nestor launches into several stories, as once again these early books look to the past.

Before examining Nestor's stories, it should be noted that by being proper hosts, Nestor and his family establish themselves as benevolent characters—they have passed the test of moral worth—and Telemachus should be able to trust them. In book 2 Athena condemned the suitors (which surely influences our judgment); here, when Pisistratus offers a cup to Athena (as the elder guest), Athena approves:

Athena was delighted with the discreet, judicious man,
for he gave her the golden cup first. (3.52–53; see also 3.352–358)

In the *Iliad*, there are no good guys and bad guys—the pains of the world touch everyone. The *Odyssey*, by contrast, demonstrates that much of human suffering results from wrongful action that could have been avoided—think of Aegisthus and the suitors (Odysseus' men also fit this category). Such ignoble action sharply contrasts with the activities on Pylos. These are the good guys in white hats.

NESTOR'S STORIES (3.102–3.403)

In telling Telemachus what he knows about Odysseus, Nestor plays the role of storyteller—again we recognize the prevalence of stories and storytellers in the *Odyssey*, though none is so brilliant as Odysseus. Some tales come in response to Telemachus' requests, revealing the dynamic relationship between storyteller (and singer) and the audience—a singer must always be ready to suit his song to the audience's interests.

We may view Nestor's recollections of Odysseus as one more "installment" of the public report concerning Odysseus, offered by various figures in the first four books. The stories are complementary: each supplements gaps found in previous or later accounts. But they are only secondhand, hearsay evidence. From Telemachus' perspective (and ours), hearing about Odysseus is not the same as meeting him in the flesh. In fact, Odysseus' reputation as constructed in books 1–4 does not prepare us for his first appearance in book 5.

Nestor is the grand old statesman of the Greeks—not so much as a fighter, but unsurpassed as a counselor to kings. When I call Nestor "old," I mean "*old!*" This is how Homer reverentially introduces Nestor in the *Iliad*:

> And then sweet-voiced Nestor stood up,
> clear-voice orator of the Pylians:
> his voice flowed from his tongue more sweetly than honey.
> During his life two generations of mortal men had died,
> those who were both born and bred in holy Pylos,
> and now he ruled among a third generation. (*Iliad* 1.247–252; see also *Odyssey*
>   3.245–246)

Nestor has ruled over three generations of men—a protracted reign!

In the *Odyssey*, Nestor recollects the sorrows of Troy, especially the loss of his son, Antilochus, who died in the war (Antilochus is a character in the *Iliad*). Here, too, the theme of homecoming is operating. For all his valor, Antilochus—like Achilles, Patroclus, and Ajax (3.109–110)—lies buried in Troy. These characters should be implicitly compared with Odysseus, who still lives.

Later Nestor names those who returned: Diomedes, Philoctetes, and Idomeneus, among others (3.180–192). When Telemachus despairs, Athena contrasts a nameless hero (who sounds an awful lot like Odysseus) with Agamemnon:

> "I would rather suffer many pains
> and then return to witness my day of homecoming,
> than to come back and die at the hearth, like Agamemnon,
> slain by the treachery of Aegisthus and his own wife." (3.232–235)

Odysseus certainly fits this profile. Once again we are asked to compare Homer's main character with heroes who achieve or fail to achieve a successful homecoming.

In praising Odysseus, Nestor emphasizes three qualities: Odysseus was preeminent among men in trickery, he was a good counselor (which apparently means that he never disagreed with Nestor—3.120–129), and he enjoyed the favor of the gods.

> "I never saw the gods so openly love anyone
> as Athena openly favored Odysseus." (3.221–222)

Nestor then focuses on the dissension among the Greeks after they sacked Troy. The brothers, Kings Agamemnon and Menelaus, couldn't agree whether to sacrifice to the gods or depart immediately. The Greek armada split up: Odysseus joined Agamemnon, while Nestor headed west to Pylos. Nestor can't tell us much more about Odysseus, because he hasn't seen him since leaving Troy.

Besides praising Odysseus, Nestor fills in considerably more detail in the "Agamemnon" story. We discover that Agamemnon's wife, Clytemnestra, at first resisted the advances of Aegisthus. In fact, she was entrusted to a singer, but Aegisthus maroons the unfortunate bard on a deserted island to die and then seduces Agamemnon's wife (3.263–272). After Agamemnon's murder, Aegisthus ruled for seven years. In the eighth year, Orestes returned and avenged his father's death (3.304–308).

Nestor draws several lessons from this story. He echoes Athena's exhortation in book 1: Telemachus should prove his bravery like Orestes (3.199–200). Nestor also advises that Telemachus not stay away from Ithaca for too long (3.313–316). Nevertheless, Nestor supports Athena's original plan: because Menelaus took so long to achieve his homecoming, he would be the best person to visit for news of Odysseus.

Nestor is a dutiful host and is reverent toward the gods. When Athena flies away as an osprey, Nestor recognizes the gods' favor toward Telemachus and promises a sacrifice to Athena, hoping to capitalize on the goddess' presence (3.380–384).

SACRIFICE AND TELEMACHUS' JOURNEY TO SPARTA (3.404–497)

On the morning of Telemachus' departure, Nestor sacrifices a heifer (a young cow) with gilded horns to Athena. Note the detail Homer delights in when describing a sacrifice:

A "Typical" Scene: Sacrifice to Athena (3.417–476)

• Heifer's horns are gilded

• Ax and basin are brought.

• Water and barley made ready.

• A prayer is offered.

• The victim's hair is burned in the fire.

• Nestor's son, Thrasymachus, cuts the heifer's neck muscles.

• The women, including Nestor's wife, Eurydice, cry out.

• The animal is slaughtered as its dark blood runs on the ground.

• They cut up the meat, wrapping it in fat.

• Nestor pours a libation (wine) into the ground.

• They cook the souvlaki (or shish ke-bab) for the meal.

This is what is known as a typical scene, typical in the sense that it follows a set pattern. Each time Homer describes a sacrifice, he will follow this pattern with minor variations (every detail is not always included). Such typical scenes, including sailing, bathing, prayer, sacrifice, and meal, and so on, are part of an oral poet's repertoire upon which he draws as the occasion rises. Typical scenes are a feature of the traditional style of epic and offer illuminating insights into everyday life.

Telemachus makes the journey to Sparta by land, accompanied by Nestor's son, Pisistratus. They stop overnight at Diocles' home in Pherae and reach Sparta the next day. I should mention that all of Telemachus' journeys are "on the map" in the minds of Homer's audience—these are real places known to many Greeks, unlike the fantastic locales Odysseus will describe.

In Pylos, Telemachus learns something about his father and begins to experience life outside Ithaca. Athena even hopes he will win a reputation for himself (3.76–78). Nestor's kingdom shows Telemachus what a well-run household looks like—the young man can only hope such order may soon be restored in Ithaca.

BOOK FOUR

In book 4 Telemachus reaches Sparta, home of King Menelaus, accompanied by Nestor's son, Pisistratus. In antiquity, Sparta was famous for its powerful army, but in Greek mythology, it is best known as the spot where Paris stole Helen. While she is often known as Helen of Troy, in fact, she is wife of King Menelaus (and Queen of Sparta). At this point, Helen and Menelaus have been reunited and Telemachus arrives at their daughter Hermione's wedding.

The purpose of Telemachus' journey is to learn of his father: indeed, both Helen and Menelaus recollect their experiences of Odysseus. While the book focuses on these stories, we shouldn't ignore the fact that Homer closes the book by switching scenes back to Ithaca where the suitors set up an ambush against Telemachus and Penelope learns that her son is gone. In book 5 Homer will turn his attention to Odysseus himself. The poet wishes to remind us of the situation in Ithaca, for the next time we return to Ithaca will be Odysseus' arrival home after twenty long years (in book 13).

Book 4 may be divided into five sections: Arrival, Hospitality, and Luxury; Helen's Recognition and Egyptian Drugs; Helen's and Menelaus' Short Stories; Menelaus' Egyptian Tale; and the Suitors' Plot and Penelope's Tears in Ithaca.

ARRIVAL, HOSPITALITY, AND LUXURY (4.1–120)

Telemachus arrives in Sparta at a double wedding. Menelaus and Helen had a single child, Hermione, "beautiful as Aphrodite" (4.14). In addition, we learn that

Menelaus had a son, Megapenthes, born to him by a slave. Whenever Helen (or her sister Clytemnestra) is around, it's hard for us not to think about marital infidelity. Here we learn nothing more than that Menelaus has an illegitimate son.

There's a slight hitch concerning hospitality in Sparta. One of the lords, Eteoneus, sees the two young men (Telemachus and Nestor's son, Pisistratus) and goes to Menelaus, asking:

> "Tell me, should we unhitch their swift horses for them
> or send them to someone else to host them?" (4.28–29)

Menelaus, however, reinforces the golden rule of hosts:

> "Just think of all the hospitality we enjoyed
> from other men before we made it here—Zeus save us
> from such misery hereafter! Quick, unhitch our guests' horses
> and bring them in to share our feast." (4.33–36)

The welcome goes smoothly—Menelaus knows how to be a good host. The travelers are bathed; then food and drink are offered before any questions are raised about their identity.

In contrast to Ithaca, Sparta—like Pylos—is a well-run kingdom. But Menelaus' kingdom is almost dripping with wealth and luxury. Telemachus and Pisistratus wash with a golden pitcher and silver basin (4.52–54). At the wedding there is a singer—and two tumblers (4.17–19). Later Helen's three servants bring in her chair, coverlet, and basket; we hear of Menelaus' gifts from Egypt: two silver baths, two tripods, and ten talents of gold (4.123–129)!

Clearly Ithaca is in a different league. The young men marvel at the splendor of Menelaus' palace, imagining that Zeus' place on Olympus must be like this (4.74–75). Ithaca and Pylos must fall far short by comparison. Menelaus disputes the comparison—at least with the gods.

> "Dear boys, no mortal man could rival Zeus
> for his home and possessions are everlasting.
> But few men, if any, could rival me in possessions." (4.78–81)

To be sure, these riches have cost Menelaus much suffering and this leads him to ponder his exotic travels—to Cyprus, Phoenicia, and Egypt—and the many men who died in Troy. In the course of this lament, Menelaus singles out one warrior:

> "For all those comrades, pained as I am,
> I don't grieve as much as for one man who makes sleep and food hateful,
> as I pore over his memory, since no one of the Achaeans labored as hard
> as Odysseus labored or achieved so much. Yet there was to be
> suffering for him—and for me, unrelenting grief felt
> for him. He's long gone now—we don't know
> whether he lives or is dead." (4.104–110)

Menelaus' quick picture stresses Odysseus' self-sacrifice, hard work, and success. Yet it appears that Menelaus will be unable to answer the crucial question for Telemachus, for he has no idea what's happened to Odysseus.

HELEN'S RECOGNITION AND EGYPTIAN DRUGS (4.121–232)

As Telemachus weeps for his father and hides his eyes in his robe, Helen makes her entrance. Here she is compared to Artemis, a virgin goddess—a somewhat surprising comparison given her past. Nevertheless, Helen is one of those people who command everyone's attention. Immediately she asks whether this visitor could be Telemachus (4.140–146). Menelaus concurs:

"As you say, wife, I see the likeness now too,
for Odysseus' feet were like the boy's, his hands,
the cast of his eyes, his head, and the hair on top." (4.148–150)

In addition to the hospitality theme (which puts Menelaus in a good light), the identity theme recurs. Athena first raised the question in book 1, which has important implications about Penelope's fidelity: Is this truly Odysseus' son? Helen's and Menelaus' reactions confirm Telemachus' lineage.

Also of great interest is that Helen proves herself adept at recognition. Just looking at Telemachus is enough for her to guess his identity. A skill often needed by characters in this epic is figuring out when to reveal oneself and when to withhold that information. Yet here's a clear risk: someone may guess who you are before you choose to make your identity known. There's no danger for Telemachus in this case, but Odysseus' success in many situations will depend upon his concealing his identity—and thwarting the suspicions of others.

As soon as everyone, including Pisistratus, is introduced, they all weep: Telemachus, Menelaus, and Pisistatus, who remembers his lost brother, Antilochus, slain in battle at Troy (4.187–189). Pisistratus, Telemachus' road buddy, is certainly a minor character, but the suffering they experience for a missing father and a dead brother forms a bond between them.

At their meal, Helen drugs their wine with something acquired in Egypt, capable of removing pain and anger.

Whoever drank it deeply, mixed in wine,
could not cast a tear down his cheeks that day,
not even if his mother or his father should die,
not even if right before his eyes some enemy slew
with sharp bronze a brother or darling son. (4.222–226)

This is impressive, to be sure, and quells everyone's tears. It also gives Helen an exotic, magical quality. But once more it seems to be almost excessive—shouldn't we weep when our parents, children, or siblings die? Weeping in the *Odyssey* demonstrates suffering to be sure, but it is also a mark of Odysseus' humanity—and ours (notice that Telemachus still grieves—4.291–293). Just as Menelaus has almost superhuman wealth, life in Sparta seems to approach a godlike existence (more on this later).

HELEN'S AND MENELAUS' SHORT STORIES (4.233–305)

Now that everyone is feeling good, Helen suggests "delighting in old stories." She tells of a time during the war when Odysseus disguised himself as a beggar—by scarring his own body and wearing rags—and made his way into Troy itself. In spite of Odysseus' skill in disguise, Helen brags that she alone was able to identify him (4.250–257). Ultimately, after she swore an oath, Odysseus told her the Greeks' strategy to take Troy. Helen was elated:

> "My spirit
> rejoiced, since my heart yearned to sail back
> home again! I regretted the madness which Aphrodite
> gave, when she led me there, away from my dear fatherland,
> abandoning my own child, my bridal bed, and my husband,
> who lacked for nothing—neither brains nor looks." (4.259–264)

In the *Poetics*, Aristotle praises Homer as a poet who speaks little in his own voice, and this is simply one instance. Indeed, Homer never condemns Helen when speaking in his own voice as the poet. Instead, in her own words, Helen describes what she did as madness, sent by Aphrodite. Earlier she called herself "shameless" (literally, "dog-faced"—4.145). Her regret is plain.

Homer has rejected the mythological variant that Paris abducted an unwilling victim. And he reveals his genius for depicting characters in a psychologically plausible manner. Ask yourself if you know any married couples who separate, one of them takes a lover, and whether years later there isn't often some regret. True, Helen is Zeus' daughter, but Homer is on the mark in portraying familiar human emotions in recognizable situations.

Menelaus then tells his story, praising Odysseus for his planning and intelligence. He gives a brief account of the wooden horse that led to Troy's fall. According to Menelaus, Helen went around imitating the voices of the wives of Greek heroes—Menelaus attributes this contradictory behavior to a "dark power which desired glory for Troy" (4.274–275). When Diomedes and Menelaus were about to emerge from the horse, Odysseus intervened to maintain their hiding place. One foolish warrior, Anticlus, is about to cry out and Odysseus muzzles him, thus preserving the ambush.

It's been long day, and Telemachus insists that it's time for bed. A royal guest room is made ready and the scene ends with Menelaus in bed with Helen, his wife, beside him.

MENELAUS' EGYPTIAN TALE (4.306–624)

The most important information comes the next morning in Menelaus' Egyptian tale, perhaps the most amazing story in the whole epic other than Odysseus' tales in books 9–12. Besides the specifics on Odysseus—he's stuck on Calypso's island—its relevance concerns the gods, homecoming, and the possibility of immortality.

After the war, Menelaus tells Telemachus, he got stuck in Egypt on the island of Pharos. (Note how Homer doesn't repeat what Nestor told Telemachus about the aftermath of the war—brothers quarreling, storms, and Menelaus' wanderings—again, the stories are complementary.) Menelaus is helped by Eidothea, the daughter of Proteus, the powerful old man of the sea. Menelaus needs to know which god blocks his return (sounds a lot like Odysseus, doesn't he?). Eidothea explains that he needs to catch Proteus while he's napping, and then hold on for the ride of his life. Proteus is "protean" in our sense of the word—our word comes from this mythological figure—he'll change into wild beasts, fire, and water, but if Menelaus holds on, all his questions will be answered.

Eidothea even plots Menelaus' ambush and provides disguises. She brings sealskins for Menelaus and his men to hide in, since each day Proteus comes ashore, counts his seals, and lies down for a nap. She even rubs ambrosia in each man's nose as protection against the seal stench.

Everything transpires as Eidothea predicted. They wait in their sealskins all morning; at noon Proteus comes out of the sea, counts his pod of seals, and lies down to rest. Menelaus and his men rush up like warriors and hold on, as the old man of the sea becomes a lion, serpent, panther, boar, rushing water, even a tree. Finally, Proteus surrenders and answers Menelaus' question: how can he reach home?

In situations like these, it's often a forgotten sacrifice—"oh, you forgot the gods!"—and this case is no exception. In fact, Zeus and the other gods demand this honor. Once he learns about his own way home, Menelaus asks a second question.

"Did all the Achaeans reach home in the ships unharmed,
whom Nestor and I left behind coming from Troy?
Or did any die a bitter death in his ship
or in the arms of loved ones, when they wound up the war?" (4.487–490)

Proteus first mentions Ajax, who taunted the gods and was destroyed by Poseidon. (This Ajax is not the big Ajax, son of Telamon, who committed suicide; this Ajax is an archer and son of Oileus.) Second is Agamemnon, who does make it home, but is murdered by Aegisthus, Clytemnestra's lover. We know this story, but again additional details are added. Aegisthus' spy, at his post for an entire year, spotted Agamemnon's ship and a trap was set. With the help of twenty hitmen, Aegisthus invites Agamemnon to feast.

> "Aegisthus led him to his destruction—Agamemnon suspected nothing—he
>   killed him as
> he dined, as someone slaughters an ox at the feeding trough." (4.534–535)

This is the first Menelaus has heard of his brother's death. He kneels in the sand and weeps, as Proteus foretells Orestes' vengeance (4.543–547). In spite of his grief, Menelaus asks about the third man, and for the first time, Telemachus hears the truth about his father. Proteus tells Menelaus that Calypso keeps Odysseus on her island, captive and against his will (4.555–560).

From the poet's perspective, several goals are achieved. First, this is the last installment of the public report of Odysseus, begun in book 1. A full, complimentary portrait emerges of Odysseus as clever, loved by the gods (and some of his fellow Ithacans), wise in counsel, brave, capable of disguise and trickery, and so on. This gifted individual, our hero Odysseus, will be barely recognizable when we first meet him in book 5. Second, we are reminded of the importance of gaining the gods' favor—and the difficulties in returning home if a god opposes you. Menelaus needs to sacrifice for his voyage home; we have already learned of Poseidon's hostility toward Odysseus. Third, we continue the series of implied comparisons with Odysseus regarding the homecoming theme. Menelaus (who himself makes it, after much wandering) asks explicitly who else has failed to achieve a homecoming. In addition to those who died at Troy, there is Ajax, Agamemnon, and Odysseus—who still lives.

Before turning to the situation back in Ithaca, let's look at three other fascinating features. First, as Telemachus hears more about his father (and we as readers learn further details), the reliability of all such tales appears somewhat suspect. Many of the reports given are second- or thirdhand (Proteus' tales appear in a story-within-a-story), and not all the particulars agree. An entertaining or heart-rending tale may be true, but from Telemachus' perspective, how can he tell? He certainly enjoys Menelaus' story (4.597–598), but which story should he believe? As Mentes in book 1, Athena told one version; here, he hears something different—and it's thirdhand, at that! My point is that not only are there countless tales, but there's a lesson for us: we must be critical of everything we hear. Homer encourages us to empathize with Telemachus, as we listen along with him.

Second, Homer introduces the first of several lion similes describing Odysseus. When Telemachus first mentions the suitors, Menelaus denounces them as cowards and predicts that Odysseus will deal with them like a lion finding fawns bedded down in its den: it'll be a ghastly, bloody death (4.333–346). Odysseus is a multifaceted character: here, with Odysseus as wild animal, we anticipate a vengeful beast who slays intruders without remorse. Keep your eyes peeled for more lion similes describing Odysseus.

Third, the fascinating possibility of immortality arises, again with later implicit relevance to Odysseus himself. Proteus answers a question Menelaus didn't ask: what will his own future be?

> "But it is not decreed, god-nurtured Menelaus,
> for you to die and meet your fate in horse-nurturing Argos.

No, the immortal gods will send you to
the Elysian Field and the ends of the earth, where gold-haired
    Rhadamanthys waits,
where life is most easy for mortal men.
There's no snow, no big storms, or rain—ever—
but always the river Ocean sends up the breezes
of whistling Zephyrus which refresh mankind.
All this because you are Helen's husband and the son-in-law of Zeus." (4.561–569)

Death apparently does not await Menelaus. Instead he will go to the ends of the earth. (Ocean is a river that runs around the rim of a disk-shaped earth: think "earth-as-frisbee"!) This is the promise of paradise, the Elysian Fields, elsewhere in Greek myth called the Isles of the Blessed.

Why should we care? As always, we need to ask what Menelaus' future has to do with the main event: Odysseus or his family. We are about to learn in book 5 that Calypso has promised immortality to Odysseus—if he will stay with her as her husband. The principle of "characterization-by-comparison" insists that we contrast the godlike existence awaiting Menelaus, as son-in-law to Zeus, with the lot of Odysseus. Odysseus, too, has the option for immortality, yet he rejects it. Who wouldn't want to be a god? What could be better?

THE SUITORS' PLOT AND PENELOPE'S TEARS IN ITHACA (4.625–847)

After Homer brings us along on Telemachus' journey to Pylos and Sparta, we are returned to Ithaca. The scene switches several times between the suitors and Penelope. The suitors are lounging around hurling javelins, when someone comes up and innocently asks whether Telemachus has returned yet. The two leaders of the suitors, Antinous and Eurymachus, are nonplussed but finally seek details. Antinous makes immediate plans:

"Quick, get me a swift ship and twenty men—
I'll watch and ambush him as he returns
in the straits between Ithaca and rocky Same,
so that his voyage to find his father will end miserably!" (4.669–672)

This plot erases any doubt the reader may have about the morality of the suitors—they have declared themselves enemies of Telemachus and thus Odysseus' family.

Penelope has also been unaware of Telemachus' absence. When she learns that her only child has gone off, her knees get weak, her eyes brim with tears, and she laments her misery: not only is her husband gone, but now her son is away. With the suitors' plot, who knows what will happen to him?

The servant Eurycleia admits her role in helping Telemachus—but she swore an oath not to reveal that he was gone. On Eurycleia's advice, Penelope prays to Athena:

> "Hear me, daughter of aegis-bearing Zeus, Atrytone,
> if ever here in his halls, resourceful Odysseus
> burned the rich thighs of oxen or sheep in your honor,
> remember it now for my sake, and save my darling son.
> Defend him from these evil, overbearing suitors!"
> So speaking she cried out, and the goddess heard her prayer. (4.762–767)

This is a typical Homeric prayer. The suppliant (a) addresses the deity with uniquely distinguishing names, such as Atrytone; (b) then either reminds the divinity of past help (as here) or promises future sacrifices; and finally (c) makes a specific request. Homer almost always indicates the divine response. Here when it is said that "the goddess heard her prayer," this means not only that the request reached her, but that Athena would respond and grant the prayer.

In book 4 Homer offers his fullest portrait yet of Penelope—we didn't learn much about her in book 1. She recollects Odysseus as a fair king (4.687–693), a lion simile links her to Odysseus (4.791–793), but perhaps the most striking insight comes from her response to hearing about Telemachus' absence. She goes into the house, and is unable even to sit in a chair.

> Spirit-breaking woe overwhelmed her, nor could she bear
> to sit on a chair—there were many in the house—
> but she sat on the floor of the well-made room,
> weeping pitifully. The servant-women, young and old,
> all whimpered around her. (4.716–720)

Penelope laments the pain Zeus has given her: a lost husband and a son in great danger. Homer presents Penelope as a pathetic figure—pathetic in its original Greek sense of "suffering," but also inducing shared suffering (*pathos*) in us. It's a hard-hearted reader who fails to sympathize with Penelope.

Yet Athena continues to watch over Odysseus' family in his absence. She sends a phantom of Penelope's sister, Iphthime, to the sleeping Penelope who promises that her son will return, for he is escorted by Pallas Athena (4.825–829). Yet when Penelope asks about her husband, the phantom insists that she can reveal nothing more.

The mood is ominous. Penelope is still desperate though the gods are assisting her. In spite of Penelope's prayer, the suitors present a real danger to Telemachus. We now have to ask whether he will achieve his homecoming. Indeed, Odysseus himself must face the suitors who have now declared themselves to be his enemies. The final lines of book 4 remind us that the suitors lie waiting in ambush.

BOOK FIVE

There are three episodes in book 5. The gods hold an assembly; Odysseus takes his leave of Calypso after many years; then while sailing the seas, Odysseus encounters the wrath of Poseidon, but finally makes it to shore. This near-death experience at sea offers a second chance—a rebirth that allows Odysseus to start over again as he reenters the world from which he had vanished.

We finally encounter Odysseus—in person—in book 5. Homer presents a character who has suffered greatly and—like Penelope—has almost given up hope. In the first four books, various people offered recollections about Odysseus. We heard of a hard-working, dedicated soldier with many tricks up his sleeve. In books 5–12 Homer presents a different sort of portrait of Odysseus, who proves himself to be a sort of jack-of-all-trades, a man with many skills: he can build a ship, swim, be an effective orator, hurl a discus, and sing spell-binding songs.

ASSEMBLY OF THE GODS (5.1–43)

It may seem odd that the gods must call a second assembly, and that Athena must remind Zeus a second time that Odysseus is still kept captive on Calypso's island. Once again Zeus grants permission to help Odysseus return home; yet it is only now that Zeus actually sends Hermes to Calypso's island to inform her of the will of the gods: release Odysseus now. All this had been decided in the very first scene of the epic when Athena said:

> "Let us then dispatch the guide and giant-killer Hermes
> to the island, Ogygia, to announce at once
> to the nymph with lovely braids our fixed decree:
> the homecoming of stout-hearted Odysseus, so that he may return!" (1.84–87)

In book 1, Zeus ratified Athena's double plan: she would go to Ithaca to mentor Telemachus and Hermes would instruct Calypso to allow Odysseus' departure. The first half of this plan was presented in books 1–4, but now Homer needs to kick-start the second half. His solution is to replay the assembly, at least the part where Zeus approves of Athena's words and then actually sends off Hermes.

The best explanation for the repetition in book 5 is that this is Homer's way of showing simultaneous action. He requires that a "second" assembly be called for Hermes' trip to Ogygia, Calypso's island. Notice the emphasis: Odysseus will return; it is his destiny to see his loved ones; he will pay back the suitors (5.23–42). From our point of view, these two activities (Telemachus' journey and Odysseus' release) may be viewed as happening at the same time. This is hardly a failure by Homer—his narrative is extremely sophisticated—yet while any epic poem moves forward with its narration, in a sense Homer has backed up in book 5, turning now to those events that concern Odysseus.

ODYSSEUS LEAVES CALYPSO'S ISLAND (5.44–268)

Hermes flies to Calypso's island, which is near the ends of the earth. She has a mysterious, magical home. Homer describes her singing, the fragrance of cedar, owls in attendance, four bubbling springs, lush meadows. Even the god Hermes marvels at this delightful spot (5.59–76). Calypso remarks that Hermes' visits are all too rare ("When was the last time you came to the ends of the earth?"), but Hermes gets right down to business. He tells her that Zeus commands her to send back Odysseus to his home in Ithaca.

The Amazing Greek Language

The name "Calypso" comes from a Greek verb, *kalypto*, which means "to hide," which is precisely what this goddess has done with Odysseus—he's been hidden away. The verb *kalypto* also gives us the word "apocalypse," which means to "un-hide" or "reveal what was hidden." The subject of the final book of the New Testament, Apocalypse (or in Latin, Revelation), reveals (or un-hides) the future of the world.

At first, Calypso argues with the god's decree. After all, she saved Odysseus and offered to make him immortal. This is her side of the story:

> "Then all the rest of his loyal shipmates died,
> but the wind and current drove him on, bearing him here.
> And I welcomed and nourished him, even vowed
> to make him immortal and ageless, all his days." (5.133–136)

Yet Calypso recognizes the futility of opposing Zeus' command and goes to find Odysseus. Our first encounter with Odysseus tells us a great deal. He is gazing out to sea—indeed, this is his dilemma. The sea, or at least the sea god Poseidon, is his enemy. Yet it is only by crossing the sea that he will ever make it home.

> Calypso found him sitting on the headland. His eyes were never
> dry from tears, his sweet life was flowing away
> as he lamented his homecoming, since the nymph no longer pleased him.
> (5.151–153)

This is hardly the hero we have been hearing so much about. Odysseus is truly wretched, weeping and hopeless. Even when Calypso passes along the news, he suspects treachery and won't believe her until she swears a great oath that she's not plotting some new trick against him (5.173–179).

Finally convinced that Calypso will let him go, Odyssseus has a meal with the goddess. Although we have heard that he has been making love to the goddess as an unwilling partner, they spend a night of love together (5.226–227). Then he gets down to the business of building a boat.

Several observations are worth making at this point. First, Odysseus demonstrates his skill: he can build (and later sail) a boat. This requires cutting down trees, boring planks, constructing decks, fashioning a mast, and setting up the sails. This is basically a one-man operation and Odysseus finishes it in four days. The boat appears to be somewhat box-like and roughly constructed, though it's more than a raft (as it's sometimes translated). Be on the lookout for Odysseus' other remarkable skills, especially in books 5–8.

Second, in the fascinating exchange between Odysseus and Calypso at dinner, we return to several major themes: surrogates, immortality, fidelity, and hospitality. First, there is an explicit comparison between the goddess Calypso and Odysseus' wife, Penelope. When Calypso claims to be Penelope's equal in beauty and figure, Odysseus admits that in many ways it's no contest:

> "Mistress goddess, don't be angry at me for this. I know very well
> that wise Penelope falls far short of you in appearance,
> with respect to beauty and stature.
> For she is mortal and you are immortal and ageless.
> Nevertheless I wish and desire all my days
> to travel home and see my homecoming day." (5.215–220)

There is simply no possibility that Odysseus' mortal wife Penelope could be as beautiful as any goddess. And yet Odysseus—when faced with these two options—chooses to return to his wife. As we shall see, Calypso is the first in a series of what we might call "surrogate wives," women who in one way or another try to take the place of Penelope. In this case Calypso has attempted to usurp the role of Odysseus' wife. (Earlier we saw Athena play the surrogate father to Telemachus—again explicitly noted by Telemachus—"you have spoken to me the way a father speaks to his son.")

But there's more. Not only is Calypso a goddess; she offers Odysseus the possibility of immortality, if he will stay with her. In book 4, Menelaus heard that he and Helen would go to the Elysian Field, to paradise, as Zeus' son-in-law and daughter. That sounded kind of fantastic, but here Odysseus is offered a similar chance. As we shall see, Odysseus rejects this offer with full knowledge of what this decision entails.

On the other side, Odysseus' insistence upon returning to Penelope and his home in Ithaca must be balanced by questionable fidelity on Odysseus' part. He does reject staying with Calypso forever, but no one can deny that Odysseus sleeps with her—sometimes as a willing partner. The whole question of marital fidelity is central to the epic: Will Penelope remain faithful to Odysseus or will she prove to be treacherous like Clytemnestra? (And is Telemachus actually his son?)

The explanation offered here may not satisfy many modern readers, but the fact is that there's a double standard in ancient Greece (and throughout much of human history). Men, like Odysseus, may still be loyal to their wives (Odysseus chooses to go home, after all), and yet these men sleep with goddesses without the stigma that a woman would suffer. In patriarchal societies—where property and kingship are passed down to sons from their fathers—men insist that their wives remain utterly faithful. Rulers don't want to pass on their inheritance to some other guy's son. This isn't a fair world and in fact Calypso attacks the double standard at the divine level. There's no problem if a male god sleeps with a mortal woman (check out Zeus' list at *Iliad* 14.315–328); it is only, Calypso claims, when goddesses sleep with men that everyone gets upset (5.118–129). Nevertheless, Odysseus is granted an indulgence in Homer's epic while Penelope, in order to be praised and prove herself worthy, must be true to Odysseus.

One defining feature of Odysseus is his suffering—and this is no ordinary suffering. When first seen, Odysseus is weeping; later when Calypso warns him of future trouble if he leaves, Odysseus replies:

"And if a god will smite me again on the wine-faced sea,
I will endure that too, with a sorrow-bearing spirit in my chest.
For already I have suffered much and labored hard
in the waves and in war. Let this be added to the total!" (5.221–224)

Like Penelope, Odysseus has undergone almost unendurable pain, but he is not yet broken.

Finally, what may be an obvious point. With respect to the theme of hospitality, Calypso plays a fine host to Hermes, offering him nectar and ambrosia, the drink and food of the gods. But she has refused till now to let go of Odysseus, who washed up on her shore. I insisted above that hospitality is the touchstone of someone's character: the suitors are terrible guests, the Cyclops as a host eats his guests—these are clear signs of violating the code of hospitality. Still Calypso is not particularly evil. She has helped Odysseus; in a sense, she's saved his life. She offers him love and the gift of immortality, and in the end—when the gods insist—she helps him on his way, bathing him, and giving him fine clothes, wine, water, and food. Nevertheless, for seven years she has been a hostess who has forcibly kept her guest from leaving. Judging Calypso's role as hostess then is more complicated than it was with previous characters.

The Amazing Greek Language

The drink and food of the gods, nectar and ambrosia, are served to Hermes; later Calypso helps herself, while offering Odysseus "food which mortals eat" (6.197). Interestingly both words, nectar and ambrosia, derive from the idea of immortality. "Ambrosia" comes from *a*- ("not") plus *brotos* ("mortal")—immortality itself. (*Brotos*—believe it or not—is related to an even earlier root, *mrotos*—which gives us the word *mortal*, or "subject to death.") The origins of "nectar" are subject to more speculation, but it may mean *nec*- ("death") plus *tar* ("overcome"), or "overcoming death." Thus nectar and ambrosia are appropriate for the gods' consumption (also they don't have blood running through their veins—it's *ichor*). Homer never explicitly says this, but Calypso may have been offering nectar and ambrosia to Odysseus as part of her promise of immortality, much as Adam and Eve had access to the Tree of (Everlasting?) Life in the Garden of Eden. Once they were expelled from the Garden, they became mere mortals, subject to death.

ODYSSEUS' OCEAN VOYAGE (5.269–493)

Odysseus sails for eighteen days, never sleeping, watching the stars (including the Bear, our Big Dipper). Just as land appears, Poseidon spots Odysseus and sends a terrible storm: clouds clash, waves churn, and hurricane-force winds blow.

Mythological Geography

Calypso is a daughter of Atlas, the Titan who holds the vault of the sky up off the earth. If we were to locate Atlas' spot on a map, it would be at the western end of the Mediterranean, at the so-called "Pillars of Heracles," or—to us—the Straits of Gibraltar between Spain and Morocco. To the Greeks of Homer's day, this was at the far end of the known world. Calypso's island is presumably nearby. Hermes comments that no city of men lies near (5.101) and later we discover that Odysseus must sail eastward (that is, from the westward end of the Mediterranean) for eighteen days to reach the Phaeacians' island, all the while keeping the Bear (our Big Dipper in the north) on his left hand (5.271–281).

Odysseus foresees his own death (5.304–305) and envies the warriors who died at Troy (5.306–309; Vergil adapts Odysseus' words as Aeneas' first speech in the *Aeneid* 1.94–101). A lot of action ensues. Lightning splits the boat; the clothing Calypso gave Odysseus holds him underwater. Like Menelaus, Odysseus is saved by a sea nymph, Leucothea (called Ino when she was mortal), who tries to offer this advice.

> "Strip off these clothes and leave your craft
> for the winds to hurl, and swimming with your arms, strive for your arrival
> on the land of the Phaeacians, where it is your destiny to escape.
> Here, tie this immortal scarf around your chest—
> have no fear of suffering or death.
> But when you touch land with your hands,
> untie it and throw it back into the wine-faced sea,
> far from shore, but you—turn your head away!" (5.343–350)

Leucothea is only trying to help, but Odysseus is at first undecided.

There are numerous interventions by the gods in this book. The hostile Poseidon sends the storm that breaks up Odysseus' boat. On the other side are Leucothea, Athena, and the river god who help Odysseus to safety. Yet we shouldn't view Odysseus' ups and downs wholly as the consequences of a divine chess match. Homer demonstrates Odysseus' autonomy and the importance of his decisions, most prominently with monologues. In this case, Odysseus fears a divine trap (he's still suspicious) and holds onto the damaged boat. When Poseidon demolishes it, Odysseus is left with no choice. He strips off the clothing, ties the scarf around his chest, and swims for it. Later he must decide how to approach the island (5.408–423) and where to spend his first night on shore (5.465–473). Odysseus is no puppet. He needs the advice and favor of the gods if he's to return to Ithaca—without it, he'd still be with Calypso—but Homer makes it clear that Odysseus contemplates his options and makes independent decisions.

This is an exceptionally vivid book. Homer's descriptions are enhanced by a handful of similes. Odysseus' boat is driven like thistle blown by an autumn wind (5.327–332); the boat's planks are scattered like chaff (5.366–370). After Odysseus has floated for two days, he spies land. Homer introduces a "family" simile to evoke Odysseus' joy.

> As when a father's life joyfully appears to his children,
> a father who suffered powerful pains and lay in sickness,
> wasting away for a long time; a hostile spirit hurt him,
> and the gods now released him from suffering;
> so did land and woods appear joyfully to Odysseus. (5.394–398)

Later Odysseus tries to approach the island. He grabs onto a reef but is in danger of being smashed under a wave. Here a simile compares the chunks of skin torn from his hands to the pebbles caught in an octopus' suckers when it's pulled from its lair (5.430–435). Each simile adds a new dimension to our appreciation of Odysseus' predicament. He has suffered like a stricken father (given up for dead?); and he's tenacious like an octopus torn from its lair.

At last, Odysseus finds a river outlet. He prays to the river god to halt the outward-flowing current and the god complies. Odysseus swims in, crawls onto shore, and collapses. Upon reviving, he unties the scarf, throws it into the sea, and kisses the earth. Faced with a tough choice about where to spend the night,

Odysseus decided to climb a tree to avoid wild animals (Robinson Crusoe does the very same thing when he is first shipwrecked).

It is hard not to view what's happened to Odysseus as a symbolic rebirth. He must remove his clothes and swim for his life: he emerges from the sea naked, swollen with brine, and desperate. (Some have seen the river's current—in its narrow channel—as representative of labor pains!) Odysseus has been lost and now must start over. He can rely only on his skills, ingenuity, and toughness in order to survive and get home. This new beginning, however, poses its own threats. This scenario—a naked solitary man in an unknown land—not only allows Odysseus to withhold his own identity, as we shall see, but also enables the poet to explore new potential roles and relationships for Odysseus. He's not in Ithaca yet! (See Newton in "Further Reading.")

Odysseus covers himself up with leaves and Homer introduces a final simile, which contains a spark of hope—literally.

> As when someone buries a torch in black ash
> at a country hearth, to which no other neighbors go,
> saving the seed of fire, so that he wouldn't need to kindle it elsewhere,
> so Odysseus was hidden in the leaves. (5.488–491)

Odysseus' life is like that torch that could so easily go out—he's nearly lost it—yet from that "seed" of fire, he might "rekindle" his life.

BOOK SIX

In book 6, a young princess, Nausicaa, enters the epic. She goes to the beach merely to wash some clothes, yet proves instrumental for Odysseus' homecoming. This book contains one of the all-time great scenes in Homer: Odysseus emerges naked from the woods, with only a branch to cover him, seeking the help of this adolescent girl. Two wonderful similes contrast the veteran sailor and the innocent girl. Odysseus also demonstrates one more skill: he's very good at giving a speech. Most interesting of all in terms of the plot is Nausicaa's ambiguous role. At one level, she's the hostess who helps a desperate traveler. Yet she also plays the role of a surrogate wife who threatens to take the place of Penelope. In a variety of ways, Homer suggests the likelihood of marriage between shipwrecked stranger and young princess—it's practically a fairy tale! As we shall see, Homer offers no resolution for a considerable time before finally interrupting this potential romance and returning us to Odysseus' quest to regain his kingdom.

There are three scenes in book 6. The first two are quite short: Athena speaks to Nausicaa in a dream; then the princess visits her parents; the third scene occurs at the beach where Odysseus has come ashore.

NAUSICAA'S DREAM (6.1–47)

Athena intervenes again, this time by going to the house of King Alcinous (four syllables: see Appendix 1). In the guise of one of the princess' friends,

Athena appears to the king's daughter, Nausicaa, as she sleeps. Athena instructs Nausicaa to wash clothes first thing in the morning. The underlying point, however, is that marriage is on Nausicaa's mind.

> "Your fine clothes are lying here neglected,
> yet your marriage is near. You must wear the best,
> and provide elegant dress to those who escort you.
> That's how a woman gains a good name among the people
> and father and queenly mother rejoice.
> Yes, let's go wash at daybreak.
> And I'll go along as your companion, so you may
> get to work quickly, since you won't be a maiden for long.
> Already the noblest Phaeacians in the country—from the same stock as you—
> are courting you." (6.26–35)

Notice how Homer links a concrete item—dirty clothes—to the goal obsessing this young girl: her imminent marriage.

FATHER AND DAUGHTER (6.48–84)

Upon awakening, Nausicaa goes straight to her parents, asking for mules and a wagon to do the laundry. Although she refrains from mentioning her own wedding plans—she speaks only of her brothers—her father intuits what's on her mind (6.66–67). King Alcinous shows himself to be an indulgent father—remember, he has five sons and a single daughter. He promises to grant her every wish and orders the mule team for Nausicaa and her servant-women (they are actually slaves!). The servants load up the dirty clothes, a picnic lunch is packed, Nausicaa cracks the whip, and they're off.

THE BEACH (6.85–331)

Athena makes no immediate move: the details of her plan are never explicit. Arriving at the river near the beach, the young women do the laundry, bathe, and eat lunch while the clothes dry. So far, so good. At this point, they take off their veils and start to play ball. Now Athena intervenes by making one of them miss the ball. It lands in the water, they scream, and Odysseus wakes up.

Before we get to Odysseus' reaction, notice the remarkable simile Homer uses to describe Nausicaa and her companions as they play ball: the princess is compared to the goddess Artemis.

> White-armed Nausicaa led their play,
> like the archer Artemis striding down the mountains—
> either down towering Taygetus or Erymanthus—
> delighting in wild boar and swift deer.
> With her, nymphs—the daughters of aegis-bearing Zeus—
> played in the fields. And Leto rejoiced in her heart.
> She stood head and shoulders above the rest,

quite conspicuous, though all are lovely;
so the unwed maiden Nausicaa stood out prominently among her servants.
(6.101–109)

In the *Iliad*, Homer frequently compares his warriors to the Olympians gods: "Diomedes entered battle looking like Ares," for example. Here the poet likens Nausicaa to Artemis, a virgin goddess associated with the woods and hunting. In the scene within the simile, Artemis is surrounded by beautiful nymphs—just as Nausicaa is surrounded by her servant-women—yet Artemis stands out: she is taller than the rest, conspicuous among them. The highest compliment anyone could give to a mortal woman, of course, is that she looks like a goddess.

Homer and Vergil

Vergil's Roman epic the *Aeneid*, written 700 years after the *Odyssey*, alludes (indirectly refers) back to Homer in many ways. In the first book, Aeneas and his men are driven by a storm to north Africa on their way to Italy. When Dido, the Queen of Carthage, first appears, she is compared to Diana (the Roman equivalent of Artemis) with practically the same simile Homer uses here to describe Nausicaa (see *Aeneid* 1.496–504). Vergil wants us to recall the parallel scene in the Homeric epic, in particular, the potential for romance between hero and royal lady. (Aeneas' mother, Venus, cloaks him in a protective mist on his way to Carthage just as Athena does for Odysseus in the seventh book of the *Odyssey*.)

When Odysseus awakens, his first question concerns the inhabitants of the island. His thoughts reveal the vulnerability of shipwreck survivors:

"O, cursed me! Whose land have I come to now?
Are they violent, savage, and lawless,
or kind to travellers with a god-fearing heart?" (6.119–121)

Despite his uncertainty, Odysseus hopes he may finally have reached human society. He then makes his way out of the woods:

Godlike Odysseus crept out of the bushes,
and with his massive hand broke off a leafy branch
from the thick brush to shield his body's private parts. (6.127–129)

We recall that Odysseus has lost everything—even his clothes—in the shipwreck brought on by Poseidon.

Odysseus is naked and covered with sea scum, as he confronts the young women. When they see him, all the women scatter in panic, except Nausicaa who stands firm—Athena has planted courage in her heart. Homer has just provoked our anticipation of the coming encounter by comparing Odysseus with a hungry mountain lion charging after sheep, oxen, or deer (6.130–136). Yet why would Homer introduce a lion simile in this context? Is there a threat to Nausicaa and company? Should we cue the theme song from *Jaws*?

I should note that first, Odysseus has been (and will be) compared to a lion in other similes—here the point is that hunger and desperation are driving him. Second and more important to this particular situation, the lion simile has to be something of a joke. Normally, if a hero is said to be like a lion, he's about to enter battle and attack. Here, Odysseus isn't facing enemy troops—it's a bunch of unarmed women playing with a beachball. To that extent, the simile is ironically placed, designed to offer some comic relief to Homer's audience.

Odysseus now confronts the problem of what to say upon arrival in a strange place. He's not sure whether he should throw his arms around Nausicaa's knees—the ritual gesture of supplication—but wisely decides against it. Odysseus addresses her from a distance, beginning with the highest compliment, speculating that Nausicaa may be a goddess, perhaps Artemis.

> "I beseech you, princess—are you a goddess or a mortal?
> If you are one of the gods who rule broad heaven,
> I would liken you most to Artemis, the daughter of mighty Zeus,
> in beauty, build, and bearing." (6.149–152)

Odysseus certainly proves himself intelligent and shrewd. Here, he may be seen as cleverly flattering and manipulating an innocent maiden. Homer has already made it clear that Nausicaa has been fantasizing about marriage; Odysseus appears to intuit as much, when he pursues the possibility that Nausicaa is mortal and praises her husband-to-be.

> "That man is the one more blest than all other men alive,
> that man who showers you with gifts and leads you home, his bride!
> For I have never laid eyes on anyone like you,
> neither man nor woman. I look at you and a sense of wonder takes me."
>
> (6.158–161)

In another context these words could be seen as a subtle way of courting a potential bride.

Odysseus gives virtually no information about himself other than his twenty days at sea, yet Nausicaa offers to help. Odysseus insists on washing himself and—what luck!—there are plenty of clean clothes he can wear. Athene even makes him look a bit better: taller, more muscular, and that dynamite hair—like hyacinth flowers! Odysseus now makes a very different impression. Nausicaa describes him to her companions:

> "Now he seems like the gods who rule broad heaven.
> Ah, if only a man like that were called my husband,
> lived in this place, pleased to stay right here." (6.243–245)

Nausicaa's innocent wish not only indicates her increasing interest but also raises the stakes for what may happen between princess and this shipwrecked stranger.

Girls Just Want to Have Fun

As I mentioned earlier, there was a double standard in ancient Greece, with women having considerably less freedom than men. When aristocratic women leave the house or even enter a room filled with men, they are expected to wear a veil to cover hair and face, and should be accompanied by servant-women. This is especially true of young, unmarried women (the Greek word for such a young woman is *parthenos*; the temple in Athens, the Parthenon, is named for the virgin goddess Athena—much like naming the state Virginia for Queen Elizabeth). Thinking they are alone, Nausicaa and her companions take off their veils to play ball (6.100). Later Odysseus says he feels shame appearing naked before them (6.221–222). Once more as modern readers we are struck with how sharply men's freedom contrasts with the way women are protected—men competed at the Olympics naked, yet women were forbidden even to watch. Still, many of Homer's readers may be surprised when Nestor has his daughter give Telemachus a bath (3.464–468). Perhaps it's OK in that case because it takes place in Nestor's own home and Telemachus is an honored guest (Helen recalls bathing Odysseus in Troy—4.252–253).

Odysseus is given food and drink; Nausicaa then addresses him directly. She will lead him to town, but insists that they split up once they get near the town's harbor. Who knows what the gossipy sailors may say? Nausicaa vividly imagines an old salt mocking them:

> " 'Now who's this tall, handsome stranger with Nausicaa?
> Where did she find him? He will be her husband, to be sure! . . .
> Or he may be a god come down from heaven,
> an answer to all her prayers, to have her all his days.' " (6.276–277, 280–281)

In this ingenious manner, Nausicaa proves herself as skilled as Odysseus in offering compliments. Indirectly she describes Odysseus as handsome, her prospective husband—and possibly a god!

One way of understanding Odysseus' encounter with Nausicaa's is to think in terms of two mutually contradictory plots. From Odysseus' point of view, the poet suggests the plot of *female benefactor aids hero's return*, a story familiar from countless fairy tales. We can understand what Odysseus does as self-interested—he seeks help that will bring him closer to Ithaca. And in terms of her actions, Nausicaa lives up to the role of the perfect hostess. She welcomes Odysseus, offers food, drink, clothes, and will take him to town. She even rebukes her servants for running away.

> "All travelers and beggars are
> under the protection of Zeus!" (6.207–208)

And yet things are not so simple. From Nausicaa's point of view, the plot appears to be *princess marries handsome stranger* (we might think of other Greeks myths, such as Theseus arriving to kill the Minotaur in Crete where Ariadne falls in love with him; or Medea, who falls in love with Jason in quest of the golden fleece). Homer has evidently put into play both plots, suggesting two possible outcomes to his audience. The consequence of promoting both plots is dramatic suspense: we, as readers, must contemplate the possibility that Odysseus may stay with Nausicaa (see Felson-Rubin and Morrison in "Further Reading").

Of course, this would violate the epic tradition (Odysseus needs to return) and even earlier foreshadowing in the epic, for the gods have promised that Odysseus will see his family once again. Nevertheless, in this scene each character acts in such a way as to promote this possible romance and Odysseus refrains from revealing who he is—or even that he already has a wife and family. Odysseus could easily nip this in the bud. All he has to do is tell Nausicaa who he is or at least that he has a wife and son, yet Odysseus declines to do so. Once more the theme of identity proves of critical importance, yet the effect here is to suggest an alternative outcome to Odysseus' adventures. Odysseus will refrain from revealing who he is for an inordinately long time, until finally in book 9 he announces his identity. Until then Nausicaa—and soon her parents—envision this shipwrecked traveler as a potential groom.

BOOK SEVEN

In book 7 there are two scenes: first, Athena—in disguise—leads Odysseus to King Alcinous' palace; then Odysseus mysteriously appears at the knees of Queen Arete and seeks help from her and her husband, Alcinous.

Many questions are raised this book. Why does Athena remain in disguise when she speaks to Odysseus? What is their relationship? And where has she been for the past seven years? Regarding the Phaeacians, they are of great importance to Odysseus, for they're the ones who can take him home. But we wonder: Are they trustworthy hosts? Will they help him reach Ithaca? How strong is their desire for Odysseus to stay and marry Nausicaa? They seem to take their time in fulfilling their promise of escort to Odysseus. Also, why is it so important that Odysseus go to Arete rather than the king? If Alcinous is in charge, why must Odysseus gain the queen's favor? Part of this puzzle includes the recurring role of the surrogate (Nausicaa as potential "wife") as well as the theme of identity. Not only does Athena disguise herself, but Odysseus refrains from revealing who he is for an extraordinarily long time. Why?

ATHENA TAKES ODYSSEUS TO THE PALACE (7.1–132)

As Odysseus waits in the grove of Athena, Nausicaa continues on to the palace with those freshly washed clothes. Athena then surrounds Odysseus with a heavy mist so that no Phaeacian would see him on his way to the palace. The mist will protect Odysseus:

> So that no swaggering Phaeacian might encounter him
> with taunting words and ask who he was. (7.16–17)

Hospitality on Scheria is evidently not guaranteed. A few lines later, just as Odysseus is about to enter the town, Athena appears to him, looking like a young girl. Odysseus asks her to guide him to Alcinous' palace. Athena agrees yet warns him not to glance at anyone.

> "The men here do not tolerate strangers,
> nor do they greet kindly whoever comes from elsewhere." (7.32–33)

Odysseus' success in returning home depends upon the hospitality of the Phaeacians, yet this is no travelers' paradise. In book 6, Nausicaa already expressed concern about what the locals might say if they saw her with Odysseus; now both the narrator and Athene have mentioned potential conflicts with the local residents. This adds to the suspense as Odysseus makes his way to town.

The Sea People

The Phaeacians play an ambiguous role in this epic. They will take Odysseus home, and this makes perfect sense: they pride themselves on their seafaring skills. Indeed, many of them are named for the sea. Some incorporate the Greek word for ship (*naus*) or sailor (*nautes*), such as Nausicaa and her grandfather, Nausithous (literally, "swift ship"—an astronaut is literally a "star sailor"). In book 8, we are introduced to Phaeacians whose names could be translated in English as "Topship" (Acroneus), "Quicksea" (Ocyalus), "Oarsman" (Eretmeus), and "Broadsea" (Euryalus—8.110–117). Later we hear the king boast of their prowess in sailing, dancing, feasting, fresh clothes, warm baths, and beds (8.246–249). Yet there is an underlying atmosphere of menace. Regarding the code of hospitality, the Phaeacians receive at best a mixed report. Alcinous, as we shall see, is quite sensitive as a host. Yet Nausicaa and Athena both warn Odysseus of the lack of friendliness to outsiders on the part of at least some Phaeacians (this is also confirmed by the narrator: 6.273–288, 7.16–17, 7.30–33). Most troubling of all is the Phaeacians' connection with the god Poseidon, who is Odysseus' antagonist. Not only have the Phaeacians set up a shrine to Poseidon (6.266)—naturally they must rely on the favor of Poseidon for their success as a sea people—but the fact is that Alcinous is Poseidon's grandson and Arete is his great-granddaughter (7.56–66)! This is enough to unsettle Odysseus' confidence in his hosts. (The Phaeacians' island, Scheria, was identified in antiquity with Corcyra—modern Corfu—a Greek island in the Adriatic Sea off the northwest coast of Greece.)

There are three puzzles we need to ponder. First, Athena remains in disguise and never reveals herself as a goddess. We recollect that she concealed her identity from Telemachus in the early books; here with Odysseus, she never lets on that she is actually the goddess Athena. To put it bluntly, should Odysseus be counting on her? Remember Odysseus' prayer to her at the end of book 6:

"Hear my prayer now at least, for you didn't hear me before,
when I was shattered and the famous earth-shaker wrecked my craft." (6.325–326)

As readers, we know that Athena did help Odysseus, yet she seems loath to openly declare herself. Let's keep an eye on both Odysseus and Athena, who in many ways are alike, especially their inclination to conceal their identities.

Second, like Nausicaa, Athena specifically instructs Odysseus to go to the queen of the house, Arete, rather than King Alcinous.

"If she will take you to her heart,
then there's hope that you will see your loved ones and reach
your high-roofed house and your native land." (7.75–77)

The double standard in Greek society has already been made obvious: men get to go out of the house, while women generally remain within. It's King Odysseus, King Agamemnon, King Nestor—the men apparently rule. So why is *Queen* Arete so critical to answering Odysseus' prayers?

Third, we need to appreciate Homer's description of Alcinous' palace and estate. The palace gleams like the sun or moon: its walls and doors are covered with bronze, gold, silver, and lapis lazuli. Gold and silver "immortal" watchdogs guard the house—like some sumptuous Beverly Hills mansion! And, like California, the island's an agricultural miracle. Orchards of pear, apple, fig, and olive offer fruit all year round. Raisins are baking in the sun, gardens are thriving, springs are bubbling. Odysseus has seen the world, yet here he gazes in wonder at "the marvelous gifts of the gods in Alcinous' home" (7.132).

What's up with all that? I have a guess. Earlier, Odysseus had the chance to become an immortal god and live with Calypso on her island of paradise. As we have seen, one of the options for Odysseus here in Scheria is to stay on as husband of Nausicaa—her father, in fact, is about to suggest it. In the end, Odysseus will make his way to Ithaca, but when he does, it will be a deliberate choice. In each case he gives up something extremely enticing—living forever with Calypso in one instance, or life in la-la land in the other. Ithaca's more of a gritty, rock-strewn Maine village, and to say no to this golden-age land cannot be easy for Odysseus. Note what he says when he begins his story: nothing is sweeter than your homeland, "even if you live in a rich house far from home" (9.35–36). Once more characterization-by-comparison highlights the differences between Odysseus' home in Ithaca and—in this case—the enticing Eden of Scheria.

THE KING AND QUEEN MEET ODYSSEUS (7.132–347)

You'll have to admit, it's a great entrance. Odyssues comes into the palace unseen and flings his arms around Queen Arete's knees; at that moment Athena dispels the mist that has hidden him. Odysseus asks for help:

"Arete, daughter of godlike King Rhexenor!
After many trials I come to your husband and your knees
and all these feasters here. May the gods grant them fortune
all their lives, and may each hand down to his children
the riches in his house and the status the people have granted him.
But for myself, grant me a rapid escort to my native land,
since—long apart from my loved ones—I have suffered greatly!" (7.146–152)

An awkward silence follows. Finally, good old Echeneus insists that this is no way to treat a guest: Odysseus should be offered a chair, wine, and food. This rebuke jolts Alcinous into action and now at least Alcinous and his wife prove to be good hosts. Could they be just a bit rusty at entertaining out-of-towners?

After Odysseus washes and begins to eat, Alcinous announces that there'll be an assembly the next day in which the Phaeacians will figure out how to escort this stranger home. The king even speculates that Odysseus may be a god, but Odysseus insists that he is just a mortal man, who has had more than his share of toil and grief. Odysseus even requests peace while he eats, for "there is nothing more shameful than a hateful stomach" (7.216–217). The crowd takes no offense at these earthy remarks and heads home to bed. Odysseus' brief comments are typically Homeric in zooming in—without embarrassment—on the necessities of life: without food, you die. Later Homer will remind us that Odysseus hasn't had a warm bath since Calypso's island (8.450–453). Homer neglects no aspect of our humanity, from ideal cities and beautiful songs to the cooking of food and the importance of blankets on a bed.

At this point, we gain our first insight into Arete—in brief, she's as sharp as a Minoan axe. Once Odysseus has eaten, it's appropriate to ask questions. Arete has three: Who are you? Where do you come from? And where did you get those clothes? This is a queen who gets right to the point.

Homer is saving Odysseus' life story for later. In response to Arete, Odysseus concentrates on his time with Calypso. He happens to mention the offer of immortality (what we might call "immortality-dropping," like name-dropping) and his various shipwrecks: the first that brought him—the lone survivor—to Calypso's island, Ogygia; the second that brought him to the Phaeacians. Finally he answers her third question—the clothes are from Nausicaa—yet he declines to say anything about his identity and homeland.

The effect of Odysseus' speech is wholly remarkable. Despite not knowing this guy's name, Alcinous offers his daughter in marriage, with a house and Swiss bank account thrown in for good measure (7.311–315). The surrogate wife motif reappears and once more Odysseus has an opportunity to interrupt the possibility of marriage by revealing who he is. Once more Homer delays that scene of revelation. The effect is that Odysseus remains anonymous to the Phaeacians (identity theme) and the marriage is still on offer (surrogate wife).

Odysseus is certainly selective in telling his story, yet his only lie concerns Nausicaa. When Alcinous insists that she should have brought Odysseus to the palace herself, Odysseus fibs by saying that Nausicaa offered to do so but Odysseus didn't want to embarrass her (remember she actually wanted to avoid the unruly sailors). In fact, it's this lie that triggers Alcinous' proposal of marriage. The book ends with a well-earned night of sleep. Odysseus is apparently one step closer to Ithaca. Yet he will need deftly to refuse Alcinous' offer—he can't afford to upset his host.

This is a logical spot to pause and consider Homer's presentation of the character of Odysseus. Think how far Odysseus has come since the beginning of book 5—when he was truly a sorry sight! Odysseus has proved himself to be an able builder and sailor; his tenacity was emphasized by the octopus simile as he escaped the reef off Nausicaa's island. In book 6, he showed his oratorical skills by complimenting Nausicaa and alluding to a marriage that was never far from her mind. With Arete and Alcinous in book 7, he is able to ignore two of Arete's questions apparently without seeming to be rude. Odysseus also neatly compliments their daughter, remarking how unusual it is for a young person to act so maturely (7.292–294)—what parent wouldn't love to hear such things said about a child? In the first line of the epic, Odysseus—though unnamed—is called *polytropos*, which we could translate as "much-turning," "much-turned," or perhaps "many-sided." Homer is doing a wonderful job of showing the different sides of Odysseus, which in these books include his skills and determination. Soon we will meet Odysseus as athlete and singer; indeed, Homer is keeping more in store for the second half of the epic when he will reveal new depths in the character of Odysseus.

Does Arete Rule the Roost?

Many of the remarkable figures in Homer's *Odyssey* are female characters, both mortal and divine. Arete is just one example—she is said to be highly honored by her husband and the Phaeacians; she's an effective politician in her own right who can resolve disputes (7.67–74). Yet for all that, Alcinous is apparently in charge: he's the one who runs the kingdom. So why, according to Nausicaa and Athena, must Odysseus approach Arete rather than Alcinous and gain her support?

An ingenious answer has been proposed (I borrow here from Newton, "The Rebirth of Odysseus"—see "Further Reading"). Homer is evidently treating Odysseus as what the Greeks called a deuteropotmos ("man with a second fate"). This is someone who has been absent so long that many—including his family—assume him to be dead. When such a person reappears, the Greeks had a ritual that symbolically permitted such a person to return to the community of the living. A Greek author from late antiquity, Hesychius, describes how someone "who has been reported to have died abroad but then returns . . . tumbles through a woman's lap, as was the custom of the second birth among the Athenians." The ritual must take place at the lap (or knees) of a woman: it represents a second birth for the long-absent traveler.

This interpretation fits wonderfully with what we have already seen of Odysseus' symbolic rebirth in book 5: he emerges naked from the ocean, brine pouring from his nostrils as he collapses on the beach. For Homer to evoke this Greek ritual in book 7, Odysseus must appear at a woman's lap or knees—thus the importance of Arete rather than her husband—only a woman can give "rebirth." (The movie *The Return of Martin Guerre* tells a similar story. A man appears after many years at war, claiming to be the soldier the townspeople had long given up on. But alas, there's no rebirth ceremony at the knees of a mother-figure in this movie.)

BOOK EIGHT

Book 8 may be divided into four sections: the Assembly; Feast and the First Song; the "Olympics," the Second Song, and Gifts; and the Third Song and the Big Question. At the assembly Alcinous promises an escort to Odysseus, ordering a ship and fifty-two men to get ready. After a feast, some competition, and a second feast, Alcinous finally asks the big question. He insists upon learning Odysseus' name—no man is nameless, he remarks—and this leads to the mini-epic of books 9–12 in which Odysseus tells his own personal history since the sack of Troy.

Perhaps the most fascinating aspect of book 8 is the singer Demodocus and his three songs. Not only are the subjects of these songs thematically significant with respect to the rest of the epic; we also learn about the mechanics of singing songs and the dynamics of performer-audience interaction. Indeed, many have thought that Demodocus, the blind singer of Alcinous' court, is our best evidence for knowing something about Homer himself. It's hard not to speculate that this fictional singer is based to some degree on the actual composer of the *Iliad* and *Odyssey*.

THE ASSEMBLY (8.1–55)

As we have already seen, Athena is quite intent on helping Odysseus return home. As day breaks, Athena plays a herald who gathers a crowd before King Alcinous and his guest; she also pours "charm and grace" upon Odysseus to make him appear taller and more powerful. After promising a ship and crew, Alcinous makes an invitation to the feast and orders the singer to be present.

Beauty in the Eyes of the Greeks

Athena is always improving on Odysseus' looks, in particular, by making him look taller. Greek assumptions regarding the gods help explain these repeated manipulations. Among the ancient Greeks, the gods provided standards for many ideals, especially beauty. Yet the gods were thought to be larger than human beings—the statue of Athena in the Parthenon was thirty-five feet high! Aristotle even remarks that a small person might be well proportioned and attractive, but to be beautiful (or handsome), you have to be tall—like a god. When Odysseus is described elsewhere, he is broad but on the short side (see *Iliad* 3.191–224, for example). To give the impression of being "god-like," Athena has to add a little extra height if Odysseus is to dazzle the crowd.

FEAST AND THE FIRST SONG (8.55–104)

At the feast, Alcinous is a generous host: twelve sheep, eight pigs, and two oxen are sacrificed and prepared for eating. It is at this point that a herald leads the blind singer Demodocus into the banquet hall and shows him where his lyre is hung, and where food and drink are. Apparently on his own initiative, Demodocus launches a song about the Trojan War, in particular an episode in which Odysseus and Achilles quarrel. The leader of the expedition, Agamemnon, rejoices, for the quarrel jibes with an optimistic prophecy offered by the god Apollo (whose oracle is in Delphi).

The "Biography" of Homer

We have no certain knowledge about Homer's life. We don't know his dates or his homeland. Some have thought that different singers composed the *Iliad* and the *Odyssey* (I strongly disagree!). It is largely because of this lack of reliable evidence that we look to the figure of Demodocus to learn about Homer himself. We should distinguish between the mechanics of singing as represented here—which are helpful for understanding a live performance—and the possibility that Homer has bestowed autobiographical details upon Demodocus. Regarding the mechanics of singing, the solo singer who accompanies himself on a lyre seems right. At times, the singer responds to requests from the audience; at other times, the singer chooses the subject; the lord of the house—in this case, Alcinous—may interrupt the song at any time. An effective singer who brings delight to his audience is highly honored with food, wine, and other presents. As to Homer's "autobiography," there is a famous

---

line in the "Homeric Hymn to Apollo" that refers to the blind singer of Chios, which jibes with the tradition that Homer was a blind singer (it *could* be true—John Milton wrote *Paradise Lost* while blind); several islands along the west coast of Asia Minor—including Chios—claimed him as a native son. This, however, will remain speculative. In book 8, blindness is said to balance the gift of song bestowed by the gods. Remember the issue raised in Zeus' first speech: What causes mortal suffering? Here we learn that the Muse, one of the goddesses who inspire poetry:

"loved Demodocus greatly and gave him both good and bad.
She took sight from his eyes, but gave him sweet song." (8.63–64)

Odysseus reacts to Demodocus' song by hiding his face and weeping. Only Alcinous notices Odysseus' groaning and immediately interrupts the song. The Phaeacian King suggests they turn to athletic competition:

"So our guest can tell his friends,
when he reaches home, how far we excel others
at boxing, wrestling, jumping, and speed of foot." (8.101–103)

THE "OLYMPICS," THE SECOND SONG, AND GIFTS (8.105–448)

Odysseus witnesses many competitions: a footrace, a wrestling match, boxing, and so on. But tension rises when one of Alcinous' sons, Laodamas, challenges Odysseus to join one of the contests, "if you have skill in any" (8.146). We might recall that this is Alcinous' favorite son, the one who had to give up his seat to Odysseus the previous evening. Odysseus rejects the challenge at first—hasn't he suffered enough?—yet Odysseus' refusal provokes an insult, from Laodamas' friend Euryalus (or "Broadsea"):

"Stranger, I never thought you looked like someone skilled
in games, the kind men play everywhere!
No, you look like one who sits in a many-benched ship,
a captain of sailors, who are traders,
mindful of cargo, watching for paths
of profit and gain. You look nothing like an athlete." (8.159–164)

Odysseus will not let this putdown pass. In anger, he calls Euryalus a reckless fool, and grabs a discus—an extra-heavy one. Odysseus' cast flies past all the others (Athena helps measure it). Odysseus' fur is up and now he starts looking for a tussle—he'll box, wrestle, or race any challenger.

The *Odyssey* and the Olympics

Homer describes athletic competitions that sound very much like the Olympic games (see also the funeral games honoring Patroclus in *Iliad* book 23). If we are right in locating Homer in the eighth century B.C.E., this makes chronological sense, for the traditional dating for the start of the Olympic games was 776 B.C.E.—perhaps in Homer's own lifetime. We are told that the first competition was a footrace and other contests were added later. Both the Olympics and Homer's description of games derived from the military training all Greek men underwent. The competition on Scheria is one of many reflections in the epic from Homer's own historical period.

Alcinous effectively defuses the tension. He praises Odysseus, acknowledges that the earlier taunts were out of place, and insists upon a dance and song that will impress his guest. Demodocus sings a second song, this time concerning the Olympian gods on the subject of love, not war. Aphrodite, the goddess of love, shares her bed with Ares, the god of war. Aphrodite's husband, Hephaestus (the blacksmith god), learns of the affair and constructs invisible chains that capture his wife and her lover in the act. All the male gods are called to witness Aphrodite's infidelity and break out in laughter. Hephaestus has won some measure of revenge, yet Apollo and Hermes joke that they would gladly exchange places with Ares—caught in chains with everyone watching—if only they might sleep with golden Aphrodite. Demodocus' audience, including Odysseus, is delighted with this second song. I'll return to its significance in a moment.

An elaborate dance follows with leaping and rapidly throwing a ball to and fro. Odysseus marvels and declares that the Phaeacian dancers are the best in the world. Alcinous responds that "our guest is a man of real taste" (8.388) and promises that he and the twelve lords on the island will bring parting gifts for their guest: clothes, gold, an elaborate chest from Arete, a cup from Alcinous— Euryalus even offers a sword to make amends for his earlier insult. Alcinous is successful in leading the entire company toward mutual harmony.

THE THIRD SONG AND THE BIG QUESTION (8.449–586)

The sun goes down, and after a bath, Odysseus finds Nausicaa leaning against a column. She asks that Odysseus remember her and he promises:

"Even at home I'll pray to you as to a goddess
all my days to come, for you saved my life, dear girl." (8.467–468)

This is Odysseus' farewell to Nausicaa—and she still doesn't know his name!

At the evening's feast, Odysseus approaches the singer Demodocus, and, offering a select cut of roasted boar, praises his skill.

"Surely the Muse has taught you—Zeus' daughter—or Apollo.
How true to life you sing the fate of the Achaeans,

all they did and suffered and toiled,
as if you were there yourself or heard from another who was." (8.488–491)

There's a powerful irony in this scene: the singer, who is blind and presumably has never left the Phaeacians' island, sings as though he has witnessed the Trojan War itself—as if he were there. Of course, only one person in the hall actually experienced the Trojan War—the anonymous traveler Odysseus!

After this compliment, Odysseus makes a specific request: he asks Demodocus to sing about the wooden horse and the trap Odysseus set against the Trojans. Demodocus obliges him and sings of how the famous horse stood before the Trojans, packed with armed Greek soldiers. The Trojans debated whether to push it off a cliff, open it up by force, or—their fateful decision—bring it into the city as an offering to the gods. Once inside the Trojan walls, Greek soldiers stream out to wreak destruction: Odysseus himself, like the god Ares, marched with Menelaus to Deiphobus' house, presumably to retrieve Helen (8.517–518).

This third song again makes Odysseus break down in tears. We must think of how soldiers today react when hearing about a battle or reliving it themselves in their own minds. Homer introduces a most remarkable simile to describe Odysseus' state of mind. Odysseus weeps like a woman trying to embrace her dead husband who died defending his homeland. The woman in the simile:

sees her husband dying and gasping for breath;
she clings to him and shrilly cries out. But those behind her
dig spear-butts into her back and shoulders,
and drag her off to slavery to have toil and misery.
Her cheeks were wasted with the most pitiful pain;
so Odysseus wept pitiful tears from his eyes. (8.526–531)

All similes build on an explicit point of comparison: in this case, Odysseus weeps like a woman in a defeated city. But there's always more to an Homeric simile than the most obvious connection between the narrative and the world of the simile. This simile is nothing short of amazing: on the face of it, Odysseus could not be more *unlike* the person to whom he's being compared—other than the fact that they both weep. Consider the details. First, Odysseus is compared to a woman. Also, Odysseus was on the winning side at Troy, yet this woman has seen her husband die, her city sacked, and is being led off to slavery. Homer doesn't explicitly say that this is how Odysseus felt, but that's the suggestion of the simile. The implication is that, although Odysseus is a man and a victor and she's a woman of a conquered city, for us to understand what Odysseus is going through as he hears Demodocus' song, we must imagine him in a situation like hers.

The subject of the first and third songs is war. Although the Greeks were victorious, Odysseus reacts with great pain in reliving that experience. So great is the effect of war (see Shay, *Achilles in Vietnam* in "Further Reading"); so great too is the effect of song. As represented in song, Odysseus is heroic, clever, and successful—much like the recollections Telemachus hears in books 1–4. Yet the simile that follows Demodocus' third song suggests the reality behind such heroic endeavors. Odysseus toiled for ten years in Troy and now for nine more years has failed to reach his home and family. Even Demodocus' second song—which provoked laughter—has a serious side. The themes found in this song of a divine love triangle are adultery and trickery. An unfaithful wife takes a lover: we think of Clytemnestra and again wonder about Penelope. The husband Hephaestus, slower than Ares, gains a victory over his male rival, but it's a bittersweet triumph. Odysseus can laugh—the gods are in some ways remote—but Homer's audience may appreciate that even these songs-within-songs are integrated with the larger thematic concerns of the epic.

A second time Alcinous notices Odysseus' weeping. This time he insists upon learning his guest's identity and guesses that Odysseus may have known someone at Troy—perhaps a relative? Suspense has been building for the Phaeacians and finally they will learn who sits at their feast.

BOOK NINE

In books 9–12, Odysseus tells the Phaeacians of his adventures from the past ten years involving unusual creatures, narrow escapes, and even a journey to the "underworld." In a sense, Odysseus has become the singer. Although he doesn't play the lyre, he demonstrates yet another skill and is praised for his ability as a riveting storyteller.

The structure of book 9 is easy enough. After identifying himself, Odysseus tells three stories: the Cicones, the Lotus-Eaters, and Polyphemus the Cyclops. The first two are shorter and less elaborate; the third is more expansive and clearly is the most significant. This same pattern of two short episodes followed by one long story is also found in books 10 and 12 (see "The Structure of the *Odyssey*," pp. 7–10).

The three major themes of identity, homecoming, and hospitality dominate almost every episode in books 9–12; also significant are the role of the surrogate, the possibility of immortality, and a redefinition of heroism. Because books 9–12 are a flashback (or "retrospective" narrative), we are offered Odysseus' own view of what has happened to him. The narrative sequence is at odds with the chronological sequence: we learn about what actually took place *before* book 1. Homer asks us to find explanations for Odysseus' behavior in books 5–8—his suspicions of Calypso, his reluctance to identify himself to the Phaeacians, the lament over his sufferings—in these earlier events. In addition, the reasons for Poseidon's hostility to Odysseus are fully clarified.

Most important perhaps is the question of Odysseus' leadership and responsibility. Remember Zeus' claim: mortals suffer because of their own recklessness. Is that true? When Odysseus and his men succeed, who deserves the credit? When there is failure—and ultimately Odysseus will lose all his men—what role does Odysseus play? In what sense can we call him heroic?

IDENTITY (9.1–38)

Odysseus finally reveals who he is: Odysseus, son of Laertes, from Ithaca, famous for his trickery (9.17–27). Why has Odysseus waited so long to disclose his identity? Why does he reveal it now? A number of factors help to answer these questions.

First, Odysseus' delay in revealing his identity calls attention to the theme of identity, especially Odysseus' ability to decide when to conceal and when to reveal his name. If every time he met someone, Odysseus said, "Hi, I'm Odysseus, King of Ithaca," there would be no interest in this whole question. But Homer makes it an issue by *not* naming the hero for the first twenty lines of the epic, by having Athena and Odysseus appear in disguise at various times, and so on. In addition, the audience experiences dramatic suspense in awaiting the moment of revelation. As we have seen, the refusal to indicate his name also has the effect of promoting a potential marriage with Nausicaa.

In addition, there is a psychological reason from Odysseus' point of view. I'm anticipating here, but the adventures Odysseus is about to recount will help to explain why he may be reluctant to reveal who he is; also we learn the consequences of revealing one's name and the advantages of concealing it. Odysseus may well have learned from his previous mistakes.

When we consider the grand design of the entire epic—the architecture of the *Odyssey*—we appreciate the parallelism to the upcoming situation in Ithaca. When Odysseus arrives home, no one knows who he is; he chooses when to reveal his identity and to whom (for the most part). In Scheria, he demonstrates his skill in concealing his identity—a skill he will need in Ithaca—but from purely an aesthetic viewpoint, Homer delights in parallel situations. We recall the correspondences between Agamemnon's household and Odysseus' in Ithaca: a wife courted by a lover (Aegisthus) or lovers (the suitors), a single son, and so on. In a similar manner, Homer never shies away from emphasizing comparable situations or figures. This may be an instance where the poet promotes a parallelism between arriving by shipwreck in Scheria and a nighttime arrival in Ithaca: in both, Odysseus keeps his identity secret.

So why does Odysseus reveal himself now? As the Phaeacians finally learn who their guest is, Odysseus is in a position to influence their reaction by telling *his* version of the past. Lots of people have been talking about Odysseus: there are rumor, inaccuracies, and singers' tales. Now Odysseus has the opportunity to set the record straight.

THE CICONES (9.39–81)

Homer does not want to reduplicate what his audience has already learned about the final events at Troy from Nestor and Menelaus, so Odysseus begins his story just as he leaves Troy. Odysseus and his men cross over to the land of the Cicones, in Thrace on the European side in what is now northern Greece. Odysseus and his troops sack a city and divide up the spoils. When Odysseus urges his men to set sail, the men resist and a large force attacks them at dawn. Dozens of men lose their lives, yet Odysseus and the survivors succeed in sailing away.

We might briefly note that sacking a city of Cicones is not very different from sacking a city of Trojans—this is life as usual for the Greek warrior-on-the-go. The "mutiny" by the crew is troubling, but the world is much as they found it in Troy. Things are about to change.

THE LOTUS-EATERS (9.82–104)

Powerful winds afflict the ships, but Odysseus is within reach of Ithaca, "doubling Cape Malea" (9.80), when relentless winds drive the ships for nine days to the land of the Lotus-Eaters. Cape Malea is part of the known world—it's at the southern tip of the Peloponnesus, near Sparta. Once blown farther to the west, Odysseus enters a fantastic world of magic and monsters, a place where the normal rules of society no longer operate (see Map 1).

At their first stop to draw fresh water, Odysseus sends three men to explore the territory. The native people are not violent or devious: in fact, they are good hosts and offer food—the lotus—to Odysseus' men. The effect of the fruit, however, is to erase all thought of homecoming. Odysseus' men are content to simply go on eating lotus (this lotus is a sweet fruit from a tree, not our familiar water-lily lotus). Odysseus has to use force to get them back to the ships: they weep and only want to get "stoned," if that's the correct analogy. At the Cicones' land, men died in battle and lost any chance of returning to Ithaca. Here, the lotus threatens the homecoming of Odysseus' men in a new and troubling way: the very thought of home vanishes. These men who have fought abroad for ten years no longer think about Ithaca.

The *Odyssey* and Greek Colonization

The historical period of Homer's *Odyssey*—the eighth century B.C.E.—is a period of vigorous colonization for the Greek world. Following a population increase, many Greeks departed the cities of their birth to establish new city-states to the northeast along the Bosphorus and in the Black Sea and especially in the west: on Sicily, southern Italy, even as far away as what is now France. Such travelers doubtless brought back to the Aegean world many tales of unusual peoples, wonders of nature, and unbelievable events. Odysseus' fantastic stories are in part a reflection of sailors' tales from this period of Greek expansion over the Mediterranean world in Homer's lifetime (see Malkin in "Further Reading").

THE CYCLOPS (9.105–566)

The third and longest adventure in book 9 takes place in the land of the Cyclopes. (Yes, that's the plural: one Cyclops, many Cyclopes—with three syllables! Generations after Homer, the Lotus-Eaters were located in north Africa, the Cyclopes on the island of Sicily near Mount Etna.) Odysseus takes one of his twelve ships to Polyphemus' island where they discover a cave, large flocks of sheep and goats, and a splendid array of cheese. The crew wants to grab and run: take the cheese, kids, and lambs, and head back to sea. Yet Odysseus resists, insisting that they wait to receive a "guest gift" from the cave's owner—something a guest would normally expect to receive from his host (as Odysseus does from Alcinous and company).

Polyphemus' entrance terrifies Odysseus' men: they scamper to the corner of the cave. When the giant lights a fire to prepare his dinner, he sees the men and asks who they are and where they come from. Odysseus speaks in general terms: they are Agamemnon's men, who sacked Troy. Then Odysseus mentions his hope of a guest gift, but Polyphemus is not "into" hospitality:

> " 'Stranger, you are a fool, or come from far away,
> bidding me to fear or watch out for the gods!
> For we Cyclopes have no regard for aegis-bearing Zeus
> or the other blessed gods, since we are more powerful by far.
> I'd never spare you to avoid Zeus' hatred,
> neither you nor your comrades, unless my spirit bid me.'" (9.273–278)

Polyphemus then proceeds to seize two of Odysseus' men, smash their brains on the ground, and eat them.

Talk about bad manners! We have already encountered bad hosts and guests, but the rules of hospitality clearly have no validity in the land of the Cyclopes. Odysseus' men may not be the best guests—they contemplated stealing Polyphemus' cheese—but to eat your guests simply isn't done.

In a sense, it's Odysseus' fault that they're all stuck in the cave, but now he figures out a plan of escape. The next day they sharpen a staff of the Cyclops, harden it in the fire, and hide it under sheep dung in the cave. That night Odysseus offers some strong wine to Polyphemus. The Cyclops asks Odysseus his name and Odysseus answers: "My name is Nobody." Pleased with the wine, Polyphemus promises a "gift" to Nobody: he will eat Nobody last of all! (9.364–370).

Mixing Water and Wine

The wine Odysseus offers Polyphemus is extremely powerful. Greeks normally mixed wine with water in a proportion of two or three parts water to one part wine (their wine was stronger than ours is today). The exclusive vintage Polyphemus imbibes would require twenty parts water to one of wine (9.208–210), but Odysseus gives it to Polyphemus straight. It's like a bucket full of Bacardi rum 151 proof—no wonder Polyphemus passes out!

The Cyclops eats two more men and passes out in a drunken stupor. At this point Odysseus and his men get to work. They get out their huge stake, heat the sharp point in the fire, and drive it into the monster's single eye. The blinded Polyphemus calls out for help, but when the other Cyclopes come to his cave, he tells them, "Nobody is killing me!" (9.408) His fellow Cyclopes assume Polyphemus has gone crazy and tell him to pray to the gods for help.

Odysseus and his men have won the battle—yet they still have to get out of the cave. Odysseus puts each of his men under the middle of three rams tied together, for in the morning Polyphemus will let them out to graze. Odysseus must hold onto the single largest ram and there's a moment of anxiety as Polyphemus strokes his favorite old ram, asking why he's the last to leave. In the end, the rams exit, Odysseus unties his men, and they race to their ship.

At this point, they appear to be home free, yet Odysseus insists on taunting the Cyclops. First, he calls out that Zeus has punished Polyphemus for dishonoring his guests, yet his voice gives the blinded Cyclops an idea of where to toss a mountaintop to smash Odysseus' ship. He just misses and waves drive the ship back to shore. They row out again and a second time Odysseus shouts:

> "Cyclops, if any mortal man should ask you
> about the disgraceful blinding of your eye,
> say Odysseus, sacker of cities, blinded you,
> son of Laertes, who has his home in Ithaca!" (9.502–505)

Odysseus' decision to call out his own name has profound consequences. It triggers Polyphemus' recollection of a prophecy that he would be blinded at the hands of Odysseus—but he expected a giant, not a pipsqueak. More significantly it gives Polyphemus enough information to invoke a curse against Odysseus:

> "'Hear me, Poseidon, earth-holder, god of the sea-blue mane!
> If I truly am yours and you claim to be my father,
> grant that Odysseus, sacker of cities,
> son of Laertes, who has his home in Ithaca, does not reach home.
> But if he's fated to see his family and reach
> his well-built house and his native land,
> let him come home late, in bad circumstances, having lost all his companions,
> in a stranger's ship, and let him find trouble in his home.'
> So he spoke in prayer and the god of the sea-blue mane heard him."
>
> (9.528–536)

If all Polyphemus had known was that this guy's name was Nobody, he couldn't have made such a specific request. But once Odysseus reveals his name, father, and homeland—this is like adding a ZIP code or social security number—Poseidon can torment Odysseus for years to come in response to his son's request.

Odysseus sails on to more adventures in book 10, but this elaborate episode deserves a further examination. We note, of course, the role of the three themes:

Illustration 4. *The Blinding of Polyphemus.* On a vase from ca. 670 B.C.E., Odysseus is helped by two of his men to blind the seated Cyclops. By permission of the Ministry of Culture of Greece (Eleusis Museum, Eleusis, Greece). © Archaeological Receipts Fund.

hospitality, identity, and homecoming. While Polyphemus fails the test of hospitality, Odysseus' invention of a new name ("Nobody")—which masks his true identity—is essential for securing any hope of reaching Ithaca.

As to the issue of heroism, the common practice in battle is that when you've defeated an enemy, it's all right to taunt him—everyone does this at Troy, as seen in the *Iliad*. It's one way of proclaiming your glory in war. Yet this more traditional notion needs to be rethought in such new circumstances. To be a hero in Troy or against the Cicones is one thing—on Polyphemus' island all the rules need to be rewritten. This new unfamiliar world requires a different sort of heroic behavior: less blunt and more restrained. It's true that while Odysseus got his men into trouble in the first place, he also got them out of the cave. But Odysseus' insistence that the Cyclops know who it was who blinded him brings on the wrath of Poseidon—the last thing they need while sailing the seas. We now see the cause of Poseidon's anger against Odysseus, which had previously been only briefly alluded to before (1.69–70)—he's avenging the blinding of his son.

There's more. Homer has set up a contest between the brute force of Polyphemus and the intelligence of Odysseus. Though there's no way even thirteen men can oppose the Cyclops' strength, Odysseus shows how to outwit the monster: he lies by saying their ship was wrecked; he realizes that if he stabs the Cyclops in his sleep, they'll never get out of the cave—the door-stone is too massive to budge; he invents the name of "Nobody;" and devises an escape from the cave for his men. But this isn't simply a battle between power and wit. It's also a cosmic bout between civilization and a more primitive "Golden Age" existence.

The Bible tells of Eden, a paradise where Adam and Eve lived before humans suffered from birth pains or toiled for food. The Greeks had a similar story about what they called the Golden Age, when the first race of men lived. There was no sickness or toil, crops sprang up from the earth, honey dripped from trees, and everyone lived a pain-free existence (see Hesiod, *Works and Days* 109–126). Of course, it's true that the Cyclopes are man-eating monsters who reject the Olympian gods and the code of hospitality: they're savage and live solitary lives in caves. But there's another side to the life of Polyphemus. He's a herdsman, watching over his flocks, making cheese; he has no need to plow fields or sow seed, and lives without concern for sailing the seas (in antiquity, the sea was always terrifying—better left alone). The character of Polyphemus is a curious amalgam, but the simple, pastoral side of Polyphemus' life echoes many characteristics of the Golden Age.

A great many short similes punctuate Odysseus' encounter with Polyphemus: the Cyclops is as big as a mountaintop (9.191), he grabs Odysseus' men and dashes out their brains "like pups" (9.289–290), he puts the door-stone in place "as someone puts the lid on a quiver" (9.314), the staff they use to blind Polyphemus is "like a mast from a twenty-oared ship" (9.320). Homer also uses two extended "epic" similes to highlight the opposition of Polyphemus' pastoral lifestyle and Odysseus as representative of human civilization. These two "technological" similes punctuate the blinding of Polyphemus—Odysseus' moment of triumph. The first describes how Odysseus and his men drove the stake into the Cyclops' eye:

> "I leaned on it from above
> and spun it, as when a man bores a ship-plank
> with a drill and the men below grasp a strap on either side
> and whip the strap back and forth, and the drill keeps whirling,
>   never stopping." (9.383–386)

We have already learned that the Cyclopes don't build ships (9.125–131): here Odysseus is likened to a shipbuilder who drives his drill into a ship plank. Homer is subtly showing how man's ingenuity—symbolized by the building of a ship—overcomes the stronger, but less inventive, Polyphemus. A second simile—evoking the sound of the sizzling eyeball—also calls attention to Odysseus' skill and by implication to man's technological progress. Polyphemus' eyeball hissed:

> "As when a blacksmith plunges a great ax or adze
> into cold water, tempering it, as it
> shrieks aloud—for the strength of iron depends on this—
> so his eye sizzled round that olive stake!" (9.391–394)

Toolmaking is a mark of civilization—in the golden age, there's no need for a plow or ships or metal tools. Yet men, though small and weak, have the capacity to learn the skill of tempering iron. With that same cleverness, Odysseus plots and executes the successful blinding of Polyphemus.

BOOK TEN

Book 10 follows the pattern of book 9: two short episodes precede a longer, more elaborate one: Aeolus and the Winds, the Laestrygonians, and Circe—Odysseus' third surrogate wife. Once again the episodes are integrated into the epic as a whole with the themes of identity and hospitality. Regarding homecoming, Odysseus' fleet is devastated, losing eleven out of twelve ships.

AEOLUS AND THE WINDS (10.1–79)

Odysseus' first stop after leaving Polyphemus almost succeeds in bringing him back to Ithaca. Aeolus, Zeus' steward of the winds, puts all the winds (except for the favorable west wind) in a bag and Odysseus appears to be homeward bound. In many ways, Aeolus is the perfect host: he entertains Odysseus and his men for a month with music and feasting; when Odysseus asks permission to leave, he immediately grants it.

We're still not in Kansas, Toto. Aeolus rules a floating island (it has no fixed location); his six sons are married to his six daughters; and of course he controls the elements with supernatural powers. Nevertheless, everything is going well when on the tenth day of sailing Ithaca actually comes into sight. It is, in fact, too good to last. Odysseus falls asleep, and the men suspect he's hidden gold or silver in the windbag. Upon their opening it, a hurricane blows them all the way back to Aeolus' island. Their reception is completely different this time: Aeolus is convinced Odysseus and his men must be hated by the gods and insists they leave immediately—they're on their own now.

In this case, Odysseus himself says, "We were destroyed by our own folly" (10.27). Falling asleep at the last moment is certainly bad timing, but Odysseus had been awake steering his ship for nine days. Although Poseidon doesn't seem to have intervened, this is the first episode since Polyphemus' curse. Until they actually land on Ithaca, the sea will remain a threat. We might also note that this is the only time Odysseus contemplates suicide (10.50–52). As he sees it, his choice is to throw himself into the sea, or get tough and endure it. He now has to earn Homer's description of him as "much-enduring."

THE LAESTRYGONIANS (10.80–132)

After six days of sailing, they arrive at a place that sounds to us like the fiords of Norway. Here the paths of days and night are close ("Land of the Midnight Sun" in the northern latitudes?) and the harbor's narrow entrance has steep mountains on either side. Let's not get hung up on real geography—this episode's right out of a fairy tale, like Jack and the Beanstalk. The Laestrygonians are man-eating giants who skewer Odysseus' men like fish. Need we say?—bad hosts! Of the twelve ships, only Odysseus' makes it away since he tied up outside the harbor. This is one of the briefest episodes in Odysseus' entire account, yet the effect is perhaps the greatest (other than Polyphemus' curse): over 90 percent of Odysseus' men are lost, eleven out of twelve ships.

It is significant that this does not follow an obvious error in leadership by Odysseus. If he had lost almost all his men after insisting on waiting for a guest gift, his claim to intelligent leadership would be subject to doubt. (One of Odysseus' men, Eurylochus, will accuse Odysseus of being rash and blame him for the loss of their men to Polyphemus—10.435–437.) We also remember that Odysseus himself is the narrator and it may be useful at this point to distinguish Homer the poet of the *Odyssey* from Odysseus the narrator of books 9–12. Homer's goal in a sense is to reduce Odysseus' fleet to a single ship and then to Odysseus alone—this allows for the various ruses Odysseus employs at Scheria (the Phaeacians' island) and on his return in disguise to Ithaca. But for Odysseus the narrator—well, it's perhaps natural that he would not want to dwell on this debacle.

CIRCE, THE WITCH (10.133–574)

In the third episode with Circe—as in Polyphemus' cave—Odysseus again proves himself a capable leader. Upon arrival on Circe's island, Aeaea, the men are dispirited, yet Odysseus goes off to investigate and kills a stag for a grand dinner. He encourages them, although his promise that "we will not go down to Hades" is disproved by the journey in book 11 (10.174–175). Odysseus also decides to split the men into two groups and sends off only half his men (twenty-two of them) under the command of Eurylochus. When this group finds Circe's home in the woods, she's singing "like a woman or a goddess" while working at the loom.

Circe comes from an interesting family: she's daughter of the sun Helius and sister of Aeetes (Aeetes is Medea's father—Medea's a witch, too, in the story of Jason and the Argonauts). Circe also *appears* to be the perfect hostess. She invites Odysseus' men in and offers food and wine—yet she's added drugs to their meal, which turn them into pigs. She taps a wand on their heads, they're transformed, and she sends them off to the pigsty. Note the distinction between outer appearance and inner feeling:

> "They had the heads, voice, bristles, and build
> of pigs, but their minds were just as they were before.
> Like this, weeping, they were penned up." (10.239–241)

Homer has already suggested that appearances may mask the "true" self. Upon their arrival, Odysseus' men meet wolves and lions, which fawn on them like friendly dogs, presumably maintaining the temperament from their former lives as humans. In the second half of the epic after arriving on Ithaca, Odysseus will take advantage of appearing to be one thing—a beggar—while inwardly maintaining his craftiness and determination.

While the men are transformed into swine, Eurylochus, who suspects treachery, makes his way back to the ship. He begs Odysseus not to force him to return, so Odysseus goes himself, setting off through the woods. Fortunately, he meets the god Hermes (in disguise!), who offers a different drug, the plant *moly*, as an antidote to Circe's magic. Hermes also instructs Odysseus:

> "When Circe would drive you with her long wand,
> then draw your sharp sword from beside your thigh
> and rush at Circe as though you're bent on killing her.
> In fright, she will bid you to sleep with her.
> Then refuse the goddess' bed
> until she promises to release your companions and to treat you well.
> Make her swear a great oath by the blessed gods
> that she will plot no other evil harm against you
> and that she will not make you weak and un-manned, once you're naked."
>
> (10.293–301)

Naturally Odysseus appreciates this valuable help.

Odysseus enters Circe's home and everything transpires as Hermes foretold. It's a great moment when Circe taps Odysseus on the head and tells him to go off to the pigsty, and Odysseus—still human in appearance—draws his sword. Circe grabs his knees as a suppliant and—even without a word from Odysseus—she realizes who this must be. Calling himself "Nobody" helped save the crew's necks with Polyphemus; here, too, it is essential that Odysseus conceal his identity to succeed against Circe, who had previously been warned (by the busy Hermes) of the coming of Odysseus. Odysseus then sticks with Hermes'

Illustration 5. *Circe Transforming the Men of Odysseus.* On a cup from ca. 550 B.C.E., Circe offers her magical meal to Odysseus' men, who have already begun to turn into wild animals. Odysseus rushes in from the left with his sword drawn. The artist has attempted to capture a sequence of events (meal, transformation, rescue) in a single frame. Reproduced with permission. © 2000 Museum of Fine Arts, Boston. All Rights Reserved.

plan. Before they go to bed, Circe swears an oath not to plot any more trickery. And later at Odysseus' insistence, his men are transformed back into human shape and rejoin Odysseus for a more conventional meal.

There's a poignancy in Odysseus' reunion with his men, particularly the simile Homer introduces:

> "So when they saw me,
> in tears, they embraced me. Their spirit was as moved
> as if they'd reached their fatherland and the city
> of rugged Ithaca, where they were born and reared." (10.414–417; cf.
> 10.419–420)

As we well know—and even the Phaeacians listening know—Odysseus is alone when he reaches Scheria. None of these men will ever see Ithaca again.

Circe is a goddess, a sorceress, and—once Odysseus' men look human again—a very good hostess. Too good perhaps, for she also plays the role of Odysseus' surrogate wife. It's a year before someone confronts Odysseus, saying that it's time to go. Odysseus has evidently been in no hurry. We recollect that Calypso offered immortality to lure Odysseus to stay; Nausicaa offered youth and innocence. What's Circe's attraction? Homer (or the storyteller Odysseus) never says, but it's clear that Circe shares with Odysseus a propensity toward trickery. It may well be this affinity for craftiness that entices Odysseus to tarry a bit longer than his men would like.

When Odysseus approaches Circe with a desire to leave, she insists she will not keep him against his will. (This may be a subtle message from Odysseus to Alcinous—don't keep me here against my will!) Yet a difficult journey must precede the return to Ithaca: a voyage to the realm of Hades, the land of the dead. Why? So that Odysseus might consult with Teiresias about his homecoming. Odysseus accepts this command, yet not everyone reaches the land of the dead by the same route. Odysseus and his men sail there—Odysseus is a man who's not afraid to ask directions, learning it's beyond the river Ocean, which lies at the edge of the world. One sailor named Elpenor, however—he's the youngest and rather undistinguished—wakes up suddenly after drinking to excess, falls off Circe's roof, and tumbles to his death. He'll be in the realm of Hades when Odysseus arrives.

BOOK ELEVEN

Book 11 of the *Odyssey* is a small masterpiece in its own right, containing some of the most memorable and profound moments in the entire epic: Odysseus' meeting with his mother, Ajax's refusal to speak to Odysseus, and the punishments of Tityus, Tantalus, and Sisyphus, to name just a few. While the ideas of identity and homecoming are significant, perhaps of greater importance is what Odysseus learns in this journey. In fact, this is the purpose of the trip: to consult with Teiresias. Let me briefly discuss the pattern found in book 11 and then turn to analysis.

Books 9, 10, and 12 all have two short episodes followed by a long one. Book 11's structure is more complex, but it's still built on patterns of three. Let's divide it into six sections. After (1) the Voyage and Rituals, (2) Odysseus speaks to the souls of *three* people: Elpenor, the seer Teiresias, and his mother, Anticleia. There follows (3) a "catalog" of famous women. (4) The spell of the story itself is broken when Odysseus remarks that he's tired and that it's time for bed. This "intermission" consists of Alcinous and Arete promising even more gifts and asking about specific encounters. (5) Odysseus then tells of meeting *three* Greek heroes who fought at Troy: Agamemnon, Achilles, and Ajax. Finally, (6) he views the punishments of *three* "criminals": Tityus, Tantalus, and Sisyphus. After a glimpse of the wraith of Heracles, Odysseus flees the land of the dead. The pattern of three sets of three—Elpenor, Teiresias, mother; three Trojan War heroes; and three punishments—undoubtedly helps the poet organize these encounters in his mind while providing the audience with a recognizable and coherent structure.

THE VOYAGE AND RITUALS (11.1–50)

Odysseus and his men reach the end of the world by crossing the river Ocean (thought of as a circular river running around the flat, disk-like earth) and reaching the Cimmerians, a people who live in perpetual mist and darkness. I should point out that Homer does not envision the dead as living in an "underworld," beneath the earth (for this, see Aeneas' journey in Vergil's *Aeneid* book 6 or Orpheus' trip in Ovid's *Metamorphoses* book 10). The spirits of the dead evidently migrate to a place beyond the limits of the world itself.

Odysseus and his men then perform rituals according to Circe's instructions: they dig a trench, and pour *three* libations of milk and honey, wine, and water while sprinkling barley. Odysseus promises sacrifices upon his return to Ithaca; finally, the blood of two sacrificial sheep flows into the trench as a type of nourishment for the spirits of the dead. Odysseus is terrified when a swarm of ghosts appears before him, but he prays to Hades and Persephone, gods of the dead, and uses his sword to ward off the dead until his interview with Teiresias.

We shouldn't skip over the setting. Homer lays out all the ingredients for a gripping ghost story: it's dark, a crowd of flittering spirits appears with a great cry, Odysseus is terrified. We should also recall that this part of Odysseus' story is told before the court of the Phaeacians in the middle of the night, as the embers of the fire glow.

ELPENOR, TEIRESIAS, AND ANTICLEIA (11.51–225)

Before Odysseus even has a chance to speak with Teiresias, the spirit of Elpenor (drunk, fell off Circe's roof) appears, begging for burial back on Circe's island, which Odysseus promises to do. It's a good 700 years before Vergil describes the "doors" of Hades being open day and night, with countless ways to "enter," but Elpenor is evidently an example of the quick trip. When Odysseus asks how Elpenor got to the world of darkness before him, his answer boils down to this: "I died."

Though seeing his mother, Odysseus insists on speaking with Teiresias next. Teiresias, the blind seer from Thebes (made famous for us in Sophocles' *Oedipus the King* and *Antigone*), drinks the blood of the sacrificial victims for strength to foretell Odysseus' future. Teiresias speaks first of Odysseus' homecoming: the problem of Poseidon's anger, the importance of *not* eating the cattle of the Sun god, and the trouble awaiting Odysseus at home—suitors devouring his herds and courting his wife.

Homer links book 11 with the rest of the epic in several ways: Elpenor appears from the Circe episode; Odysseus later asks his mother if Penelope has been faithful; Agamemnon tells his version of Clytemnestra's infidelity and his own murder. In addition, Teiresias' prediction of Odysseus' homecoming—arriving alone with trouble in his house (11.113–115)—clearly echoes Polyphemus' curse from book 9. With these links, Homer has made book 11 an integral part of the epic.

But Teiresias does not stop there, although the *Odyssey* as a whole closes with Odysseus' confrontation with the suitors. Homer uses the seer to look ahead to an accommodation with Poseidon and the end of Odysseus' life. After Odysseus' house has been put in order, according to Teiresias, Odysseus must carry an oar to a people who know so little of the sea that they think the oar is a tool for winnowing grain. When this happens, Odysseus is to plant the oar in the earth and sacrifice to Poseidon. The significance apparently is that this is Odysseus' atonement for the blinding of Polyphemus, Poseidon's son: he'll bring the worship of Poseidon to an inland people who previously failed to honor the god of the sea.

Teiresias then predicts the end of Odysseus' life:

"Death will come to you away from the sea,
a gentle death, which will take you
in rich old age. Around you, your people
will be blessed and happy. I speak these words truly to you." (11.134–137)

It is not Homer's job to give us a sequential biography of Odysseus—birth, childhood, and the rest up to his death. Instead the poet concentrates upon the return of Odysseus during a period of a few weeks, ten years after Troy has been sacked (the entire epic covers forty days). And yet in this passage Homer uses foreshadowing (a prophet's prediction) to give us some sense of how Odysseus will die, thus providing closure to Odysseus' life as a whole. The description of Odysseus' death is not very precise. In fact, the expression translated "death . . . away from the sea" is ambiguous and could be "death out of the sea" or "death caused by the sea," alluding to a role played by Poseidon. Such prophecies are frequently vague and enigmatic.

Odysseus' mother, Anticleia, appears next, and this is something of a shock. When Odysseus left Ithaca a dozen years earlier, she was still alive. Anticleia fills him in on the situation back home: Penelope is wasting away weeping for her husband, Telemachus is doing well. As a mother is likely to do, she spends the most time on Odysseus' father, who has become something of a recluse. In response to Odysseus' question about how she died, Anticleia says it was from sorrow and longing for her son. In a brief fifty lines, Homer offers insight into this relationship of a grief-stricken mother and her wandering yet lovable son.

Odysseus is filled with a desire to embrace his mother.

"Three times I rushed toward her—my heart commanded me to hold her—
three times she fluttered through my hands, like a shadow or a dream,
and each time grief cut my heart more sharply." (11.206–208)

Here Odysseus learns what death means. Your flesh and bones are gone, your spirit flitters about like a dream: Odysseus will never again hold his mother in his arms. (Later writers, most famously Vergil, use this scene of failing *three* times to embrace a loved one: see *Aeneid* 2.792–794 and especially 6.700–702 when Aeneas in the underworld attempts to embrace his dead father, Anchises.)

Life after Death?

Homer's picture of what happens after death may not always be philosophically consistent but it's a vivid portrait. Homer uses the word *psyche* for the spirits of the dead—as in psychology ("study of the soul")—but it hasn't yet come to mean "soul" in our sense of the word. These spirits live in the dark; they fly about squeaking; they're like smoke, a shadow, or a dream. They may appear as they were at the moment of death: virgins with recent grief, soldiers with bloody armor (again familiar from many ghost stories). Only after drinking blood can they speak and perceive—Odysseus' mother doesn't even recognize her son until she drinks the sheep's blood. In addition, powerful emotions endure beyond the grave. Elpenor is desperate for an heroic burial ("Remember me! Don't leave me unburied!"—10.71–72), Agamemnon and Achilles long for news of their sons, Ajax's anger has not diminished. Although there are certain punishments for the worst criminals, everyone goes to the land of the dead—heaven isn't an alternative. The only other option is to become a god (like Heracles) or live like gods on the Isles of the Blessed—this awaits Menelaus and Helen (see Vermeule in "Further Reading").

THE CATALOG OF WOMEN (11.225–332)

There follows a parade or pageant of the illustrious wives and daughters of noble men, whom Odysseus interviews. These include Antiope, who bore Zeus two sons destined to build the famous walls of Thebes; Alcmena, mother of Heracles; and the mother (and wife) of Oedipus, though Homer uses the name Epicaste, rather than the more familiar Jocasta. The list seems endless and Odysseus in fact claims that he could never name them all (11.328–329). On top of that, "the time has come for sleep," and Odysseus stops his tale.

The so-called "catalog of women" is certainly more diffuse than the rest of the book. There are some thematic connections with the epic: Poseidon uses disguise to sleep with Tyro (11.241–242), many of the women are unfaithful to their husbands (often with Zeus). This section also has the function of providing a wider view of the Greek heroic world, especially the female side. In contrast to Demodocus (two of his three songs are about war), Odysseus may be appealing to the women in his audience. If this is his goal, he succeeds admirably, for Arete is the first to praise his story.

INTERMISSION (11.333–384)

The Phaeacians are silent, until Queen Arete compliments Odysseus and commands everyone to honor him further with gifts: "This is *my* guest!"

(11.338). She's clearly been enjoying the evening's entertainment. Alcinous also promises more bounty and praises Odysseus for his skill in storytelling.

"Oh, Odysseus! We do not look upon you
and think you a liar and a rogue, many of whom
the black earth feeds in all parts, men who
compose lies, so that none could detect them.
There is eloquence in your words, and good sense as well!
You have told your story like a skilled singer—
the wretched pains all the Achaeans and you endured." (11.363–369)

There's a sense in which Odysseus is not a singer—he's no professional like Demodocus, he doesn't strum the lyre as he tells his story. But Alcinous' praise makes it clear that we should acknowledge singing (or at least storytelling) as another of Odysseus' many skills. Indeed, it's remarkable that Alcinous contrasts Odysseus' stories with the lying tales of rogues that can't be debunked—what could be more unbelievable than stories of man-eating Cyclopes, witches that change men into animals, and journeys to the land of the dead? And yet the Phaeacians swallow all this as credible. (This break in the story-within-the-story is also a clever way for Homer to remind his audience that Odysseus is still the narrator with the Phaeacians listening. Otherwise Odysseus' flashback risks dwarfing Homer's main story of Odysseus' return to Ithaca.)

AGAMEMNON, ACHILLES, AND AJAX (11.385–565)

In response to Alcinous' request (storytellers often deal with such demands), Odysseus describes his meeting with Agamemnon, Achilles, and Ajax. As with his mother, Odysseus had no previous knowledge of Agamemnon's death at the hands of Aegisthus, Clytemnestra's lover. We encounter one last version of the story of Agamemnon, whose household has so many parallels with Odysseus'. Agamemnon gives an eyewitness account of what it's like to be murdered in your own house, slaughtered "like an ox at the trough." He adds the detail that Clytemnestra killed Priam's daughter, Cassandra, and that she failed to close the eyes or mouth of his dead corpse.

Agamemnon draws a lesson from his experience: "'There's nothing more deadly and shameful than a woman'" (11.427). Although he praises Penelope, Agememnon advises Odysseus not to trust fully his own wife and insists:

"I will tell you one other thing. Bear it in mind!
Steer your ship in secret—not openly—
coming to your fatherland, since there's no trust in women." (11.454–456)

Although Odysseus has heard of troubles in his household from Teiresias and his mother, Agamemnon gives the most graphic argument for extreme caution on the part of Odysseus (or anyone) who returns home after many years away.

Don't shout to the hilltops that you're back—be sneaky! Luckily, this is one of Odysseus' talents.

Agamemnon is an unusual case. Many warriors lost their homecoming in battle at Troy or by sea, but Agamemnon actually makes it home—expecting a welcome—and he's murdered instead. Reaching Ithacan soil is not enough: Odysseus will need to figure out who can be trusted. Arriving secretly in Ithaca combines the themes of homecoming and (concealing) identity. Agamemnon also draws a sharp contrast between the impudent and deceitful Clytemnestra, who brings shame upon all women, and the patient Penelope—characterization-by-comparison is alive and well in the land of the dead.

The second hero from Troy is Achilles, in many ways the greatest warrior of the Greeks. Even in the land of the dead, Odysseus comments, Achilles is honored like a god, just as when he lived. Achilles' answer puts a damper on Odysseus' optimism.

> "Don't talk to me glibly of death, glorious Odysseus!
> I'd rather be on earth toiling for another man—
> some tenant farmer, who has little to his name—
> than rule all the dead who have perished." (11.488–491)

No man has known greater glory than Achilles—he was honored by Greeks and gods alike. Yet now Achilles says he'd rather be a serf to a poor farmer than king of the dead. The heroic code argues for risking one's life to obtain glory. Here, Achilles states a preference for life, however humble, to a glorious death. (In the *Iliad*, Achilles also questions the value of glory among men, so perhaps there's some consistency for his character in both epics.) Again we are implicitly asked to contrast Achilles' fate—glory and an early death—with that of Odysseus.

Agamemnon had asked about his son, Orestes. We know he avenged his father's death, but Odysseus is utterly ignorant whether Orestes even lives. In response to Achilles, however, Odysseus tells much of his son, Neoptolemus: his valor at Troy, the many men he slew in battle, the spoils he won from sacking Troy—he wasn't even wounded! Evidently the best to hope for in the land of the dead is news of a brave son:

> "So I spoke, and the spirit of swift-footed Achilles, Aeacus' grandson,
> went off with great strides across the fields of asphodel,
> rejoicing that I said his son was distinguished." (11.538–540)

Odysseus' third encounter is with Ajax, who committed suicide after losing the contest of arms with Odysseus (though offering a quick synopsis of Ajax's death, Homer relies upon his audience's familiarity with the story of Ajax's suicide: see "The Epic Tradition: Trojan War Stories"). Odysseus begs Ajax:

> "Ajax, son of excellent Telamon, were you not going
> to forget, even in death, your rage against me
> for those cursed arms?" (11.553–555)

Though Odysseus praises Ajax as best of the Greeks after Achilles—they grieved for him as they did for Achilles—Ajax stalks off, still angry, the only spirit that refuses to speak with Odysseus.

Homeric Allusion in Vergil's *Aeneid*

Like Odysseus, Vergil's hero Aeneas also journeys to the land of the dead in *Aeneid* book 6, which has many allusions (indirect references) to *Odyssey* book 11: for example, Aeneas seeks to throw his arms around his father three times, like Odysseus with his mother. One of the most powerful allusions occurs with Vergil's echo of Homer's scene with the silent Ajax. Dido, a central figure in the *Aeneid*, commits suicide after her lover Aeneas leaves her. In the underworld, Dido refuses to speak with Aeneas, who hopes that at least in death she might give up her resentment. Such hatred persists even beyond the grave.

PUNISHMENTS, HERACLES, AND ODYSSEUS' EXIT (11.566–640)

Odysseus doesn't seem to be walking around the land of the dead, but at this point he is able to survey some of the more interesting inhabitants—again Homer provides models that poets, philosophers, and artists have adapted for more than 2,700 years.

Odysseus sees Minos, another son of Zeus, who serves as judge over the dead. Some emphasis is then given to the punishment of three "criminals": Tityus, Tantalus, and Sisyphus. Tityus, who tried to rape Leto (mother of Apollo and Artemis), has two vultures tearing at his liver. Tantalus, who according to one tradition stole nectar and ambrosia from the gods, is thirstily standing in a pool of water. Yet each time he stoops to drink, the water vanishes. He's hungry, too, yet he can never quite grasp the pears and figs hanging from nearby trees. Each time he reaches, the wind pushes the fruit away. Tantalus is truly "tantalized"—his name and punishment provide the origin of our word. Third is the labor of Sisyphus, who works mightily to roll a huge boulder up a hill, yet each time he almost pushes it off the top, the stone rolls back down and Sisyphus must begin again.

These men suffer endlessly for crimes against the gods, yet it must be said that no one enjoys being in the land of the dead. The gap between mortals—who are subject to death—and the gods, who live forever, is made astonishingly clear. This lesson is brought home by Odysseus' vision of Heracles, for it's not actually him—it's only a phantom:

> "Heracles himself delights in the feasts
> of the deathless gods, and he has lovely-ankled Hebe as wife,
> the daughter of mighty Zeus and golden-sandaled Hera." (11.602–604)

After the wraith of Heracles addresses him, Odysseus flees the land of the dead in terror.

Two points need to be emphasized. First, we should return to the question of why Odysseus has journeyed to the land of the dead. Circe says that he must consult with Teiresias and it is true that Odysseus hears of the cattle of the Sun, the suitors, and his later years. But much of what he learns, Circe tells him again on his return in book 12. The poet's underlying goal for this journey is to show that Odysseus can do it all: he can fight like Achilles, he can sail like Jason, and—if Gilgamesh, Heracles, and Orpheus can make it to the land of the dead—Odysseus can as well. He's no less heroic than they are.

Second, I return to Heracles, the ultimate hero. Odysseus comments explicitly that the Heracles he saw in the land of the dead was a mere phantom, for Heracles himself was now with the gods—he has become immortal. This implicitly recalls the destiny of other key figures: Menelaus and Helen going to the Isles of the Blessed, and Calypso's offer to make Odysseus immortal. As we saw in book 5, Odysseus rejected that offer—he'd rather see his wife and home than live forever with the goddess. We didn't know it then, but now we are in the position to appreciate that when Calypso made her offer, Odysseus—more than any man alive—knew the consequences of his refusal. Although Odysseus' journey to the land of the dead (book 11) is *presented* after Calypso's offer (book 5), in terms of Odysseus' own life, he went to Hades *earlier*—and saw what mortality truly means. Only after losing all his men does he wash up on Calypso's shore—remember books 9–12 are a flashback. When Odysseus says "no" to immortality, he knows exactly how he'll end up—flittering around, squeaking like a bat, thirsty for blood—and yet he chooses *not* to become a god. This episode presents a stark confrontation with the sort of existence awaiting Odysseus after he dies. Yet in the end, Odysseus chooses to remain mortal and human—like us.

BOOK TWELVE

Book 12 presents three main episodes. The two shorter ones have entered our everyday conversation: we still talk about hearing siren songs or attempting to steer between Scylla (pronounced "sill'-uh") and Charybdis. As far as the *Odyssey* is concerned, the third, longer episode is the most critical: by eating the cattle of the Sun, Odysseus' men are doomed. The book concludes with Odysseus washing up on Calypso's island, where he'll be stuck for the next seven years—this closes Odysseus' stories for the Phaeacians. What is unusual is that about one-third of book 12 consists of Circe anticipating Odysseus' adventures ("previews of coming attractions"?). I'll speculate about the reasons for this in a moment, but for now let's divide the book into four sections: Circe's Instructions; the Sirens; Scylla and Charybdis; and the Cattle of the Sun.

CIRCE'S INSTRUCTIONS (12.1–141)

Leaving the land of the dead, Odysseus and his men cross the river Ocean and sail east to Circe's island (it's true that Odysseus' other stops in books 9 and 10 appeared to be in the west, but they've just come back from the ends of the earth—who knows where *that* lies on a map?). They give burial rites to Elpenor, cremating his body and erecting a mound with his oar on top. Circe plays a good hostess (no more magic), offering food and drink and promising to give directions for their next journey. She also recognizes their uniqueness, calling them "twice-dying"—other men die but once (12.22).

At this point, Circe has a private audience with Odysseus. After hearing about his latest journey, she predicts what now awaits him. First, she warns him about the Sirens and their enticing song. Circe comes up with the idea of putting wax in the crew's ears and tying Odysseus to the mast, so that he can hear the Sirens sing without danger. Then she offers Odysseus a choice: he can attempt to sail by the Wandering Rocks, which only Jason and the Argonauts succeeded in passing; or he can maneuver between Scylla and Charybdis. Circe recommends staying closer to Scylla in spite of her terrifying description as a squid-like, dog-barking, six-headed monster with three rows of teeth: it's better to lose six men than everyone. Finally, Circe gives dire warnings about not harming the cattle of the Sun or there will be no homecoming (this reinforces Teiresias' warning from book 11).

Before examining the adventures themselves, let's consider the reasons for Circe's extended anticipation of the coming events. Homer—and the narrator Odysseus—achieve several goals by including this preview. First, Homer gains suspense by predicting the challenges ahead—we look forward to seeing how Odysseus handles these challenges. Also, when the events themselves occur, the focus is on pure action and Odysseus' reactions, since the background details are already in place. Interestingly, this preview allows Circe to mention the adventure of the Argonauts, which (as we now do automatically) may be compared with the adventures of Odysseus. Both Jason and Odysseus have adventures on the sea; each is favored by a goddess (Jason by Hera, Odysseus by Athena). Yet here Odysseus distinguishes himself from Jason—he'll skip the Wandering Rocks and brave the terrors of Scylla and Charybdis. Undoubtedly, the singer Homer is also contrasting the *Odyssey* with the *Argonautica* in order to distinguish himself from other singers who have sung of the Argonauts.

Most important, there are two decisive reasons for Circe's foreshadowing. First, some of these adventures could never take place without explicit instructions ahead of time: Odysseus needs to know beforehand that he should put wax in his men's ears and get tied to the mast—otherwise, they'd be wrecked on the Sirens' shore like other sailors. Also, these dangers are unavoidable: you have to face either Scylla and Charybdis or the Wandering Rocks—there are no other options. If we contrast this to earlier episodes, we realize that if Odysseus had known in advance about Polyphemus or the Laestrygonians, he would simply have avoided them—that's not possible this time.

The other key factor is that Homer—and his hired-gun narrator, Odysseus—need to explain how Odysseus loses all his men without him looking like a chump. The conversation with Circe allows Odysseus to raise the possibility of battling Scylla—as any self-respecting hero would. Circe explains that this would be counterproductive: Scylla is immortal (she can't be defeated) and anyway if Odysseus and his men take the time to arm and challenge her, she'll strike again, taking six more men. This is yet another instance in which the conventional rules of bold heroism need to be altered for Odysseus to succeed.

I mentioned Odysseus the narrator and it's worth considering his perspective. He is telling his adventures before the Phaeacians: he once commanded a fleet of twelve ships but now he's alone. As the man in charge, Odysseus has some explaining to do. Circe's set of instructions helps to excuse him from the blame of losing six men to Scylla (this is the best that could be expected); also the rest of his men are blameworthy for ignoring his prohibition—which has the authority of the goddess Circe and the prophet Teiresias—against eating Helius' cattle. If any hero knows something about "spin," it's Odysseus.

THE SIRENS (12.142–200)

Odysseus and his men sail away the next morning. Odysseus tells his men selectively of what's ahead: for now, they prepare for the Sirens. Odysseus puts wax in his men's ears and they strap him to the mast with ropes—they've been instructed to lash the ropes even tighter if Odysseus commands them with gestures to release him (remember, they won't be able to hear him).

Odysseus alone is able to experience the beautiful song of the Sirens, in spite of the danger: Circe has already mentioned the beach littered with the bones of rotting men (12.45–46). Not only is the Sirens' song lovely, but they hold out the promise of knowledge:

> "We know everything that happened in broad Troy:
> all that the Argives and Trojans achieved by the will of the gods.
> We know all that comes to pass on the much-nourishing earth." (12.189–191)

Odysseus is endlessly curious and this is the chance of a lifetime. Even with Circe's warning, Odysseus can't restrain his desire to listen to their song and commands the crew (with nods) to release him. They respond by tying him even tighter. After they've rowed away, Odysseus is released. Once again Odysseus is the hero who can do it all: journey to the land of the dead, hear the Sirens' song, sleep with beautiful goddesses—and live to tell about it! You have to admit, it's an extremely impressive resumé.

Swan Song?

Homer doesn't describe the Sirens, but later artists portrayed them as half-bird, half-woman, always with wings and frequently with a harp (to accompany their song). They have been compared to the German Lorelei, or mermaids who lure sailors to their death.

SCYLLA AND CHARYBDIS (12.201–259)

The Sirens are a walk in the park compared to what follows. Even before the vision of Scylla's hungry heads, Odysseus' crew is terrified by smoke, waves, and booming thunder. Odysseus gives them an encouraging speech:

> "Friends, we are by no means unacquainted with trouble.
> This danger is no greater than when the Cyclops

Illustration 6. *Ulysses and the Sirens.* In Ancient Greece, the Sirens were often portrayed with wings, feathers, and even webbed feet—half woman, half duck! This early twentieth-century dreamy vision might be seen as an improvement. Ferens Art Gallery, Hull City Museums and Art Galleries, UK/Bridgeman Art Library.

held us in his hollow cave with brute force.
But even then we escaped by my successful and ingenious plan,
and I think perhaps one day we will remember these things." (12.208–212)

Vergil models one of Aeneas' most famous lines upon this speech: *forsan et haec olim meminisse iuvabit* ("perhaps one day we will remember even these things with pleasure"—*Aeneid* 1.203). The situations are different in significant ways: Aeneas' men have just escaped a storm at sea, while Odysseus and his men are about to face Scylla and Charybdis. They are between the proverbial rock and a hard place.

Odysseus watches as Charybdis on one side sucks down the ocean and sand appears; when he looks back, Scylla already has six of his men suspended in the air, like fish on a hook—"the most pitiful death I saw" (12.258). Six men are lost, but they row on, away from the narrows.

THE CATTLE OF THE SUN GOD HELIUS (12.260–453)

Still out at sea, Odysseus hears the herds of the Sun god Helius mooing and baaing on the island of Thrinacia. He attempts to dissuade the men from landing, but Eurylochus insists: they're all tired, they don't want to sail at night, and he promises they'll leave in the morning. Odysseus yields, but only on the condition that all the men swear an oath not to kill cows or sheep on the island.

But the odds are stacked against them. In the night, Zeus sends a contrary wind, which lasts for a month. The crew runs out of provisions and resorts to catching fish and birds (a truly unheroic menu). In the end, Odysseus goes off to pray to the gods, falls asleep, and Eurylochus convinces the men that famine is the worst death of all. His idea is to sacrifice to the gods, while promising to build a temple to Helius upon their return to Ithaca. Otherwise, Eurylochus is resigned to his fate:

"If in anger at our eating his straight-horned cattle
Helius wishes to destroy our ship, and the other gods join in,
I would rather die swallowing a wave all at once
than to waste away slowly on a deserted island." (12.348–351)

The other men are persuaded and they set to work, slaughtering the cattle. Odysseus comes back only after the meat's on the fire. Clearly these are not your ordinary cattle: they're immortal and when they've been slaughtered, the skins crawl and the flesh bellows—freaky! Odysseus rebukes his men but it's too late. A nymph, Lampetia, tells Helius ("who sees and hears all") and Zeus promises to destroy their ship.

It's no surprise that when the adverse winds die down and the men sail off, Zeus splits their ship with a lightning bolt. As Odysseus says, "God took away their homecoming" (12.419). Odysseus constructs a makeshift raft, by lashing together the ship's keel and mast. He is driven back to Charybdis, and when she sucks down the sea (including his raft), he hangs suspended from a fig tree branch "like a bat" (12.433), and waits all day until Charybdis spits out his keel and mast. He paddles off and after another nine days reaches Calypso's island. At this point, Odysseus the storyteller calls it a night.

Looking over this book and Odysseus' adventures more broadly, we need to address the epic's themes and especially the issue of responsibility. First, regarding identity, hospitality, and homecoming, in book 12, it's only the last of these that is significant. Odysseus doesn't disguise himself from the Sirens, it doesn't make much sense to talk about Scylla's lack of hospitality, but homecoming comes center stage. The Sirens present one type of threat to returning to Ithaca—if Odysseus comes too close to shore, they'll die as many have done before—no homecoming! Also, there'll be no homecoming for the six men grabbed by Scylla. And clearly, by breaking the oath and eating the cattle of Helius, Odysseus' crew have forfeited any chance of return—this was anticipated in the first nine lines of the epic:

> For they lost their lives by their own recklessness—
> fools!—who ate the cattle of Helius, Hyperion's son,
> and he took away their day of homecoming. (1.7–9)

Only Odysseus avoids the dangers of the sea to arrive at Ogygia and—seven years later—at Scheria, Alcinous' home.

So much is clear. But the reasons are not. Zeus blamed the sufferings of mortals upon their own recklessness (1.32–34) and it's possible to say that what happened on Thrinacia was the fault of Odysseus' men. Two earlier cases, however, were more clear-cut. In the first episode after Troy, Odysseus' men reject his orders to leave the land of the Cicones and some pay for this insubordination with their lives—that is their own fault. Then in book 10, within sight of Ithaca, Odysseus' crew opens the bag of winds, driving them back to Aeolus' floating island—again, they are to blame.

My feeling is that eating Helius' cattle is morally more ambiguous. Eurylochus argues effectively that it made no sense to sail through the night (12.284–290). Zeus' contrary winds drive the men to the brink of starvation. In performing their rituals to honor the gods, Odysseus' men do their best: there's no barley, so they use leaves; there's no wine, so they make offerings of water—at least, they're trying! They promise a temple dedicated to Helius in Ithaca. What other options were there? I acknowledge that they swore an oath and then proceeded to willfully break it. But it's hard not to sympathize with their situation—I would at least argue that these are extenuating circumstances. To be sure, it's not Odysseus' fault—he's off the hook (although he does fall asleep at the darnedest times!).

More than anything else I would emphasize Odysseus' remarkable ability to survive—Eurylochus says that Odysseus is (metaphorically) made of iron (12.280). When everything around him has collapsed—his men are dead and the ship lies floating in splinters—Odysseus does not give up. He grabs the mast and keel, and fashions a raft (another Odyssean skill!). When Charybdis sucks down his puny craft, he hangs on for what seems like an eternity until his raft is belched forth. Then he paddles off and it's another nine days to Calypso's island.

Odysseus has a tenacious will to survive. We see this trait captured by the brief simile—he's "like a bat," hanging to the fig tree—and we've seen it before. In Polyphemus' cave, Odysseus clung to the underside of the big ram, waiting for their morning escape. And even on the Phaeacians' island—after his other shipwreck—he has the presence of mind to climb a tree to avoid wild animals. There, too, Homer used a simile to express Odysseus' stubborn drive: he was like a torch hidden in black ash at a hearth, "saving the seed of fire" (5.490). In a technical sense, we can absolve Odysseus of wrongdoing—he didn't eat any of Helius' cattle and did everything in his power to restrain his men. But even more important than ethics and the letter of the law is Odysseus' capacity to determine his goal and stick to it. "Much-suffering Odysseus" endures a great deal, but he also succeeds where others might have given up.

BOOK THIRTEEN

Book 13 is a book of transition and transformation. These changes include Odysseus finally reaching Ithaca after twenty years, the Phaeacians getting out of the taxi business, and the alteration of Odysseus' appearance. Athena's divinely engineered disguise allows Odysseus to return to his palace with virtually no one knowing it's him. After reaching his island, Odysseus now faces the task of reestablishing himself as king and husband.

Homer's three themes are still in operation. While in a sense, Odysseus has achieved his homecoming, Agamemnon's murder teaches that setting foot on your home soil is not enough—you must also test the loyalty of those who remained at home. In addition, Telemachus—still in Sparta—needs to achieve his own (less dramatic) homecoming.

Homer's other two themes become especially dominant: identity and hospitality. Although he has returned, Odysseus must keep his identity secret. Indeed, much suspense in the second half of the epic results from a set of recognition scenes in which Odysseus reveals himself to only a very few figures before confronting the suitors (see "The Structure of the *Odyssey*"). In addition, hospitality will continue to be the touchstone that reveals character: how will this beggar (Odysseus in disguise) be treated?

Book 13 may be divided into four sections: Farewell; Journey and Arrival; the Gods and the End of the Line; and Athena's Plan.

FAREWELL (13.1–69)

Book 13 begins with the end of Odysseus' tale and the effect is more than any singer could hope for.

> Thus he spoke, and they were all struck with silence,
> held by the spell of his words in the shadowy halls. (13.1–2)

Odysseus' song has had a magical effect upon the Phaeacians—they are "spellbound."

There is much ceremony and speech preceding Odysseus' departure. Alcinous announces that the time for Odysseus' escort has come, although he asks his aristocratic peers to add a few extra gifts for their guest. At dawn, a ship is made ready as the Phaeacians offer one final feast to Odysseus. The wait is just about over, but even this last meal makes Odysseus anxious (it's a lengthy, all-day affair). As he watches the sky for sunset, Homer uses a simile to compare Odysseus to a man ploughing a field waiting for dinnertime to arrive (13.31–35).

Odysseus gives a gracious farewell speech. He thanks his hosts, wishing all the best for them—and for himself, for he hopes to find his wife waiting for him in Ithaca. Odysseus also says a special goodbye to Arete, urging her to find delight in her home, her children, her people, and her royal husband. Just about everything has been taken care of: the gifts and provisions have been stored on the ship and there's even a spot on board for Odysseus to take a nap.

JOURNEY AND ARRIVAL (13.70–125)

Like Odysseus' tales, the voyage home is also magical. The ship is swifter than a hawk as its speeds across the sea. Homer suggests that Odysseus' arrival in Ithaca might be thought of as a "rebirth" or at least a "return to the land of the living." Upon departure, Odysseus falls into a deep sleep: "the sweetest, unwakable sleep, most like death" (13.80—the idea of Odysseus being symbolically "born again" at his arrival in Scheria has already been discussed in books 5 and 7). This new stage of Odysseus' life is also signaled by Homer's synopsis of the past twenty years:

> So the ship ran along swiftly, cutting the waves of the sea,
> bearing a man with god-like wits,
> who had already suffered so many pains in his heart
> cleaving his way through the wars of men and painful waves,
> but then he slept peacefully, oblivious of all he had endured. (13.88–92)

Odysseus has now left behind the Trojan war and his adventures at sea; he is entering a new stage of his life.

Book 13 offers some especially vivid descriptions of sea and land. Homer uses two similes to describe the ship's motion and speed (13.81–88). The morning star (the planet Venus) is sighted upon their arrival at Ithaca (13.93–95). An extremely detailed portrait is offered of the Bay of Phorkys in Ithaca, with its twin headlands protecting the harbor from adverse winds.

Landing in Ithaca, the Phaeacian crew puts Odysseus' loot by the trunk of an olive tree near the cave of the nymphs (13.120–123). The cave itself is quite fascinating—bees store honey there, it has flowing springs and two entrances (one for gods, the other for mortals)—but the olive tree links Odysseus' arrival to other key incidents. Remember that upon his arrival in Scheria, Odysseus climbed an olive tree to avoid attack by wild animals (5.476–487); later (actually earlier in his life), he sharpens an olive staff to blind Polyphemus (9.319–320). I don't want to give too much away, but there's a very special olive tree awaiting you in book 23. My point is that the poet has used the olive tree to mark out the stages of Odysseus' trials and achievements—here, the olive tree is linked to his arrival home (even if he is asleep).

THE GODS AND THE END OF THE LINE (13.125–187)

After the crew carries Odysseus and his treasures onto the strand, they depart and Homer switches in the midst of a poetic line to Poseidon's dialogue with Zeus (13.128–158—remember the divine assemblies at the start of books 1 and 5). Poseidon acknowledges that he knew Odysseus would ultimately make it home—Zeus had promised this after all—but the sea god feels his honor has been wounded. Zeus tries to reassure his brother—he's a powerful god without question—but then tells him, "Do what you wish." Poseidon's idea is to smash the Phaeacians' ship and cover their city with a mountain as punishment for conveying mortals by sea (Odysseus, in particular). Zeus then offers a more restrained response, which Poseidon adopts.

Within sight of Scheria, the Phaeacian ship is turned to stone and rooted to the earth. While the Phaeacians on shore are bewildered, Alcinous remembers an earlier prophecy that Poseidon in anger would smash a ship and cover them with a mountain (think of the predictions remembered after the fact by Polyphemus and Circe). Alcinous quickly resolves to put an end to their escort service and hopes that a sacrifice of twelve bulls to Poseidon may save their city (13.172–183). Odysseus is the last man to be ferried by the Phaeacians. We never find out if the sacrifice mollifies Poseidon, for Homer turns his attention to Ithaca as Odysseus wakes up.

ATHENA'S PLAN (13.187–440)

In past instances, the identity theme concerned people and whether they revealed or concealed who they were. When Odysseus wakes up, it's his homeland that is "disguised"—Odysseus doesn't recognize his own island! Homer offers two explanations—Odysseus has been away so long and Athena has wrapped him in a protective mist—but the effect is almost tragic. Odysseus assumes the Phaeacians have acted treacherously and brought him to the wrong place. This is a good example of dramatic irony. Odysseus laments, while we in the audience know he's actually in Ithaca. What's unusual is that frequently in the *Odyssey* Odysseus shares our knowledge—we know he's Odysseus, he knows he's Odysseus, but the Phaeacians or Circe or (soon) the suitors don't know. Here— for once—even Odysseus is in the dark. On top of this, Athena arrives to help, but she's disguised as a shepherd boy (a more typical example of concealing one's identity). Here's a puzzle. What is her motivation? Why not just tell him who she is?

Odysseus asks where he is and Athena reveals the land to be Ithaca, though she uses a big buildup first (many know it, it's rugged, grapes and grain grow there—can you guess yet?). Odysseus rejoices, yet his response is to lie: he tells Athena he's from Crete, but has gone into exile for killing a man. Athena's reaction is to smile and stroke Odysseus' hand—an unusual mark of intimacy between deity and human (13.287–288). "Will you never stop scheming?" she asks him and sheds her disguise, appearing now as a goddess.

What's most important about this scene is that we learn about the relationship between Athena and Odysseus. Goddess and hero are two of a kind—smart and devious with a strong inclination to lie and conceal their identities. Athena makes this link explicit:

> "It would be a clever trickster who could surpass you
> in all sorts of trickery, even if it were a god meeting you.
> Stubborn, devious-minded, full of wiles, you were not likely—
> even in your own land—to cease from lying
> and deceptive words, which are so dear to you.
> But come, let us talk of this no longer, for we both know
> deviousness, since you are by far the best of all mortals
> in plotting and speeches, while I am famous among all the gods
> for craft and trickery." (13.291–299)

In this lonely spot, nothing much is at stake if one deceives the other. But soon Odysseus' skill at disguise and trickery will be essential for defeating the suitors. Indeed, this is the next obstacle facing Odysseus (foreshadowed by Homer at 13.193). No sooner does he arrive home than Odysseus must plan for his next labor.

Odysseus' actions in the second half of the epic follow Athena's detailed strategy—she's got it all figured out. First, Odysseus must not tell anyone it's him.

> "Endure by necessity,
> and do not reveal to any man or woman
> at all that you have returned after your wandering, but in silence
> suffer those many pains as you receive the brutality of men." (13.307–310)

Second, Athena is just as concerned about Odysseus' riches as he is: she advises they hide them in the nymphs' cave. Third, she will alter Odysseus' appearance so that he'll look like an old beggar. Finally, Athena instructs him to go first to Eumaeus, the swineherd (pig farmer), while she retrieves Telemachus from

Sparta. Once more we see the intertwining plans and actions of gods and mortals—this will be Odysseus' victory, but he will only achieve it with the help of the gods.

Odysseus acknowledges his debt to divine aid. When he's finally convinced this actually is Ithaca, he kisses the earth and greets the nymphs of the cave: only with the help of Athena will he survive and aid his son (13.353–360). Odysseus says that with Athena standing by his side, he would fight 300 men (13.389–391). Odysseus may be cocky at times, but he is always humble with respect to the gods.

There is an awkward moment. We recall that it's taken Odysseus ten years to get back. Odysseus says he recollects Athena's help in Troy and she helped him much later in Scheria, but in the intervening period—where has she been? After the sack of Troy:

> "Then I didn't see you, daughter of Zeus, nor glimpsed you
> having come on my ship, so that you could ward off suffering from me.
> But always my heart was torn in my chest
> as I wandered, until the gods released me from evil." (13.318–321)

Odysseus isn't exactly challenging Athena, but in a roundabout sort of way he's asking why she didn't help him those nine long years.

Athena has a response. First, she knew he'd get back to Ithaca. And more important, she found it hard to fight against Poseidon and his anger for the blinding of Polyphemus (13.339–343). This is always a problem in a polytheistic world—what happens when one god opposes another? In this case, Athena gets what she wants in the end—Odysseus' return—but Poseidon's honor cannot be ignored. The sea god has the power to grant Polyphemus' prayer: "if it is fated that Odysseus return, may he come home late, alone, in another man's ship, and find trouble in his house." In the end, when gods clash, it's mortals who suffer.

The book closes with the actual metamorphosis of Odysseus, courtesy of Athena. She uses a wand to shrivel his skin, make him bald, dress him in old tattered clothes, and outfit him with a staff and beggar's sack (13.429–438). She even dims his eyes, taking the spark out of them. Now looking like an old man, Odysseus is ready to meet the people of Ithaca, who won't know it's Odysseus—home after twenty years.

BOOK FOURTEEN

Book 14 introduces the character of Eumaeus, the swineherd (or pig farmer), who welcomes Odysseus into his modest home. Eumaeus proves himself to be a loyal servant who has been watching over Odysseus' property; he is also a good host and, as we'll later learn, of royal birth (reflecting Homer's aristocratic bias).

There are four sections: Dogs and the Beggar; the Swineherd's Hospitality; Odysseus' Cretan Tale; and Odysseus' Trojan Tale. Much of book 14 consists of storytelling—false tales told by Odysseus—yet the most striking feature of this book is the suspense and irony that results from Odysseus' disguise and the question of when he may reveal himself.

DOGS AND THE BEGGAR (14.1–47)

In book 13, there was quite a bit of description of the journey, the Bay of Phorkys, and the Nymphs' Cave. In this book, too, Homer is in no hurry. He lingers over details in describing the construction of Eumaeus' house and enumerating the 360 pigs in the pens and the four dogs and four men helping Eumaeus. We are even given a glimpse of what Eumaeus is doing when Odysseus arrives: cutting out oxhide for a new pair of sandals.

The aggressive watchdogs catch wind of Odysseus and rush noisily forward. Odysseus drops his staff and crouches on the ground, but Homer remarks that it could have gotten ugly if Eumaeus hadn't scattered the dogs by throwing stones. Elsewhere dogs have represented a true—or a false—home (two dogs accompany Telemachus to the assembly in book 2; the Phaeacians have golden dogs at their gates), but Eumaeus' dogs offer no welcome to Odysseus on his return—he's a stranger to them.

Virtually the first words out of Eumaeus' mouth are a lament for his absent master, Odysseus, and a criticism of the suitors for their endless feasting on pork. He then acts as a perfect host and invites Odysseus in for food and wine.

THE SWINEHERD'S HOSPITALITY (14.48–184)

There's no question that Eumaeus is one of the good guys in this epic. He cites the proverb "travelers and beggars are under Zeus' protection" (14.57–58—also quoted by Nausicaa at 6.207–208). The swineherd insists that he would never dishonor a guest in his home and even gives Odysseus his own mattress to recline on. Odysseus is extremely pleased with Eumaeus' hospitality.

It's also remarkable how often Eumaeus mentions Odysseus, who, he says, is absent and probably dead.

> "He treated me kindly and bestowed possessions on me,
> such as a gentle lord gives his servant:
> a home, a piece of land, and a much-desired wife." (14.62–64)

Later Eumaeus says he'll never find such a kind master, for he considers Odysseus both lord and brother (14.138–147). After initially hesitating, Eumaeus finally names his absent lord: "A longing for absent Odysseus seizes me" (14.144).

In contrast to his own observance of the code of hospitality, Eumaeus denounces the suitors as bad guests, who have no reverence toward the gods. Assuming Odysseus' death, the suitors are wooing Odysseus' wife and wasting his livelihood.

> "They unjustly woo his wife,
> and never go to their own homes, but at their leisure
> outrageously devour his possessions without restraint." (14.90–92)

Certainly Eumaeus has proven his loyalty and trustworthiness: he is devoted to Odysseus and his family. Right now he's worried about Telemachus, Odysseus' only child—if the suitors succeed with their ambush, the family line would be extinguished (14.174–182).

Yet Odysseus delays revealing the big news in this subtle exchange. The irony is hip deep. Eumaeus is going on and on about how dogs and birds have ripped Odysseus' bones or fish have eaten him, while Odysseus sits right in front of him, chatting away. At one point, Eumaeus even says, "my master, who is not here" to his master who *is* there (14.145). We are kept wondering when Odysseus will reveal himself to Eumaeus. The most he'll do is swear an oath that

Odysseus is coming back, but Eumaeus wishes to change the subject for such remembrance is painful.

ODYSSEUS' CRETAN TALE (14.185–409)

After they have eaten, Eumaeus asks some direct questions: Who are you? Where do you come from? Who are your parents? What ship brought you—for surely you didn't get here by foot? This is an opportunity for Odysseus to come clean and say who he actually is.

For reasons that are not wholly clear at this point, Odysseus will not confide in Eumaeus. He's finally home, obviously he can count on Eumaeus, but instead he fabricates an elaborate tale, lying to his faithful swineherd. Odysseus may simply be cautiously following Athena's directions, but he almost seems to be enjoying himself.

There was a proverb in antiquity: "All Cretans are liars." (As a paradox, this tormented later philosophers. What if a Cretan says, "All Cretans are liars"— true or false?) Most likely this saying was current in Homer's day, but—if not— we may be witnessing the birth of a proverb, for every time Odysseus says "I'm from Crete," we know he's about to tell a tall, tall tale. The story Odysseus tells Eumaeus is much more elaborate than the lies he told Athena in book 13. Of particular interest are the adaptations of his own personal history.

Odysseus describes himself as a Cretan wanderer, the illegitimate son of a wealthy man who died. Nevertheless, he made a good marriage, but preferred sailing and raiding—a life of adventure!—to life on the farm. After ten years at Troy, he comes home for only a single month and then takes off again, this time for Egypt.

Attacked by the Egyptian army, he survives by supplicating the king who pities him. After seven years of work in Egypt, he leaves for a year in Phoenicia. His next sea voyage meets with a storm and ends in a shipwreck, which lands him as sole survivor in Thesprotia (in northwest Greece, near Ithaca). A kind king there receives him, but during his final trip, he is robbed by sailors. Before they sell him into slavery, he escapes when they land in Ithaca.

First, we should appreciate the wonderfully compelling details Odysseus includes in his story of the Cretan wanderer. His father was Castor, son of Hylax; he led nine overseas raids before Troy; they feasted for six days before journeying to Egypt; when he escapes in Ithaca, he describes how he wades in the water up to his chest with a cloak over his head, before swimming along the shore to freedom. I should also note that every spot mentioned is well known to the Greeks of Homer's time—there are no vignettes about Cyclopes or witches or six-headed monsters. Such invention of particulars adds a feel of realism to what we know to be a patently false yarn.

Second, the point of the story is largely that—from his wanderings—the Cretan wanderer (Odysseus in disguise) has heard from the Thesprotian king that Eumaeus' master, Odysseus, is on his way home. Odysseus was just stopping at the oracle in Dodona to learn whether he should return home openly or in secret (14.321–333—see Map 1). Eumaeus says his heart is torn listening to such suffering and he believes it—except for the part about Odysseus. Even before Odysseus began this tale, Eumaeus warned him that many imposters have come to Ithaca to tell of Odysseus' imminent return, inciting tears from Penelope and winning a cloak or tunic as reward (14.121–132). There's no need for this beggar to lie about Odysseus—Eumaeus has given up hope—and besides, he'll respectfully pity his guest without such fanciful tales (14.374–389). The noble swineherd has heard enough guff to make him cynical.

Finally, it's hard not to notice the eerie echoes of Odysseus' own life in the tale of the Cretan wanderer. In the Egyptian episode when his men start raiding against orders, we might think of Odysseus' men in Thrace recklessly attacking the Cicones (9.43–61). Eumaeus is told how during the storm off Crete, a lightning bolt splits the ship and leaves the Cretan wanderer as the only survivor—this episode is told in language almost identical to Odysseus' story of the shipwreck after his men ate Helius' cattle (compare 14.301–317 with 12.403–419)—once more he hangs onto a floating mast for dear life. Even his arrival at Thesprotia echoes Nausicaa's rescue on Scheria. In the Cretan tale, it's the king's son—not daughter—who gives him clothes after the shipwreck and leads him to his royal father for escort by sea. Odysseus once again proves his skill at storytelling, but part of what we're witnessing is the way in which a storyteller constructs an effective, yet fictional tale, based in part on real-life incidents. With a moment's reflection, we are in a better position to appreciate Homer's art found in the first thirteen books: the realistic detail, artistic design, and willful invention.

ODYSSEUS' TROJAN TALE (14.410–533)

Odysseus and Eumaeus have another meal with Eumaeus' men. This includes a sacrifice to the gods and a prayer that Odysseus might return (14.418–456). In spite of his skepticism, Eumaeus insists that "the gods are capable of anything" (14.445). The swineherd has already proved his loyalty to Odysseus and his respect for travelers—in this scene, he demonstrates due reverence for the gods.

It's a cold, rainy night and when they lie down for sleep, Odysseus tells another tale—this one's set in Troy. During the Trojan War, "our man from Crete" and Odysseus set up a nighttime ambush. On that frigid evening under the walls of Troy, he nudges Odysseus, fearing he'll die from exposure. Odysseus sends a man back to camp, gaining a cloak for the Cretan warrior. Eumaeus immediately grasps the point of the story. He gets up and makes a soft bed near the fire for the beggar. We discover that nothing is too good for a guest in Eumaeus' home—and that Odysseus never passes up a chance to test those he meets with his roguish charm.

BOOK FIFTEEN

In book 15, upon Athena's prompting, Telemachus returns to Ithaca. Athena also lays out a plan for Telemchus: first visit Eumaeus, and then send Eumaeus to Penelope with news of his arrival. Athena's plan coincides nicely with Homer's goal, for the poet is about to reunite father and son, dovetailing his two stories of Telemachus and Odysseus into a single narrative. This book shares some features with book 13, which told of Odysseus' departure, voyage, and arrival in Ithaca—here, too, there is much ceremony and travel. We then switch back to Ithaca, where Eumaeus tells his guest the story of his life and how he became part of Odysseus' household.

Homer now begins a series of omens that foreshadow Odysseus' return and vengeance. And there's no better way to introduce omens than to have a resident fortune-teller, which is precisely what happens. In a great cameo role (played by David Carradine?), Theoclymenus is the hitchhiking seer whom Telemachus brings to Ithaca.

It is clear to many readers that books 13–15 develop slowly, certainly in contrast to the exciting adventures of books 9–12. Still Homer sensitively addresses any potential impatience on the part of his audience. Besides, Homer knows what he's doing: he needs to put all the pieces in place before shifting to Odysseus' palace. He wants Odysseus and Telemachus to return; Eumaeus needs to be established as loyal and trustworthy. In books 17–20, Homer will demonstrate the collective guilt of the suitors. Once all this is established, the time comes for action: a life-or-death struggle.

Book 15 may be divided into four sections: Telemachus' Departure from Sparta; Theoclymenus and the Sea Voyage; Eumaeus' Tale; and Telemachus' Return.

TELEMACHUS' DEPARTURE FROM SPARTA (15.1–182)

The last scene with Telemachus was in book 4, where we left him in the care of Menelaus and Helen in Sparta. Eleven books later, Athena arrives at the side of a sleepless Telemachus and instructs him to go home. She warns him of the suitors' ambush and even tells him that Penelope is being pressured by her relatives to marry (we have no other evidence for this). The effect is immediate. Telemachus wakes his companion, Pisistratus, and suggests leaving right away in the dark. Pisistratus persuades the impetuous youth to wait until dawn, so they might say good-bye to their host, Menelaus.

Much like Odysseus' last day among the Phaeacians, Telemachus receives gifts and a fine meal from his hosts. Menelaus offers a silver *crater* (wine-mixing cup), which is gilded; Helen presents a glistening dress for Telemachus' bride when he marries. At his departure, Telemachus graciously praises Menelaus' hospitality:

> "So when I return
> to Ithaca, if I should find Odysseus at home,
> I would tell him of the full friendship I have received from you
> on my journey, for I bring many, fine treasures." (15.156–159)

At the mention of finding Odysseus at home, there's an omen: an eagle flies past carrying a large, white goose in its talons. Helen interprets:

> "Just as this bird, coming from the mountains where its birth
> and offspring are, has seized the goose fattened at home,
> so will Odysseus return home and take vengeance,
> after great suffering and many wanderings—if he isn't already
> at home, planting trouble for all the suitors." (15.174–178)

We know Odysseus is already at home plotting revenge, yet these scenes of dramatic irony will proliferate until the final confrontation with the suitors. Homer repeatedly introduces the hopes and predictions of Odysseus' allies.

THEOCLYMENUS AND THE SEA VOYAGE (15.182–300)

Telemachus and Pisistratus take two days to reach Pylos, Nestor's realm. Once more Telemachus hopes to leave immediately: he speaks of his friendship with Pisistratus, yearning to skip a final (long!) farewell with the loquacious Nestor. Pisistratus endorses this plan, instructing Telemachus to depart before they reach his home.

Telemachus gets right to work, making ready for the sea voyage home. Just as he's sacrificing to Athena, a seer named Theoclymenus shows up. First, Homer tells us his genealogy: evidently, divination is part of the family business. One of Theoclymenus' famous relatives is Amphiareus, a seer who died at Thebes while fighting at the side of Polyneices, one of Oedipus' sons. Being a seer, Amphiareus knew he'd die, but fought anyway. As usual, Homer quickly alludes to these stories that were familiar to his audience.

Theoclymenus then tells his own story. He's in exile for killing a relative, and is being pursued by those who seek vengeance. His desperation shows:

> "Please, put me on your ship, since I come to you as a suppliant in exile!
> Don't kill me! I think I'm being pursued." (15.277–278)

This has to be pretty exciting for Telemachus, who's been royally entertained of late, but has yet to face real danger. He quickly agrees, seats Theoclymenus next to him on board, and they set sail—first by day, then by night—approaching Ithaca and the suitors' ambush.

EUMAEUS' TALE (15.301–495)

Homer abruptly switches to Eumaeus' house, where once more it's mealtime. Homer notes another of Odysseus' "tests": he tells Eumaeus that the next day he plans to go to town, visit Odysseus' house, and beg for supper from the suitors. Eumaeus talks him into waiting for Telemachus' return. Odysseus responds by attributing men's troubles to their stomachs. No one until Shakespeare's Falstaff is quite as eloquent about eating as Odysseus: he insisted on eating in Alcinous' palace; even in the *Iliad*, when Achilles finally agrees to return to battle, Odysseus demands that they eat first (*Iliad* 19.155–183).

Odysseus then interviews Eumaeus, asking first about his own (Odysseus') parents and then about Eumaeus' life story. We learn more about Laertes, Odysseus' father, and how he grieves for both his dead wife and missing son. We also learn that Odysseus had a sister who was raised with Eumaeus, but—now married—lives across the sea. With apparent innocence, Odysseus asks how Eumaeus came to Ithaca: Was his city sacked or was he kidnapped by pirates?

Eumaeus' early childhood sounds idyllic. He was the son of a king who ruled an island, Syria, a place untouched by disease. Yet his nanny—herself kidnapped by Taphian pirates—sleeps with a visiting Phoenician trader, who promises to take her home to Sidon (on the Phoenician coast). On a prearranged signal, she scoops up little Eumaeus (and some gold) and rushes to the harbor. They sail off, but she dies within a week and the traders sell Eumaeus to Laertes.

It could be said that this story doesn't advance the plot at all. In part, that's true. Yet it does establish the bond of suffering between Eumaeus and Odysseus (much like that between Telemachus and Nestor's son, Pisistratus). More significant perhaps is how Homer instructs his own audience in the art of listening to stories. Before telling of his own childhood, Eumaeus reflects on the odd experience of finding delight in hearing sad stories.

> "Listen now in silence and delight; sit there and drink your
> wine. For the nights are immense. It is a time to sleep,
> or to listen to delightful tales. And why should you
> lie down before it's time? A long sleep is tedious . . .
> Let us two drink and eat in the tent,
> and delight in the painful sorrow of each other,
> remembering. For a man, who suffers much and wanders much,
> delights afterwards even in his own past sorrows." (15.391–394 . . . 398–401)

Writers and philosophers have long wondered why we enjoy reading sad stories or watching tragedy. Homer has no answer, but he recognizes the fact that—with distance—there is a pleasure in remembering even the hardest parts of our lives.

This is what we are doing in our experience of the *Odyssey*: reading (or hearing) about Odysseus' many troubles—his mother dies while he is away, his wife is beset by aggressive suitors, and so on. And yet in the right circumstances, we enjoy this and want to hear more. Homer cleverly suggests that those who aren't interested should take a hike and sleep outside—within the epic, Eumaeus suggests as much to his men who may already know his biography. But the advice applies just as well to Homer's audience: "If you want to sleep, go outside and do it. But we're going to enjoy ourselves in reliving the sorrows of long ago" (my paraphrase of 15.395–401).

TELEMACHUS' RETURN (15.495–557)

As dawn approaches, Telemachus is dropped off on Ithaca. He's avoided the suitors' ambush and sends the ship to town. In saying farewell to Theoclymenus, Telemachus worries about the suitors who are attempting to seize Odysseus' kingdom. This time a hawk appears clutching a dove. Theoclymenus interprets.

> "There is no family more kingly than yours
> in Ithaca, and your family will always hold sway." (15.533–534)

This second favorable omen also foreshadows the suitors' defeat, while endorsing Telemachus as rightful heir to his father's kingdom. Telemachus then entrusts Theoclymenus to one of the crew and heads to Eumaeus' home where his father waits in disguise.

BOOK SIXTEEN

Book 16 is an important book. (I know, they're *all* important, but this one is *especially* crucial.) It is here that Homer brings together Odysseus and Telemachus. In terms of the *Odyssey*'s structure, this reunion allows Homer to simplify his narrative: from this point on, he tells a single story of father and son plotting together.

Telemachus learns that the beggar is actually his father: this is what we call a "recognition scene"—the first of quite a few. Soon Odysseus' servants, wife, father, and the suitors will learn of his return—but all in good time. In addition to Telemachus' realization, Homer uses this series of recognition scenes to construct Odysseus' identity. From the start of the epic, the question has been: who is this man (unnamed in the first twenty lines of the poem)? In the first four books we heard many second- and thirdhand reports that offered a portrait of Odysseus built on public reputation. In books 5–8 we met a man of many skills: shipbuilder, sailor, orator, and athlete. In books 9–12, Odysseus the storyteller and adventurer—the man who has done it all—comes center stage. In the second half of the epic, Homer approaches the question of Odysseus' identity somewhat differently. In book 16, we learn that part of Odysseus' identity is that he is the father of Telemachus.

Book 16 may be divided into four parts: Reunion; Recognition; Plans of Father and Son; and News Reaches the Palace.

REUNION (16.1–153)

The dogs signal Odysseus that a visitor, well known to Eumaeus, approaches. There is no barking, as the dogs fawn over Telemachus. When he walks in, Homer presents the reunion in vivid detail. Dropping his pail, Eumaeus stands up in amazement and—ready to weep—greets Telemachus by kissing his head, eyes, and hands. Homer highlights this meeting with the following simile:

> As a father fondly welcomes his own son
> coming from a distant land after ten years,
> his beloved only son, for whom he toiled endlessly,
> so then the noble swineherd showered kisses upon
> godlike Telemachus, as if the young man had escaped from death. (16.17–21)

Clearly, these two have an intimate relationship. Eumaeus and Telemachus speak affectionately to one another: Eumaeus calls the youth "sweet light," while in turn the swineherd is addressed as "pop."

This scene illustrates Homer's dramatic daring. We have been waiting the entire epic for Odysseus and Telemachus to be reunited. Now with Odysseus a few feet away, Homer uses a simile to compare *Eumaeus'* welcome with that of a father who hasn't seen his son in ten years. Not all the details of the comparison fit the narrative itself—in the simile it's the son who has been away for ten years, not the father for twenty—but Homer pursues at least two goals here. First, he subtly foreshadows the *true* reunion of father and son, which he'll present a hundred lines later. Second and more important, the poet is able to reactivate the idea of the surrogate, the figure who fills a role when someone is absent. Earlier Athena played surrogate father to Telemachus ("you have spoken to me as a father speaks to his son"); the various women in Odysseus' life became surrogate wives (Circe, Calypso, and Nausicaa). In book 16, Eumaeus is cast as the surrogate father to Telemachus, a young man who has never known his real father. As we come to expect from a genius like Homer, he doesn't come right out and say "Eumaeus was like a father to Telemachus in Odysseus' absence." Instead the poet suggests as much indirectly with this brilliant simile, just as we're expecting Telemachus' real father to greet the son he hardly knows.

Telemachus and the swineherd exchange fond words amidst their worries about Penelope and the suitors. As expected, the host Eumaeus serves food and wine to the young traveler. All the while, the disguised Odysseus looks on. Telemachus is still well trained in the rules of hospitality: he insists that the beggar keep his seat and asks where he's from. By this time, Odysseus has Eumaeus passing along his deceitful stories ("Oh, he's from Crete, kidnapped, ran away . . . ").

Telemachus will do what he can for this pitiable beggar. He offers a tunic, cloak, sword, and sandals; he'll even have food sent to Eumaeus' place. But Telemachus doesn't see how he can receive the stranger in his own home: his guest would risk sacrilegious abuse from the hellish band of suitors. Odysseus feigns ignorance (in fact, some of his curiosity may be sincere) and asks why no one has helped Telemachus: Is he hated by the people of Ithaca? Why don't he and his brothers league together? Odysseus comes dangerously close to revealing his own identity when he imagines himself as Odysseus' son or Odysseus himself, back for vengeance (16.99–101): "I'd rather die than see their daily outrage" (16.107). Odysseus' anger is directed against the suitors and what they have done to his home: they've wasted his property, and abused the guests and servants.

The best reply Telemachus can muster is to say there are simply too many of these rogues—plus Penelope won't decide: she neither refuses nor accepts. "All this lies in the laps of the gods," he says. Nevertheless, Telemachus cares enough for his mother to send Eumaeus with news of his own return. He also has not wholly given up on Odysseus:

> "If somehow all things in life could be decided by mortals,
> my first choice would be for my father's homecoming day." (16.148–149)

Telemachus' wish is about to be granted.

RECOGNITION (16.154–219)

As Eumaeus heads off, Athena moves into action—she's thought out each stage of the plan. Appearing like a tall woman to only Odysseus (and the dogs), Athena signals him to go outside. The goddess says it's no longer necessary to conceal his identity from Telemachus. At this point, Odysseus undergoes a reverse transformation: he becomes younger with darker skin, a longer jaw, and a dark beard. When he goes in, Telemachus is convinced Odysseus is a god—the metamorphosis was so rapid!

Odysseus insists that he is Telemachus' father, returned home after twenty years. He then kisses his son and weeps. When Telemachus is skeptical, Odysseus attributes the magic to Athena and puts it this way:

> "There will not be another Odysseus coming here,
> No! this is me—after much suffering and wandering,
> I've come to my fatherland in the twentieth year." (16.204–206)

At this point, Odysseus sits down. Telemachus' resistance vanishes and he embraces his father: together they moan like vultures who have lost their chicks.

There are two points worth making here. First, in the later recognition scenes, there will be a token (or sign) of recognition—something tangible Odysseus can point to as evidence to prove he truly is Odysseus and no other. Yet Telemachus was an infant when his father left—what token could possibly convince the youth? While in a sense there is no proof, Odysseus employs what parents (perhaps especially fathers) have used for generations: he is Telemachus' father, BECAUSE HE SAID SO! All of us have had such experiences: "Why do I have to do that?" "Because I said so!" And for Telemachus, this is enough.

The other interesting feature is Telemachus' skepticism. At first, he doesn't trust what Odysseus says, however much he'd like to believe it. As we will see, this is a family trait, shared by Penelope, Odysseus, and even old Laertes. People in this family need to be convinced, even that their fondest desires are being fulfilled. This is simply more evidence that Telemachus is truly Odysseus' son (and therefore that Penelope is faithful).

PLANS OF FATHER AND SON (16.220–321)

Odysseus reveals Athena's plan for the suitors' defeat. Telemachus enumerates over one hundred suitors, yet Odysseus insists that—with Athena's and Zeus' help—they will prevail. Odysseus then gets down to specifics: Telemachus should return home and put up with whatever outrage he (Odysseus in disguise) suffers from the suitors; at a certain signal, Telemachus is to remove the weapons from the hall with a plausible excuse; finally, Telemachus must tell no one of Odysseus' return—they must first test the servants' loyalty. On this last point, Odysseus is adamant:

> "If you truly are mine and of our blood,
> let no one from now on hear that Odysseus is within,
> do not let Laertes learn this nor the swineherd,
> nor any of the servants, nor even Penelope herself." (16.300–303)

Telemachus is to prove his lineage not only by his skepticism, but also by his ability to conceal Odysseus' true identity. He, too, must be devious—like father, like son.

NEWS REACHES THE PALACE (16.322–481)

Telemachus' ship reaches the town of Ithaca, and a herald announces Telemachus' safe return. The two leaders of the suitors, Eurymachus and Antinous, respond with more threats. After lamenting their hard work maintaining the ambush at sea, Antinous believes they must kill Telemachus now, before he gains sympathy from the townspeople or tries to drive the suitors from the palace. Another suitor, Amphinomus, rejects this idea: "It is a terrible thing to kill a royal prince" (16.401–402); he then advises that they consult the gods.

Penelope has learned of the suitors' assassination plot. She now appears and berates Antinous, recalling how Odysseus protected Antinous' father in the past. Eurymachus, the more devious leader, insists that no one will attack Telemachus while he lives, for Odysseus was like a father and "Telemachus is most dear to me" (16.441–446). Of course, he says this while plotting Telemachus' death. Penelope retreats to her upstairs chamber to cry herself to sleep.

That evening Eumaeus' return requires that Athena transform Odysseus into the old beggar once more, preventing Eumaeus from telling Penelope (16.454–459). After hearing Eumaeus' report, Telemachus smiles at his father without the swineherd noticing—by this time, father and son see eye to eye.

The final third of the epic offers a more precise account of the identity and diversity of the suitors. Books 1–4 emphasized the two leaders, Antinous and

Eurymachus. Penelope's rebuke offers some historical background on the relationship between the suitors' families and Odysseus. We also meet the "good" suitor, Amphinomus, who is praised explicitly for pleasing Penelope with words and his good sense—and for at least initially opposing Antinous' idea of killing Telemachus. Even he, however, would kill Telemachus if the gods so advise. Odysseus' desire to test the loyalty of the servants also anticipates a more detailed exploration of the household staff. In the next few books we will learn more of Odysseus' household: previously, Homer introduced the singer, Phemius (in book 1), and Telemachus' confidante, Eurycleia (especially in books 2 and 4). We are also reminded of the herald Medon, who passes along information to Penelope (16.412–413; see also 4.677–679).

By reuniting father and son, Homer tightens up his narrative. In fact, we now have parallel conspiracies: the suitors plan to kill Telemachus while Odysseus and his son plot against the suitors. Both must lie and be devious, but if the matchup is between Odysseus and Eurymachus' associates, the suitors are clearly out of their league.

BOOK SEVENTEEN

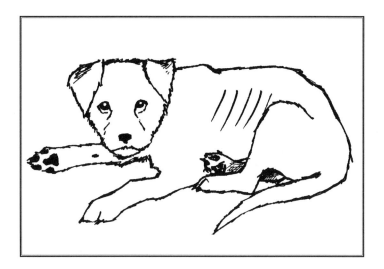

Book 17 gathers Odysseus, Telemachus, and Penelope in the same house for the first time in twenty years. The danger now concerns Odysseus' identity: Will the suitors or Penelope recognize him? There are two memorable events: first, the unexpected recognition scene with the dog Argus; second, as Odysseus begs in his own home, Antinous hits him with a stool. Homer makes crystal clear who the good guys are and who deserves to be punished.

Book 17 may be divided into six sections: Telemachus Greets Penelope; Telemachus in Town; Hospitality at the Palace; Odysseus and Eumaeus Encounter Melanthius; the Dogs Knows; and a King Begs in His Own Home. This staccato pattern results from three separate arrivals at the palace: first Telemachus; then Telemachus with Theoclymenus; finally Eumaeus and Odysseus.

TELEMACHUS GREETS PENELOPE (17.1–60)

Arriving at the palace early the next day, Telemachus is greeted by Eurycleia and his mother. Penelope says what we might expect a mother to say:

"I never thought
I'd see you again, when you went by ship to Pylos
secretly." (17.41–43)

Telemachus briefly advises Penelope to pray to the gods and heads into town. This book offers greater insight into the relationship of mother and son—except for Telemachus' orders to Penelope to go upstairs in book 1, these two haven't yet been presented together. But Telemachus' quick exit suggests this is a young man still seeking to establish his independence.

TELEMACHUS IN TOWN (17.61–84)

As Telemachus travels to town with his two dogs, Athena pours "grace" upon him. The townspeople gaze in wonder, yet the suitors, complimenting him publicly, continue to plot against him. Telemachus associates himself with Halitherses and Peiraeus—the better sort of townsfolk (Halitherses predicted Odysseus' return after twenty years)—and takes charge of the seer Theoclymenus. When asked about his treasures from Menelaus, Telemachus tells Peiraeus to hold onto them: if he's killed, he doesn't want the suitors to seize these presents as well.

HOSPITALITY AT THE PALACE (17.85–182)

Telemachus returns to the palace a second time, now with Theoclymenus. Mother and son both show due respect to their guest. Telemachus gives Theoclymenus a bath, clothes, and food. Penelope waits until after the meal to ask her son of his adventures. Telemachus quickly recapitulates what he learned in Pylos and Sparta: Nestor was like a father to him (17.109–112), but it was Menelaus who predicted Odysseus' vengeance and passed along Proteus' tale of Odysseus trapped on Calypso's island.

Theoclymenus breaks in with a prophecy:

> "Know now—by Zeus first of the gods and the table of hospitality
> and the hearth of blameless Odysseus to which I have come—
> that Odysseus is already in his fatherland
> (he is here or coming) and, learning of these evil deeds,
> he plants trouble against all the suitors." (17.155–159)

Penelope promises recompense if the prophet's word proves true. As always, the suitors are living the easy life. Medon, the herald, interrupts their discus competition to call them to dinner. The only guest yet to arrive is the king in disguise.

ODYSSEUS AND EUMAEUS ENCOUNTER MELANTHIUS (17.182–290)

Odysseus and the faithful swineherd now make their journey to town. Homer describes a mountain spring, sacred to the nymphs, where they encounter a goatherd, Melanthius. It's difficult to discover any good qualities in this man. He insults Eumaeus and Odysseus ("it's scum leading scum"), kicks Odysseus without provocation, and hopes for the death of Telemachus.

We might note that Homer has now set another character test in addition to hospitality: How do people speak of Telemachus and his father? Loyalty is proved by a desire for Telemachus' safety and Odysseus' return; the opposite hope—"may Apollo strike Telemachus and Odysseus never come back"—distinguishes the bad guys in this epic. The episode with Melanthius demonstrates that not only is Odysseus' household in disarray, but the island kingdom rests on the verge of anarchy: travelers are abused by violent herdsmen with no fear of retribution. And we wonder: Eumaeus is faithful, Melanthius is not. What about the rest of the servants? Who remains true to Odysseus?

When Odysseus is kicked (though not toppled) by Melanthius, he makes a decision. At first, the choice appears to be between killing Melanthius with his walking stick or by dropping him on his head, but Odysseus follows another path: he restrains his anger and merely endures Melanthius' abuse. Earlier Odysseus had to choose whether to hang onto the remnants of his boat or swim for it (book 5) and whether to supplicate Nausicaa by grabbing her knees or from afar (book 6). As he approaches his own household, the test for Odysseus is whether he is disciplined enough to ignore insult and outrage in order to maintain his disguise. This time he succeeds.

THE DOG KNOWS (17.291–327)

Approaching the house, Odysseus and the swineherd are spied by Argus ("Flash"), a dog raised by Odysseus before he left for Troy—this is one ancient dog! Odysseus asks Eumaeus about the neglect this dog now suffers, as it lies in dung, covered with fleas. Eumaeus praises Argus: he was strong, fast, and superb at tracking animals. Odysseus lets a tear fall (without Eumaeus seeing), Argus recognizes his master has finally returned—wagging his tail and putting down his ears—and then the old dog expires.

This may seem a trivial vignette, but once more Homer has prepared us for appreciating this episode. The dog has remained faithful to Odysseus in spite of his long absence—this augurs favorably for the rest of Odysseus' servants. In addition, this is the second in a series of recognition scenes. In book 16, Telemachus discovered his father had returned; now the dog learns as much. In a sense, there is little risk—the suitors aren't there and Eumaeus seems oblivious to what is happening on the dung heap—but it is significant that while feeling pity for the lonesome pooch, Odysseus steels himself to conceal his emotions. This is a recognition scene that is not of Odysseus' own choosing—there's always a danger that someone will learn Odysseus is back before the appropriate time. So far, so good.

A KING BEGS IN HIS OWN HOME (17.328–606)

In the *Poetics*, Aristotle emphasizes the dramatic power of recognition scenes; he also mentions "reversals" (*peripeteia* in Greek), which consist of a rapid change in fortune. For example, at the beginning of Sophocles' *Oedipus the*

King, Oedipus dynamically rules the city and is admired by all; by the end of the play, he's blind, driven into exile, utterly without power, and his wife is dead. Such reversals of fortune make a strong emotional impact upon us. This isn't quite what happens in the *Odyssey*, but it is striking that one of the Greek heroes from the Trojan war should be reduced to begging in his own home. He's a sorry sight: dressed in rags, leaning on the doorpost, ready to beg for food. It's a far cry from Agamemnon's triumphal return, but Odysseus' goal is success—however he can get it.

After Telemachus offers food, Odysseus makes his way around the suitors, soliciting scraps. Interestingly, we learn that Athena spurs him on so that he might learn which of the suitors are innocent and which are blameworthy—though either way death awaits them (17.360–364). There's some squabbling among Antinous, Eumaeus, and Telemachus: Antinous blames Eumaeus for bringing in another mouth to feed; Telemachus accuses Antinous of always stirring up trouble and sarcastically says:

> "Antinous, how kindly you care for me—like a father for his son—
> by bidding me to drive this guest from our dining hall
> with a harsh command." (17.397–399)

Antinous, of course, is no father surrogate: he's more like the evil twin of Odysseus.

Odysseus plays his part flawlessly. He walks right up to the suitors and says, "Give," sometimes with success. Homer focuses on his approach to Antinous. Odysseus praises the suitor's aristocratic appearance and tells him a short version of his life: he once lived in a rich house, he was taken prisoner in Egypt, and sold to a man in Cyprus (17.415–444). This elicits no sympathy: Antinous calls Odysseus the bane of their dinner. He also explains that the other suitors are only giving food because it's not theirs. At this point, Odysseus provokes a confrontation.

> "Unbelievable! Your wits surely do not match your looks!
> Sitting now in another's home, you would not even give
> a grain of salt to your own retainer, nor would you
> take a bit of bread and give it to me, though there's plenty." (17.454–457)

Antinous yells back and strikes Odysseus in the back with a footstool.

This is a dramatic moment. Everyone reacts. Odysseus calls the suitors to witness and seeks vengeance from the gods: "May Antinous die before his marriage!" (17.476). Antinous tells him to sit quietly, but the suitors recognize that Antinous' behavior is unacceptable and dangerous. An anonymous suitor recalls the habit of gods:

> "The gods, looking like out-of-town travelers,
> assuming every sort of appearance, visit cities,
> watching the outrage and lawfulness of men." (17.485–487)

As agreed, Telemachus is silent, but Penelope asks that Apollo strike down Antinous (this is seconded by a faithful maid, Eurynome). In spite of everyone's misgivings, this is just the first of three times that Odysseus has something thrown at him. If you were wondering: Are the suitors really that bad? Do they all deserve to die? The answer must be yes. They are violent toward travelers and they are plotting the death of Telemachus. They are guilty! guilty! guilty!

Penelope feels pity toward the beggar and asks Eumaeus to let her meet him. She is motivated by the kindness of her heart—she's a good hostess to this wanderer—but she also hopes he has news of Odysseus. Eumaeus praises Odysseus' gift for telling enchanting stories and passes along a synopsis of Odysseus' lies ("Odysseus is in Dodona consulting Zeus' oracle"). This prompts Penelope to pray for her husband's return:

> "If only Odysseus would come back to his fatherland,
> with his son he would quickly avenge the violence of these men." (17.539–540)

Immediately Telemachus sneezes—this was viewed as an omen in Homer's day. We "knock on wood" to prevent something from happening; for the Greeks, Telemachus' spontaneous sneeze signals that Penelope's wish will be fulfilled.

The book ends in suspense. Odysseus promises Eumaeus he will visit Penelope, but only at sundown when the suitors disperse. "For I know well about Odysseus, since we have received the same misery" (17.563). For Eumaeus, this statement means both Odysseus and the beggar have suffered much in their travels. As readers, we recognize that the words are literally true—more dramatic irony! But Penelope's request to see the beggar raises a concern: of all the people who knew Odysseus, Penelope has the best chance of knowing he's her husband. If she recognizes him, will she joyfully cry out and unintentionally warn the suitors? As the suitors party on, Homer leaves us anticipating the reunion of husband and wife.

BOOK EIGHTEEN

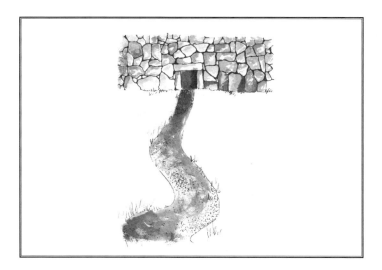

There are no recognition scenes in book 18—we must wait until book 19 to see what Penelope will make of Odysseus. In part, book 18 continues the mocking of Odysseus we saw in book 17 (another stool is thrown at him; the maids abuse him). In part, however, a new wrinkle is introduced. Penelope recollects that when her husband left for Troy, he told her to marry again when Telemachus began to grow a beard. That time has now come. This increases the urgency for Odysseus to reveal himself to Penelope and to confront the suitors (if he doesn't, she'll remarry), but it also raises questions about Penelope. While she clearly seems to miss her husband, is she actually prepared to accept one of the suitors? Or could she possibly know (consciously or not) that he has returned? Book 18 presents this enigma.

Book 18 may be divided into three sections: Battle with the Beggar Arnaeus (alias Irus); Penelope's Curious Proposal; and the Maids and Suitors Gang Up on Odysseus.

BATTLE WITH THE BEGGAR ARNAEUS
(ALIAS IRUS—18.1–157)

The resident beggar, Arnaeus, arrives and threatens Odysseus: "Either get out or I'll drag you out!" Odysseus tries to diffuse the tension ("there's plenty of room here for both of us"), but Arnaeus gets mad and the two beggars square off. Odysseus bloodies Arnaeus' face, knocks him silly, and props him up outside the door as a "guard." It turns out that Arnaeus also goes by the name of Irus, because he serves as messenger for the suitors (modeled on the name of the rainbow—and messenger—goddess, Iris). When Odysseus defeats him, the suitors make a wordplay out of his name, joking that Irus has been "un-Irused" (or in English, he has been "ironed" out)—no longer able to deliver messages.

Three quick points. First, in many ways this is a farcical combat. Arnaeus/Irus doesn't present much of a challenge to Odysseus and besides, he isn't the problem—the suitors are! In this case, the suitors are as ready to mock Arnaeus/Irus as Odysseus. Antinous even threatens to sell Arnaeus/Irus into slavery with his nose, ears, and testicles cut off! The serious aspect of all this is that beggars are under the protection of Zeus—Telemachus makes it clear that Odysseus doesn't have to fight—yet the suitors find this conflict a source of entertainment.

Second, Homer reminds us yet again that Odysseus has to be careful not to reveal himself. When Odysseus decides against quickly killing Irus, we are told he fears that the suitors might suspect something. Here Homer appears to be having it both ways. In a sense, Odysseus is profoundly changed: Athena has magically altered his appearance—he's bald with no sparkle in his eyes, and he desperately needs a new set of clothes. On the other hand, there's always a risk someone will guess who he is: this beggar is still powerfully built and (we might add) he's a gifted speaker.

Finally, Odysseus pleads with the one good suitor, Amphinomus. "You seem wise," Odysseus tells him and then fabricates a story of how he himself was once successful, but now is suffering for his wicked deeds from the past:

> "Such reckless deeds I see the suitors plotting,
> wasting the property and dishonoring the wife
> of a husband who will not long, I think, be away from his family
> and fatherland. He is quite near! But I hope a spirit
> may lead you out of here and away to your home so you don't meet up with
>   him
> when he returns home to his dear fatherland,
> for I don't think the contest between the suitors and that man
> will end without blood, when he reaches his banquet hall." (18.143–150)

This warning makes Amphinomus anxious, as he walks away shaking his head with much foreboding. The poet once more foreshadows the destruction of all the suitors. Even though Amphinomus foresees the trouble to come, Athena "binds" him to stay and pay the penalty (18.155–156).

PENELOPE'S CURIOUS PROPOSAL (18.158–303)

Upon Athena's prompting, Penelope decides to appear before the suitors: she wishes to warn Telemachus of the dangers he faces. More important, however, is her recollection of Odysseus' final words to her: if he has not returned when

Telemachus becomes a man (grows a beard), it's time to marry again and leave this house behind.

There are some pathetic moments: Penelope laments that since her husband has left, she's lost her looks. Athena doesn't disagree. While Penelope sleeps, the goddess applies divine oils and creams—the kind Aphrodite uses—to make Penelope look taller, not so wasted with grieving, and "whiter than ivory." When she appears before the suitors—accompanied by two maids, with her face modestly veiled—the suitors are bewitched by erotic longing to sleep with her.

The big puzzle, however, is her remembrance of Odysseus' last request before he left for Troy. Penelope recalls Odysseus saying:

> "When you see our son growing a beard [if I am still gone],
> marry whomever you wish, and leave your house behind." (18.269–270)

We now need to take a closer look at Homer's presentation of Penelope.

Without question, Penelope loves her husband and grieves each day he is away. In fact, she hopes that Artemis (the goddess of quick deaths) might bring a soft death to her, so that she will mourn no more for her husband (18.202–205). Penelope is loyal to Odysseus and has employed cunning to avoid the suitors' demand that she marry (recall the nightly unweaving of Laertes' funeral shroud). Yet now she seems prepared to accept one of the suitors. We know that Odysseus is already there, so the danger seems less ominous, but the question arises: What if Odysseus had returned in the *eleventh* year after the fall of Troy? When he got back, he would find Penelope, however unwilling, remarried.

I'd like to propose two approaches to this problem. The first was introduced in book 6 when we examined Odysseus' encounter with Nausicaa. In that book, it is possible to see Nausicaa playing two roles. On the one hand, she is a good hostess, who gives Odysseus food and clothes and helps him to find his way home. But she also plays another role—that of the potential lover and wife. She hints at this and her father explicitly offers her in marriage to Odysseus. What is Nausicaa's role? My answer is that Homer has given her two roles—quite contradictory—in order to create tension and to cause us to wonder whether Odysseus will accept the offer of marriage to this beautiful young princess.

Homer is doing very much the same thing with Penelope in these later books of the *Odyssey*. The poet has assigned her two roles. On the one hand, Penelope proves herself to be loyal and cunning, doing everything in her power to avoid a second marriage. Yet in a very serious manner, she here announces her willingness to marry one of the suitors. To this extent she is the bride in a contest among many wooers. Again I would argue that Homer deliberately assigns her both roles in order to create suspense and tension—in order implicitly to raise questions such as "What if Odysseus came home one year later?"

The argument above derives from analyzing potential plots and the roles that characters play in those stories. In books 6–8, Nausicaa appears to be playing both *a female benefactor who helps a wanderer to return home* AND *a princess who marries a handsome stranger*. In these later books, Penelope appears to be playing both *the faithful wife who endures the absence of her husband* AND *the wife who breaks down and accepts a new spouse*. The effect in both cases is dramatic tension, the resolution of which Homer postpones (see Felson-Rubin in "Further Reading").

But Homer is a greater poet than simply introducing contradictory plots. There's a psychological truth to his portrayal of Penelope. We can perceive this by using a second approach, by comparing Penelope's situation with soldiers' wives from recent U.S. history. Let's get beyond literature and stories and fairy tales. In terms of actual experience, we know of many wives who had husbands go off to Vietnam in the 1960s and 1970s (many fewer husbands had wives go off to war). Not all of those husbands returned. Some were killed and had their bodies brought back for burial, but a great many were classified as "missing-in-action" (the MIAs). The wives of MIAs lived their lives in a conflict terrifyingly similar to that of Penelope, another wife of a soldier. Like Penelope, these wives hoped and prayed that their husbands would return. Not a day went by without imagining that husband walking in the front door. And yet for each wife, a part of her insisted that her husband was dead, he was gone forever, and it was time to get on with her life. What I've described here is not narrative conflict; it's psychological trauma—and this is the dilemma of Penelope. Homer shows his genius by capturing what must have been—and still remains—a wrenching struggle wives undergo when their husbands remain unaccounted for in battle (see Shay's *Odysseus in America* in "Further Reading").

So where does this leave us? Is Penelope faithful or has she given up hope? At the very least, it means that we don't have to choose one view over the other. In a very real sense, both of these descriptions of Penelope are true. She remains true to her husband, yet some part of her is saying: "Put the past behind, make the best of life without Odysseus."

I might mention that readers over the years have been so troubled by Penelope's willingness to marry a suitor that some have insisted that Penelope *must* know—whether consciously or not—that he has returned. In book 19 in particular, there are moments when Penelope speaks so revealingly to her husband-in-disguise that we may wonder—does she suspect? I would argue that the wife in conflict—both hoping and despairing—is a better way of explaining Penelope's ambiguous behavior.

THE MAIDS AND SUITORS GANG UP ON ODYSSEUS
(18.304–428)

The suitors bring valuable gifts to Penelope and, when she returns upstairs, they embark on a joyous night of singing and dancing. Odysseus offers to tend the evening fires so that the maids may attend Penelope. "I am much-enduring," he tells them, which we recognize as one of Odysseus' epithets.

But just as some male servants are unfaithful to Odysseus and his family, we find the same split among the maids. Eurycleia and Eurynome are true to Penelope, but here the maid Melantho insults Odysseus (she's the sister of the goatherd Melanthius from book 17). Odysseus gets mad, calls her "bitch," and threatens to tell Telemachus. At this, the maids scatter and Odysseus takes charge of the burning braziers.

Eurymachus turns witty. He tells the suitors that they are fortunate since the beggar's bald head—reflecting the fire—shines so radiantly upon their entertainment (18.353–355). Then speaking to Odysseus, he contemplates offering him a job with good wages, but suspects that Odysseus is lazy and wouldn't be up to the task. Odysseus offers a challenge. First, he proposes various contests between the two of them: mowing hay, ploughing a field, or military combat. Then Odysseus insults the mighty Eurymachus:

> "You are arrogant and your thoughts are vicious.
> Perhaps you think you're a big lordly man,
> since you associate with feeble, little nothings,
> but if Odysseus were to come back to his fatherland,
> immediately those doors, which are quite wide now,
> would seem narrow as you fled out through them to the front porch."
>
> (18.381–386)

Eurymachus first wonders if Odysseus is drunk. Then in anger he hurls a stool at Odysseus, but it misses and hits the wine steward. There's uproar in the house: the suitors' parties used to be so much fun, but now they wish this troublesome beggar were dead.

Telemachus steps in to reestablish order, telling the suitors it's time to go home. The noble Amphinomus endorses Telemachus' suggestion and promises they won't abuse guests or servants anymore. With a libation to the gods, the suitors return to their homes—for the last time, since the next day they will realize who it is they're up against.

BOOK NINETEEN

In book 19 Homer presents the meeting between Odysseus and Penelope. Dramatic excitement results largely from anticipating this potential recognition scene. Will Odysseus reveal himself to his wife? Will Penelope recognize her husband? In addition, Homer focuses on the emotional interaction between Odysseus, who pities his wife, and Penelope, who, continuing to despair, seeks a spark of hope wherever she can.

This book may be divided into five sections: Preparing for Battle; Bad Maid/Good Maid; Husband and Wife Reunited; Odysseus' Scar; and Penelope's Dream.

PREPARING FOR BATTLE (19.1–50)

With the help of Telemachus and Eurycleia, Odysseus prepares for battle with the suitors the next day by removing all weapons from the banquet hall (Athena lights their way). Odysseus conceals his identity from Eurycleia and tells Telemachus he'll stay to test the maids and Penelope. Father and son part, as Telemachus goes to sleep until the sun rises on the day of confrontation.

BAD MAID/GOOD MAID (19.51–102)

Looking like Artemis or Aphrodite, Penelope comes in and sits down. Melantho rebukes Odysseus a second time ("Get out or I'll hit you with a torch!"), but

Odysseus warns her of Odysseus' return and Penelope's anger. Penelope calls her "bitch" (just as Odysseus did) and the good maid, Eurynome, offers Odysseus a stool.

HUSBAND AND WIFE REUNITED (19.103–316)

Homer has now set the scene for the reunion of husband and wife. It's evening. The suitors and Telemachus are gone, though Penelope is certainly not alone with Odysseus—it's unclear how many servants are present, but Eurycleia, Eurynome, and Melantho may be nearby. Once everything is in place, Penelope asks the big question: Who are you?

Odysseus begins by praising Penelope: her fame is like that of a noble king who rules over a prosperous people. In this comparison, his description very much evokes the Golden Age, a mythic time in the past without trouble—sharply contrasting with the current situation! Finally he addresses her question by exclaiming how painful it is to recall who he is and where he comes from—his life "overflows with tears" (19.122).

Penelope says that her fame would grow only if her husband returns. Then she tells this beggar the story of her life. She has been all alone, in trouble, besieged by suitors who deplete the household's resources and court her against her will. After recounting her deception involving Laertes' funeral shroud, Penelope feels she has now run out of tricks and can no longer escape a new marriage.

Odysseus then promises to tell her who he is. And we are on the edge of our chairs: given her debilitating grief, will Odysseus reveal himself as her husband? He has wandered much, the beggar begins, visiting the cities of many men. He has suffered greatly. (So far he speaks the truth.) But as soon as the word "Crete" leaps from his lips (19.172), we know that what follows will be false. Odysseus fashions himself as the grandson of Minos, one-time king of Cnossus in Crete. Indeed, he says he once welcomed Odysseus into his home when Odysseus traveled to Troy.

The effect on Penelope is heartrending. Tears stream down her cheeks like snow melting on high mountains:

> She listened, and tears poured down soaking her cheeks,
> as snow melts on lofty mountains,
> which the east wind melts after the west wind pours it down.
> As it melted, the swollen rivers flow on.
> Just so did she shed tears flooding her beautiful cheeks,
> weeping for her husband sitting beside her. (19.204–209)

Note that the force of the comparison is doubled with mention both of melting snow and the mountain-fed streams (full to bursting) rushing down. Homer makes the irony explicit: Penelope is weeping for the husband *who is right next to her*. We wonder: How cruel can Odysseus be, letting his wife go on weeping without a hint that he has returned? Is he simply manipulating Penelope by forcing these painful memories (he didn't have to tell her he had met

Odysseus)? Is there any sense that Odysseus wants to throw his arms around his wife after twenty long years?

Let's consider what Odysseus says in light of the situation. We must remember that they are not alone and that Odysseus' number one concern is that no one recognize him. While Odysseus does lie in many respects, he actually once was a wealthy man who has wandered and suffered greatly (19.75–80). Indeed, this feature of his fictitious autobiography establishes a link with Penelope. His life truly has been "overflowing with tears" just as Penelope's has. In this way, Odysseus forges a bond of shared grief with his wife. To this extent, he is successful: Penelope opens up to this apparent stranger, telling him of her desperation and past deception of the suitors (she's a storyteller like Odysseus).

Two others things must be said. First, after the snow-melting simile, Homer tells us:

> And Odysseus
> pitied his wife as she lamented in her soul,
> but his eyes stood like horn or iron—
> steady between his eyelids—as he hid his tears by stealth. (19.209–212)

Finally, after a hundred lines, Homer indicates Odysseus' inner feelings, yet we also learn that however much pain Penelope feels, Odysseus refuses to let on who he is.

Homer has also done something quite amazing. Each time Odysseus addresses Penelope he calls her *gynai* in Greek (19.107, 19.165, 19.221, 19.262, 19.336—from which we get the word "gynecology"). In two cases, this word must be translated "woman" (19.107, 19.221), but in the other instances he says "esteemed wife [*gynai*] of Laertes' son Odysseus", because the fact is that *gynai* is the Greek word for both "woman" and "wife." The effect is that what the maids (and Penelope?) hear him say is "woman," but from Odysseus' perspective, his first word to Penelope after twenty years away is "wife." Odysseus—and Homer—are both very clever, for this ambiguous address allows Odysseus to claim Penelope as his beloved without arousing suspicion.

The Amazing Greek Language: More Greek Puns

There's an even more subtle wordplay when Penelope says, "And now I can no longer escape marriage or discover yet another trick" (19.157–158). Penelope's word for "trick" is *metis*, which can mean "plan" or "trick," but it also reproduces Odysseus' pun after he tricked Polyphemus, the Cyclops: "my heart laughed, as my name and faultless trick [*metis*] deceived him" (9.413–414). But in both places, the word *metis* is another way of saying "nobody" (*me tis*—as two words), so we could read a second meaning into Odysseus' triumph: "my name and faultless 'nobody' [*me tis*] deceived him"— which is precisely how he defeated him (Polyphemus tells the other Cyclopes: "Nobody has blinded me"). If we are willing to go this far, then Penelope unknowingly is *also* saying: "I am no longer able to escape marriage or discover

---

> another nobody (*me tis*)." Yet this is precisely what she has succeeded in doing: she has found her "nobody," this beggar in disguise who conceals his own identity. He is "nobody," yet he will furnish the "trick" or "deception" Penelope requires to defeat the suitors. All this, I guess, is a good argument for learning the Greek language to enjoy Homer even more.

Penelope shares many traits with Odysseus: she tells stories, uses trickery, and has suffered greatly. She is also sheptical and tests the various claims people make. Here Penelope interrogates the beggar to learn whether he truly has met Odysseus: she asks about his clothes, physical appearance, and companions. While insisting this was a long time ago, Odysseus goes on to give extremely precise details of a purple cloak, a golden brooch (with an elaborate scene depicting a dog seizing a fawn), and a tunic of very fine fabric. Once more, Penelope wishes to weep, for she herself gave these clothes to Odysseus. Still she doesn't think she'll welcome him home again, cursing Ilium (another name for Troy).

Odysseus begs Penelope not to grieve. He imparts some true information (Odysseus is alive, he lost his ships and companions, the Phaeacians escorted him with many gifts), but once again he mixes in lies. This time he returns to the fib that Odysseus is consulting the oracle of Zeus in Dodona (on the Greek mainland, not far from Ithaca). According to this fiction, Odysseus needs to know whether—after his long absence—he should return home openly or stealthily. The beggar then swears an oath that Odysseus will return. I'm sorry to say that there's no general agreement as to *when* the beggar swears Odysseus will appear—the Greek (*lykabantos*) is difficult to interpret—perhaps "this very month" or "this day" or "this festival of Apollo" (19.306–307). Penelope remains in conflict: she hopes her husband will return, but fears she will never see him again (19.309–316).

Much of the suspense in this scene derives from the possibility that Penelope may recognize her husband. Homer has in a sense displaced an actual recognition scene with a "virtual" one. Odysseus' descriptions of cloak, brooch, tunic, and friends are called "sure signs by which Penelope might recognize Odysseus" (19.250). Penelope *does* recognize her husband, but it's the husband in this beggar's description, not the husband who sits right before her.

Though Penelope suspects nothing about the true identity of her guest, Odysseus continues to hint. Remember what he tells her: Odysseus consulted Zeus' oracle as to whether he should return home "openly or stealthily." Obviously if the god answered "stealthily," when Odysseus makes it to Ithaca, he'll hide out or be in disguise—Penelope needs to be on the lookout for such a traveler.

ODYSSEUS' SCAR (19.317–504)

Penelope now plays the good hostess. She asks that a bed be made up for her guest and suggests a bath. Odysseus insists that he only wishes that an older servant wash his feet. Penelope calls upon Eurycleia, who nursed Odysseus in his infancy.

Coming to wash the beggar, Eurycleia weeps and addresses Odysseus, her lord—who she thinks is absent—in the second person.

> "I am no help to you, child. Indeed, Zeus hates you
> with your godlike spirit more than any man alive.
> No mortal ever burned so many fatty thighs or choice hecatombs
> to Zeus who delights in lightning
> as you used to give to him, praying that you
> would reach a comfortable old age and raise an illustrious son.
> But now you alone have lost your homecoming day." (19.363–369)

This is another passage dripping with irony: Eurycleia is addressing her lord, Odysseus, whom she believes to have vanished from the face of the earth; in fact, she's about to wash his feet. Yet Eurycleia is no fool. She remarks that no other visitor has looked so much like Odysseus in build, voice, or—feet! (The distinctive feet of father and son is a running gag.) There's clearly a risk here, but Odysseus quickly remarks that many others have noticed a similarity between Odysseus and him.

Homer has played a trick on us. He had us thinking that Odysseus might reveal himself to Penelope—or that she might see through his disguise. Instead, it's the servant Eurycleia who first realizes who this is. She begins to wash Odysseus' leg—and the jig is up!—the old woman recognizes a scar just above the knee Odysseus received as a boy long ago.

On top of Homer's deception is his daring. At this highly climactic moment—Eurycleia knows it's Odysseus, she can tell Penelope, everyone might learn the truth—Homer leisurely recounts how Odysseus *became* Odysseus. Just as we learn that Eurycleia has recognized the scar, Homer interrupts his narrative to tell the story of how Odysseus got the scar—and how his grandfather, Autolycus, gave him the name "Odysseus." Throughout this flashback, Eurycleia sits there "frozen" in time. The poet begins the recognition scene, but then postpones Eurycleia's reaction and the potentially dangerous consequences.

We learn about Odysseus' name and a boar hunt near Mount Parnassus. The name of Odysseus is explained in this way. Autolycus, Odysseus' maternal grandfather, was famed for trickery (it runs in the family!). When Eurycleia puts the baby in his grandfather's lap to be named, Autolycus says that since he himself is "hated" (*odyssamenos*) by other men, let "Odysseus" be his grandson's name (19.407–409—Athena puns on this association in the first book: "Does Odysseus no longer please you with his sacrifices? Is he now so hateful [*odysao*] to you, Zeus?"—1.60–62). We then hear of Odysseus' journey to visit his grandparents on the Greek mainland, near Mount Parnassus. There's an evening feast and an early-morning hunt. A wild boar rushes out of a thicket and drives its tusk into Odysseus' leg just above the knee, as the young hero delivers a fatal wound to the animal. This episode from Odysseus' childhood anticipates brave deeds to follow.

This wonderful episode is typical of Homer's narrative economy. The *Odyssey* tells the story of how Odysseus returned home and regained his wife and kingdom. The poet refuses to begin at the beginning ("Odysseus was born on the island of Ithaca," for example) or to end with Odysseus' death. Rather by means of flashbacks (such as this one) and foreshadowing, Homer includes all the important events of Odysseus' life, but only when they become relevant. Homer wants to tell of Odysseus' childhood and how he got his name, he wants to anticipate how Odysseus' life will end (remember Teiresias' prophecy in the underworld?), but the introduction of these defining moments must be motivated by an episode in the main event: the story of Odysseus' return. We may as well sit back and enjoy this gifted storyteller's genius.

One large question pervades the entire epic: Who is this man? We have labeled this the identity theme. Through recognition scenes, we learn that this wanderer is the father of Telemachus and the master of the dog Argus and servant Eurycleia: he is also the grandson of Autolycus, who gave him his name. Homer uses this flashback to link Odysseus' name, his scar, and the bravery he showed as a child. It is now impossible to think of Odysseus without seeing the scar as an essential part of him—it symbolizes his childhood (this is how Eurycleia knows it's him) and suggests later suffering and heroism. And yet he is still nameless in his own home.

Homer returns us to the washing scene and with vivid description makes this recognition scene unforgettable.

> The old woman took the scar in the flat of her hands
> and, feeling it, recognized him—she let go of his foot.
> His leg fell into the basin, and the bronze vessel clanged
> and tipped over. Water poured out onto the ground.
> Joy and pain both seized her heart, her eyes
> filled with tears, and her voice caught in her throat. (19.467–472)

Homer's eye here is truly cinematic—you could use such a description to film this scene. Eurycleia regains her composure, holds his chin (as a sign of respect), and addresses him: "You are Odysseus, dear child." She has no doubt.

Odysseus acts quickly. Eurycleia is ready to tell Penelope (whom Athena distracts), but Odysseus grabs his nurse's throat; he even threatens her life if she reveals his identity. Eurycleia promises to be like stone or iron—utterly trustworthy—ready to denounce the unfaithful maids, yet Odysseus needs no help on this score. The old woman now conveniently leaves the scene.

PENELOPE'S DREAM (19.505–604)

Penelope has one last request for the beggar: she asks him to interpret her dream. In the dream, twenty geese eat barley and she delights in them. An eagle swoops down and kills them. Penelope is reduced to tears. But the eagle speaks to her: "The geese are the suitors and I am your husband." Penelope then wakes up. What can this dream mean?

Odysseus (calling her "wife/woman") insists that the meaning is obvious. This dream portends the death of the suitors. But Penelope rejects such an easy interpretation. She reminds her guest that not all dreams are brought to pass and speaks of two gates: one of ivory (through which unfulfilled dreams pass) and one of horn: through the gate of horn dreams that will be realized pass. Although she wishes her dream passed through the gate of horn, she fears it will remain insubstantial.

Penelope's decision to reveal her dream to the beggar once more demonstrates the trust she places in this apparent stranger. Yet she remains skeptical regarding the dream's obvious meaning. In any case, this unburdening of an intimate secret has evidently brought Penelope to a decision. The next day she will hold a contest: whoever strings Odysseus' bow and shoots an arrow through twelve axes will marry her. Odysseus endorses this decision. "Let there be no delay," he tells her, "for Odysseus will be back before the suitors succeed in this contest" (my paraphrase of 19.584–587).

Penelope has apparently given up on Odysseus' return. If one of the suitors succeeds the next day, she'll remarry and leave her home. Homer increases our anguish at her plight with Penelope's own description of her life without Odysseus (19.512–534). During the day she "delights in mourning and wailing as she goes about her tasks," but at night she lies in bed, sleepless and tormented by worry. Should she stay protecting her home and reputation or marry one of the suitors? Penelope compares herself to Pandareus' daughter, Philomela, who is changed into a nightingale after mistakenly killing her own son. This bird sings a gorgeous song at the start of spring, yet it is a song of sorrow for her lost child. Penelope's suffering matches the pain of Philomela.

In this book, Homer has given us a full portrait of Penelope. While tough and shrewd, she's also at her wits' end. Homer evokes sympathy with several arresting images: snow melting on mountaintops (and swollen rivers), a nightingale's tremulous song in springtime, and Penelope's puzzling dream (if the geese are the suitors, why does she weep when they die?). Homer has reunited husband and wife, but Penelope, a pitiable creature. is still in the dark. As the book closes, we now await two contests: an athletic one—stringing and shooting the bow— and a contest of life and death between Odysseus and his son against the suitors. His house, wife, and kingdom are at stake.

Dreams in Homer: The Twenty Geese

Finding unambiguous meaning in dreams is elusive. A recent reader of Homer, however, has convincingly unlocked the puzzle of why there are *twenty* geese: one for each year Odysseus is away. A similar omen occurs in the *Iliad*, recounted (in flashback) by Odysseus. When a bird and her eight chicks are eaten by a snake just as the Greeks depart for Troy, the seer Calchas interprets: it will take the Greeks nine years of fighting (one for each bird); then in the tenth year, they will take the city (*Iliad* 2.299–330). In the *Odyssey*, neither Penelope nor Odysseus grasps the significance of the number of geese in the dream, but in specifying that there are *twenty* geese Homer offers us one more clue—an extremely subtle foreshadowing—that the day of reckoning has come now that Odysseus' absence of twenty years has come to an end (see Pratt in "Further Reading").

BOOK TWENTY

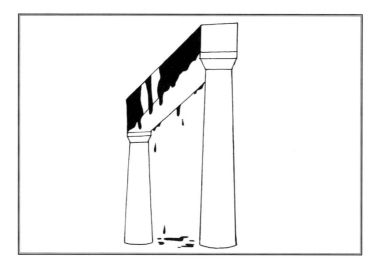

In book 20 after a restless night, the day dawns upon the bow contest, battle, and Penelope's recognition of her husband. This momentous day extends for more than three books and 1,500 lines of poetry (an eighth of the epic). In book 20, at one level Homer presents a festival honoring Apollo; at another, we move closer to the battle that will determine who rules Ithaca.

This book may be divided into four sections: Nighttime Worries; a Morning Prayer; Preparations for Apollo's Festival; and the Festival Begins.

NIGHTTIME WORRIES (20.1–90)

Throughout the evening, anxiety plagues both Odysseus and Penelope: neither can get a good night's sleep, as they anticipate the big day. Even in bed, Odysseus continues to plot against the suitors. He is also riled by the maids who go off to sleep with the suitors. He considers whether he should kill the maids now, but resolves to let them have one last night in their lovers' arms. Then as he tosses and turns, Athena appears to him and reminds him: "This is your home! Your wife and son are here!" Yet Odysseus is unnerved by the disproportionate odds (he and Telemachus against a horde of suitors). He also asks a tough question: Even if he kills them, how will he escape? Athena insists on her divine favor and sheds sleep upon him (20.30–57).

Two remarkable similes describe Odysseus' anger and concern. First, as he thinks of the promiscuous maids, "his heart barked," like a dog protecting her pups when a stranger comes near (20.13–16). Then his rolling in bed evokes a scene from the kitchen:

> But he rolled to and fro,
> as when over a large burning fire a man
> quickly turns a sausage full of fat and blood
> to and fro, desiring to roast it very quickly;
> so Odysseus rolled to and fro considering
> how he would lay his hands upon the shameless suitors—
> one man alone against many. (20.24–30)

The cliché is that epic is a lofty type of literature characterized by elevated language. That preconception has led many readers over the years to reject these similes as somehow undignified. Odysseus' heart barking like a dog; his rolling in bed like a spinning hot dog (actually it's haggis, a roasted stomach)—this is beneath Homer!

Yet Homer is continually inventing bold, memorable similes and metaphors to describe inner psychological states—this is long before Freud! Dogs are frequently associated with a true homecoming (think of Argus recognizing Odysseus)—here the comparison is between a barking dog, who will protect her own young against an intruder, and Odysseus, surrounded by suitors in his own home. Whose heart wouldn't bark? I also don't think Odysseus would be insulted by the comparison to rapid flipping over a roasting fire: the primary point of comparison is the rapid action and his constant torment. As we have seen in our earlier examination of Homer's similes, there may be secondary links: here, it's the metaphorical "hot spot" (a blazing fire) Odysseus finds himself spinning over. I say we praise—not criticize—Homer! (See Rose in "Further Reading.")

For the first time, Homer raises an ethical problem from Odysseus' point of view. The question is not whether the suitors deserve to die. But if they do, what about their families? How will Odysseus deal with them? Homer is looking ahead not only to the battle with the suitors, but also to a larger resolution that needs to take place if Odysseus is effectively to rule the people of Ithaca. Our poet will present his solution at the end of the epic.

As Odysseus falls asleep, Penelope awakens. In tears, she asks to die: "May Artemis shoot her arrow now and take my life from me" (20.61–63). Her pain is unendurable; she would like to die with an image of her husband vividly in her mind. In fact, she has had a dream that someone who looked like Odysseus was sleeping beside her (20.87–90).

In part, we may see this dream as a premonition of Odysseus' return (and subconsciously of Odysseus' actual presence?). But the dominant impression is of Penelope's suicidal thoughts. Once again she compares herself to daughters of Pandareus (different daughters apparently than the one in the book 19 comparison), who are orphaned. They enjoy all the gifts of the gods, but on the brink of marriage they are whisked away—vanished!—by the Harpies (supernatural powers that are as fast as whirlwinds). And this is Penelope's hope:

"So may the gods who live on Olympus make me vanish,
or may Artemis with lovely hair shoot me, so that
with a vision of Odysseus I might go under the hateful earth,
and not cheer the heart of a lesser man." (20.79–82)

Just as for Odysseus, Homer also uses imagery and comparison to reveal Penelope's inner psychological state: she would rather die—or vanish from the face of the earth (like Odysseus)—than be forced to marry another man.

A MORNING PRAYER (20.91–121)

It is dawn. The big day has arrived. Hearing Penelope weeping, Odysseus prays to Zeus, seeking a sign from above and on earth that he will succeed. Zeus immediately sends thunder (a favorable omen) and a feeble female servant—still working at the mill—utters her own prayer: "May this be the suitors' last day!" (20.116–117). We have already seen various means of foreshadowing that anticipate the suitors' destruction. The pace picks up now: Zeus' omen here will be matched by one at the end of this book when the seer Theoclymenus foretells imminent doom for the guests who refuse to leave.

PREPARATIONS FOR APOLLO'S FESTIVAL (20.122–239)

Much activity follows. Telemachus wakes up and checks with Eurycleia on his guest. Telemachus then goes to town accompanied by two dogs. Eurycleia gives orders to the servants for cleaning and fetching water: it's a feast day and the suitors will arrive soon. Among the various other preparations is a parade of animals brought for slaughter (with an implied parallel to the suitors' own fate). Eumaeus brings three fat pigs, Melanthius leads his goats (and threatens to fight Odysseus), and Philoetius the cowherd brings heifers to Odysseus' house.

Melanthius is a bad guy—we know that already. Eumaeus is trustworthy and true to Odysseus (though unaware his master is home). For the first time Homer introduces Philoetius, who treats Odysseus with great respect and wishes him well. Like Eumaeus, Philoetius quickly proves himself to be a faithful servant. He weeps for Odysseus, considers the situation unendurable, and prays for Odysseus to come back. With battle imminent, it's important to know who can be trusted. Philoetius promises to join against the suitors, if only Odysseus would return.

THE FESTIVAL BEGINS (20.240–394)

As the suitors plot against Telemachus, an omen appears: an eagle carrying a dove (we think of the eagle in Penelope's dream—again, anticipating Odysseus' victory). Amphinomus, the "good" suitor, then advises feasting rather than murder, and the suitors make their way to Odysseus' house. Apollo's festival continues: a hecatomb (literally, this means "100 oxen") is led to a grove of Apollo for ritual sacrifice. The suitors again prove their wickedness. This time it's Ctesippus, who sarcastically promises the beggar Odysseus a "guest gift" and hurls an ox hoof at his head. It misses and Telemachus rebukes him: "If you had hit him, I'd send you to Hades with my spear!" Two stools and now an ox hoof—it's time for vengeance!

A rich suitor, Agelaus, smoothly tells Telemachus that previously there had been no problem: they understood that Penelope and Telemachus hoped for Odysseus' return. But now obviously Odysseus is never coming back, and it's time for Penelope to choose a new husband. (I won't even mention the phrase "dramatic irony"—oops, I did.) Telemachus insists that he will in no way postpone the wedding and the suitors respond by . . . well, it's very strange what happens next.

Athena provokes weird laughter among the suitors: they laugh "with the jaws of someone else." The meat they're eating bleeds, tears fill their eyes, and they begin wailing. Are they happy or sad? At this point, the seer Theoclymenus has a vision:

> "Ah, wretches! What evil befalls you? For your heads
> and faces—and knees below—are wrapped in night;
> lamentation is blazing, tears flood your cheeks;
> the walls and fine crossbeams are dripping with blood.
> The forecourt is full of ghosts, the courtyard is full, too,
> ghosts eager to seek dark Erebus below. The sun is
> gone from the sky, and an evil mist has spread over the earth!" (20.351–357)

Now I'm not saying that we cast Jack Nicholson as Odysseus, but this is like a scene out of *The Shining* ("Heeeere's Johnny!"). Theoclymenus is possessed by the gods and has a vivid premonition of what awaits the suitors: their deaths in a bloodbath. Laughing, the suitors say he should go, but the seer needs no prompting. He leaves, knowing evil is coming and no suitor will escape. This is the last we see of the seer Theoclymenus—a great exit!

Now the suitors turn on Telemachus and complain about the disappointing guests he brings home. The book closes with Telemachus looking at his father in silence, waiting for the signal to attack—but not until the competition of the bow: contest first, slaughter after. The poet remarks that Athena and Odysseus will be serving a somewhat unpleasant "meal" for the suitors who were the first to plot their crimes (20.392–394).

BOOK TWENTY-ONE

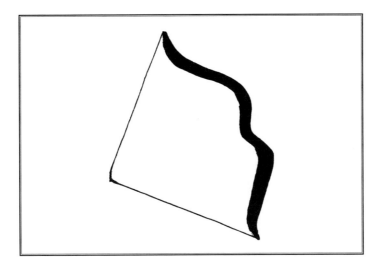

In book 21, Odysseus strings his old bow and wins (or "regains") Penelope as his bride, bringing us to the brink of battle with the suitors. The bow itself is a token of recognition—the beggar's success should be enough to make the suitors realize that Odysseus has truly returned. The bow also functions as the instrument of the suitors' destruction.

Book 21 may be divided into three sections: the Contest Begins; Plotting Outside; and the Beggar Succeeds.

THE CONTEST BEGINS (21.1–187)

At Athena's prompting, Penelope retrieves Odysseus' bow and announces the contest to the suitors. Previously unable to decide, Penelope now says she will marry whoever strings the bow and shoots through the axes. Even Telemachus tries his hand at the competition. Three times he fails to string the bow; on the fourth try, Homer tells us Telemachus would have succeeded, but Odysseus covertly signals him not to. A parade of disappointed suitors follows, each failing to string the bow of Odysseus even after heating it and rubbing tallow on it. In one sense, Homer is building suspense until the beggar—Odysseus in disguise—succeeds. But the poet has embedded several interesting features in this scene.

First, we find explicit and implicit foreshadowing of imminent battle. Athena prompts Penelope to propose the contest and "the beginning of slaughter"

(21.4). Later the poet remarks that Antinous would be "the first to taste the arrows from Odysseus' hands" (21.98–99). The first suitor to fail, the rich Leodes, comments:

> "This bow will rob many of our best
> of spirit and life, since it is much better
> to die than live, failing to win the goal for which
> we always gather here, waiting all these days." (21.153–156)

Naturally, Leodes is not asking to die, but he unintentionally foreshadows the suitors' demise with this remark. In the next section, Odysseus gives specific orders for servants to lock doors, anticipating the surprise attack upon the suitors.

Second, we may recall that even in the first book the question of Telemachus' true parents—and Penelope's fidelity—arose. "No man knows his father, but my mother said mine was Odysseus." Homer demonstrates that Telemachus must be Odysseus' son, for Telemachus is the only one (other than Odysseus) able to string the bow. Odysseus prevents him from doing so, but Homer explicitly says Telemachus would have succeeded—surely this is Odysseus' son.

Third, in addition to a detailed description of Penelope's tearful fetching of the bow—it's locked away in the attic with other treasures—Homer includes a history of the bow itself. It is a guest gift, given to Odysseus by Iphitus, son of Eurytus, long ago before the Trojan War. The poet relates that when Odysseus journeyed to the mainland "as a lad" to retrieve stolen cattle, he exchanged gifts with Iphitus. There's a tragic side to this story, for Iphitus—Odysseus' friend and host—was murdered by Heracles, who received Iphitus into his house. After serving dinner, Heracles killed his guest "with no respect for divine vengeance or hospitality" (21.28). We learn that Odysseus kept the bow locked away in memory of his dear host.

The relevance of this history is not immediately clear. Perhaps it helps to explain why Odysseus would fail to bring such a mighty weapon to Troy—out of reverence for his friend—but the circumstances of Iphitus' death are strikingly similar to what Odysseus plans to do in Ithaca. Heracles, as host, received Iphitus in his home, fed him dinner, and killed him. Odysseus has many unwanted guests in his home, they are feasting in honor of Apollo (the god of archery, among other things), and will be killed there. By now we are quite familiar with Homer's technique of "characterization-by-comparison." Homer implicitly asks us to compare and contrast Odysseus with Agamemnon, Penelope with Clytemnestra, Telemachus with Orestes, and so on. Regarding the bow's history, it is hard not to note the similarities between Odysseus and Heracles, son of Zeus. Of course, Heracles didn't use the bow to kill Iphitus, but Homer has positioned this story in such a way that we associate the bow of Iphitus with the killing of guests. Heracles, however, is condemned for "killing his guest without respect for divine vengeance or hospitality." Odysseus, too, is planning to kill men in his own house. Are we to condemn Odysseus for his plan of murder?

As I suggested in discussing book 20, while Odysseus may be justified in killing the suitors (and Athena endorses this action), harming a guest in one's home is always perilous. At the very least, the suitors' families will seek vengeance in turn—and how will such a cycle of violence end? While raising these issues, Homer does not definitively solve this dilemma on the human level. As we shall see, only the gods are able to bring closure.

Finally, a very vexed question: Once the bow is strung, where is the arrow fired? How are the axes arranged? How can you shoot "through axes"? I readily admit that I cannot confidently answer this question to which many possible solutions exist. Double-headed axes could be set up, resting on their handles so that an arrow must be shot through the topmost opening (see Sketch A). Alternatively, some have suggested that the axes rest on their ax-heads with the handle up in the air—a handle with a hole in it (try shooting through that!—see Sketch B). The ax-heads could be set vertically in the ground with the hole (through which the handle goes) as a target (Sketches C and D). Personally I prefer the solution found in Sketch A: twelve axes set up on their handles, so that Odysseus must fire through the topmost opening of all twelve axes with a single arrow, but I wouldn't bet the house on it. Without a doubt, the skill required is superhuman—heroic, in fact, and Odysseus is the only competitor to achieve success.

PLOTTING OUTSIDE (21.188–244)

As suitor after suitor fails to string the bow, Eumaeus and the cowherd Philoetius leave the house. Odysseus quickly follows and asks each one: "If Odysseus returned, would you help Odysseus or the suitors?" When the servants proclaim their unswerving loyalty to Odysseus, the beggar reveals his true identity and confirms it by showing his scar (it worked for Eurycleia). Both men embrace their long-lost king and master, but Odysseus stops them—what if someone notices? Odysseus then proposes a signal: when he asks to enter the contest, Eumaeus should bring him the bow; then order the women to lock the doors and not disturb them, even if they hear shouting and fighting.

Homer has introduced another in the series of recognition scenes, but it's not the most dramatic episode. We've already seen the scar as a token of recognition, and besides, this time Odysseus *chooses* to reveal himself (unlike the bath scene with Eurycleia). The first recognition scene (after Athena in book 13—she wasn't fooled) was with Telemachus, which revealed Odysseus as father. I would loosely gather the dog Argus and the servants, Eurycleia, Eumaeus, and Philoetius, as similar for they all reveal another side of Odysseus' identity: Odysseus as lord and master of the house. Soon Homer will show us Odysseus the warrior, husband, son, and king of Ithaca. Keep watching to see how the poet systematically makes use of these recognition scenes to answer the question: Who is this man?

THE BEGGAR SUCCEEDS (21.245–434)

The poet returns us to the gathering of suitors inside. When Eurymachus fails to string the bow, Antinous proposes sacrificing to Apollo and continuing the

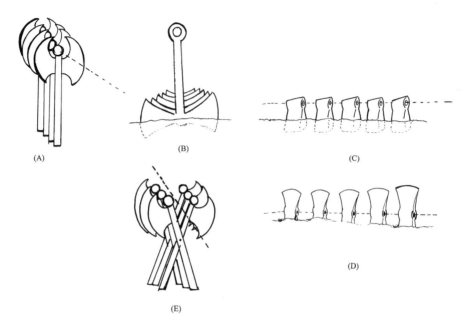

(A)

(B)

(C)

(D)

(E)

Illustration 7. *The Bow Contest.* Sketches A, B, C, D and E indicate various proposals for what the bow contest required, once Odysseus' bow has been strung. Based on *A Commentary on Homer's Odyssey*, Vol. III: 137–147.

contest the next day. At this juncture, Odysseus—the beggar in disguise—asks to enter the contest. Antinous remarks that wine must have damaged the beggar's wits and threatens to send him packing. Penelope intervenes, asking if the suitors truly think she would marry the beggar if he were to win the contest; she merely promises a nice set of clothes and weapons if he can string her husband's bow. Telemachus then asserts his authority by ordering Penelope to leave, claiming that the bow contest concerns the men of the house. This isn't really convincing—if anyone's affected by the contest, it's Penelope!—but Homer needs to clear the hall for battle. Penelope goes up to her chamber, weeps for Odysseus, and falls asleep.

There is one noteworthy aspect of this preliminary scene to Odysseus' success: Antinous' rebuke to the beggar. When accusing Odysseus of being a winesop, the suitor recalls how a centaur (half-goat, half-man) named Eurytion drank too much wine at the house of Perithous, king of the Lapiths.

> "When wine ruined his mind,
> in madness he committed evils in the house of Pirithous." (21.297–298)

Eurytion was punished, says Antinous, but from this incident strife between men and centaurs arose. This story has a special relevance for the *Odyssey*, since a well-known version of this story (known presumably in Homer's time) recounts how at the wedding of King Peirithous and Hippodamia, many centaurs, after getting drunk and lusty, attemped to carry off the bride and bridesmaids.

A battle ensued, and—with Theseus' help—the Lapiths defeated the centaurs. Although these details are not stated by Antinous (he only says Eurytion "madly committed evils"), the idea of unruly guests at a "wedding" who must be subdued by force indirectly looks ahead to Odysseus' battle with the suitors who (by implication) have madly pursued his "bride."

A Good Reason to Go to Greece

In case you ever are in London, England, or Olympia, Greece, there are two remarkable sculptural depictions of the battle between the centaurs and Lapiths at Pirithous' wedding. In the British Museum (sadly, not in Athens) are the metope sculptures from the impressive Parthenon in Athens, showing various scenes of man battling centaur or centaur abducting bridesmaid. In Olympia—a site dedicated to Olympian Zeus—on the west pediment of the major temple to Zeus was presented the battle of centaurs and Lapiths. You can now see these sculptures in the museum there.

On stern instructions from Telemachus, Eumaeus brings the bow to Odysseus. The suitors laugh, but Eumaeus tells Eurycleia to bolt the doors at the back of the hall, and Philoetius silently secures the door to the front entrance. At this point, Homer slows the pace: Odysseus examines the bow for worms that may have caused damage. While the suitors jeer sarcastically at him ("He must have one just like it at home!"), Homer compares Odysseus to a singer.

> But crafty Odysseus,
> immediately raised the great bow and looked at it on all sides,
> as when a man skilled in the lyre and song
> easily stretches a string over a new peg,
> fastening the pliant sheep-gut at both ends;
> so then without effort did Odysseus string the great bow.
> Holding it in his right hand, he tested the string,
> and it sang beautifully, like the voice of a swallow. (21.404–411)

As Odysseus examines and strings the bow, Homer likens him to a singer, someone like Demodocus from Alcinous' court. This suggests that Odysseus is as skilled in battle (with the bow) as a singer is with a lyre. But there's more. Throughout the epic, Odysseus has told riveting tales—to the Phaeacians, to Eumaeus, to Penelope—and here we find confirmation of a sort. Odysseus is like a great singer—like Homer, who is about to tell of Odysseus' great battle with the suitors! As in books 9–12, here too Odysseus momentarily merges with Homer himself.

I also find it suggestive that the string of his bow "sings" like the voice of a swallow. This brief detail apparently complements Penelope's comparison of herself to Pandareus' daughter who was turned into a nightingale. In that passage, Penelope described the nightingale's song at the beginning of spring. A

Greek proverb links the appearance of the swallow with the coming of spring; so, too, here the revealing of Odysseus, his winning of the bow contest, and his battle with the suitors are all associated with his return to Ithaca as a metaphorical spring—the rebirth of the world for Penelope and her husband.

Homer now quickens the pace. The suitors turn pale, Zeus sends ominous thunder, and Odysseus takes an arrow and shoots it through the axes. He then addresses Telemachus, using the metaphor of a "dinner of slaughter."

> "Now is also the time to fix a meal for the Achaeans
> in the daylight, and then later to celebrate
> with dance and song, for these are the delights of a feast." (21.428–430)

Then—with that remarkable eyebrow of his—Odysseus signals Telemachus to arm himself. Before our eyes, Telemachus becomes a heroic warrior, gleaming in his bronze panoply, ready to join his father in battle.

BOOK TWENTY-TWO

Book 22 presents the long-anticipated battle between Odysseus and the suitors. For the first time Odysseus speaks openly, denouncing the suitors and challenging them to fight for their lives. The token of recognition—Odysseus' bow, which identifies him as the king of Ithaca—now also brings about the suitors' destruction.

Book 22 may be divided into three sections: the First Arrows; Against an Army of Suitors; and Putting the House in Order.

THE FIRST ARROWS (22.1–200)

Homer begins cinematically. Removing some of his rags, Odysseus leaps onto the threshold and blocks the suitors' escape. He prays for Apollo's help to hit another "target," and immediately fires a lethal arrow through Antinous' throat. The poet presents these battle scenes in graphic detail. Here, Antinous flops over, the cup falls from his hand, and a jet of blood spurts from his nose.

> On the point of raising a fine goblet,
> gold with double handles, Antinous held it in his hands
> about to drink wine. Slaughter was nowhere in his
> thoughts . . .
> Odysseus aimed and hit him in the throat with an arrow.
> The point went right through his tender neck.

> He leaned back, the cup fell from his hand
> as he was hit, and immediately a thick jet of human blood
> came from his nostrils. Suddenly he struck the table with his foot
> and kicked it away, knocking food onto the ground,
> and defiling the bread and roasted meat with blood. (22.9–12, 15–21)

There's very little explicit sexual material in the *Odyssey*, but in terms of violence we might have to rate this work "R"—parental discretion advised. Homer's audience evidently enjoyed these vivid depictions of blood and guts.

The other suitors are caught by surprise, futilely looking for weapons as they rebuke Odysseus: "You'll die and the birds will eat your body!" Homer reminds us that the suitors still haven't figured out that Odysseus' shot was deliberate—or that the beggar is Odysseus—but now Odysseus speaks without pretense:

> "You dogs! You never expected me to return home
> from the land of Troy, so you ravaged my home,
> used force to sleep with the servant-women,
> and—while I still lived—wooed my wife
> with no fear of the gods who hold broad heaven,
> with no regard for retribution from man.
> Now the bonds of death are fixed upon all of you!" (22.35–41)

Odysseus quickly announces his return, catalogues the crimes of the suitors, and foretells their doom. I must say it's refreshing to hear Odysseus speak what's on his mind after so much double-talk and fiction.

Here is one of the pivotal recognition scenes: the suitors at last realize whom they're facing and look to escape. Always a quick wit and devious with words, Eurymachus acknowledges that Odysseus has rightly condemned them, but blames it all on Antinous! He pleads for the chance to make it up to Odysseus—perhaps they could replace all the food and drink, adding bronze and gold as reparation. We almost expect Eurymachus to promise that they won't do it again.

Odysseus offers a choice: fight or run for your lives! As Eurymachus attempts to lead his colleagues in battle, Odysseus kills him with an arrow through the chest—again, we are offered a graphic description of Eurymachus doubling over, his head hitting the ground, and then kicking the table in a final spasm of death. At this point, Telemachus enters the fray. He hits Amphinomus with a spear and hurries to bring shields, spears, and helmets to Odysseus and the faithful servants. Still firing arrows, Odysseus manages to arm. Although Melanthius, the evil goatherd, succeeds in helping the suitors obtain weapons, Telemachus and Eumaeus seize him, lash him to a plank, and hang him in the air.

AGAINST AN ARMY OF SUITORS (22.201–389)

Agelaus now takes over as leader of the suitors, ordering six of them to hurl javelins at Odysseus all at once. This fails: they all miss. It's hard not to think of

James Bond or Sylvester Stallone movies where an army of bad guys fire at the hero and hundreds of bullets miss, hitting the ground just in front of him. On the other side, Odysseus and his three allies hurl spears and each one cuts down a suitor as they battle toward ultimate success.

Athena plays an interesting role. First she appears looking like Mentor, Odysseus' old friend, and challenges Odysseus to fight the way he fought at Troy. She then flies up to a roof beam and sits there like a swallow. Homer remarks that she was "testing the strength of Odysseus and his son" (22.237–238). This is one more instance of how the gods support heroes and heroines in their pursuits. In a sense, Odysseus couldn't succeed without Athena's help, but in the end this will be Odysseus' victory. Mortals are *not* the puppets of the gods.

Later Athena holds the aegis over the banquet hall that has become a battle-field. This uncanny shield is wielded only by Zeus or Athena: here, it terrorizes the suitors. Homer describes their panic with a double simile. First, the suitors are driven mad like cattle tormented by a gadfly in springtime; then Odysseus and friends are compared to eagles who swoop down and slaughter feeble birds below (22.299–308). Naturally Homer doesn't depict the death of each suitor, but he does generalize: "A wretched groan arose as the suitors' heads were struck; all the ground swam with blood" (22.308–309).

Near the end, Homer introduces two supplication scenes. A prophet named Leodes rushes to Odysseus' knees and begs for his life. He swears he did nothing wrong; in fact, he tried to stop the suitors. Odysseus cuts him off—literally! Leodes' decapitated head hits the ground while he's still speaking (a similar scene—with severed head still talking—also appears in *Iliad* book 10, and finds its way onto the screen in a German film by Werner Herzog, *Aguirre, Wrath of God*).

The second supplicant is the singer Phemius. Uncertain at first whether to seek sanctuary at Zeus' altar or to plead with Odysseus, he carefully sets down his lyre and seeks clemency.

> "I beseech you, Odysseus. Have mercy and pity for me.
> Grief will come to you hereafter, if you kill
> a singer, who sings for gods and mortals.
> I am self-taught, and the god inspires all the paths
> of song in me. It is fitting that I sing to you
> as to a god. Don't yearn to cut my throat." (22.344–349)

At this point, Phemius calls upon Telemachus as a character witness, who proclaims Phemius innocent of wrongdoing. The herald Medon is also spared, although this scene is a bit comic. Medon's been cowering under a throne, hidden under an ox hide, and has to unwrap himself to appear. This provokes a remarkable response. For the first time in the entire epic, Odysseus smiles (it takes over 10,000 lines of poetry to loosen our hero up). Odysseus instructs these two to wait in the courtyard under he finishes the business at hand.

PUTTING THE HOUSE IN ORDER (22.390–501)

Once the battle is over, Homer again uses two similes to depict the defeated and the conqueror. The suitors lie dead on the floor like fish caught in nets, seeking the salty waves as they're heaped up on the sand, helpless in the hot sun (22.384–388). Odysseus, on the other hand, sits among the corpses like a lion, bloody on its cheeks and chest. This is how Eurycleia finds her lord and master—a terrifying sight (22.402–405). Yet when she wishes to raise a yell of triumph, Odysseus restrains her joy.

"Rejoice, old woman, in your heart, but hold back and don't cry out.
It is not righteous to boast over slaughtered men.
Fate from the gods and their own evil deeds have subdued them." (22.411–413)

Odysseus has certainly been relentless, but he attributes the destruction of the suitors to the will of the gods. There will be no gleeful rejoicing. (In contemplating the possibility that Odysseus may have gone too far—killing rather than banishing the suitors—it may be pertinent to recall that Athena has guided his plan of revenge.)

Apparently, Odysseus has thought out everything. There are three stages: punishment, cleansing the house, and—only then—greeting the faithful women of the house, both servants and wife. Odysseus moves to the first stage: determining the guilt or innocence of the servant-women. Eurycleia condemns twelve of the fifty servant-women as guilty of dishonoring Odysseus' family. As the women weep, Telemachus pronounces sentence. They are hanged by the neck, like birds in a net—they gasp for a bit and then die. It's a pathetic scene, but neither Odysseus nor Telemachus feels any pity toward these disloyal women. Without an order from Odysseus, the servants mutilate Melanthius by cutting off his nose, ears, testicles, hands, and feet. Again, a grim fate is dished out to one who has disregarded the gods and the authority of Odysseus.

In order to put his house in order, Odysseus has the corpses of the suitors heaped up, the furniture wiped with sponge and water, and the banquet hall is scoured with fire and brimstone. This is both a physical cleaning and a ritual purification of a house in which blood has been shed. Only after this rite does Odysseus call for Penelope and the other women of the house. Book 22 closes with Odysseus embracing the loyal servant-women, as they welcome him home. In this book we have seen Odysseus speak frankly to the suitors and smile at the cowering Medon; now he is able to give vent to his feelings openly, for he weeps as he recognizes each of the women who remained faithful in his absence.

BOOK TWENTY-THREE

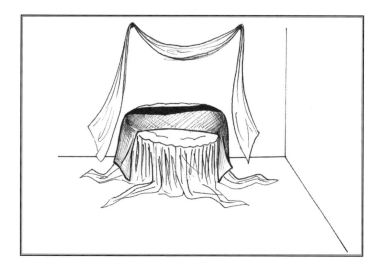

Book 22 was filled with action; book 23 consists largely of speeches as Penelope tests Odysseus. While the outcome is inevitable—Penelope recognizes her husband at last—Homer pursues two other goals in this book. First, by delaying Penelope's actual moment of recognition, the poet is able to prolong the suspense. Second, Homer uses that delay as a means of characterizing Penelope. It has been pointed out that Homer uses a number of methods to reveal character: a character's own words and actions; other characters' observations; explicit or implied comparisons (including similes); even the sequence of events can be employed to tell us something about a character. Here Homer uses a variety of methods to show that Penelope is a kindred spirit to Odysseus: both of them are tricky, cautious, wise, and ultimately successful with the help of the gods. Homer also introduces a token of recognition that confirms Penelope's fidelity to her husband.

Book 23 may be divided into three sections: a Skeptical Wife; Reunited; and Journeys Past and Yet to Come.

A SKEPTICAL WIFE (23.1–116)

This book begins with Eurycleia telling Penelope that the suitors are dead and that her husband is home. Penelope's reaction is what might be called mixed. First, she accuses Eurycleia of mocking her. When Eurycleia insists that the stranger in their home is Odysseus, Penelope leaps from the bed and embraces

Eurycleia, but persists in her questions: How could one man kills so many suitors? Eurycleia doesn't know (remember, the women were locked out) and Penelope's skepticism returns: most likely it's a god in disguise who killed the suitors, but surely Odysseus will never return. Mentioning the scar on his leg, Eurycleia wagers her life that her words are true. Penelope then descends to the banquet hall to see her son and the dead suitors.

By Penelope's own words and actions, Homer demonstrates that she is exceedingly cautious, a trait we have seen in Odysseus as well. Penelope insists on testing the validity of Eurycleia's claims, however much she would like to believe them. Penelope's idea that her savior must be a god in disguise also recalls Telemachus' reaction in book 16 when his father was revealed to him (like mother, like father, like son). Notice that Homer reinforces this feature of Penelope's personality with the observations of other characters. Eurycleia insists that "your spirit is always unwilling to believe" (23.72). Later Telemachus will accuse his mother of being pitiless with a heart harder than stone (23.97–103). Homer ingeniously uses this personality trait for a narrative function: Penelope's persistent caution produces suspense as the audience awaits her acceptance of her husband's return.

As Penelope comes downstairs, her spirit is dancing. Should she speak to the stranger from afar or grab his hands and kiss him? Penelope sits silently opposite Odysseus, looking up now and again—sometimes it looks like him, sometimes she doesn't recognize her husband at all (23.89–95). When Telemachus rebukes her for heartlessness, Penelope is firm:

> "If truly
> this is Odysseus and he has reached his home, certainly we two
> will recognize one another—even better—for there are
> signs between us, which we know but are hidden from others." (23.107–110)

This coolness from Penelope evokes another smile from Odysseus, who tells Telemachus to permit Penelope's testing to continue.

REUNITED (23.117–246)

Odysseus demonstrates his patience once more in moving on to other tasks. He proposes that the household sing and dance so that any passerby will believe there's a wedding going on and suppose that one of the suitors has finally married Penelope. Odysseus also decides to wash and put on clean clothes. Athena helps by adding charm, making him a couple of inches taller, and fixes Odysseus' hyacinthine locks.

Odysseus returns and sits opposite his wife. Although he says no other wife could stand apart from her husband after so long, Odysseus apparently won't press the point and asks that a bed be made up for him. In an offhand manner, Penelope instructs Eurycleia to move the bed that Odysseus himself built outside the bedchamber and make it up for her "guest." Here Penelope proves herself as equal to the deviousness of her husband: this is Penelope's test! Odysseus angrily objects, for the bed he built with his own hands used the trunk of a living olive tree. It's rooted to the earth—how could anyone move it outside their bedroom? This is the moment we've been waiting for. As Homer says, "Penelope recognized the sure signs"—this must be Odysseus! She runs to him in tears, throws her hands around his neck, and kisses him. Penelope asks Odysseus not to be angry, for she was afraid that some mortal would deceive her, as Helen was deceived. Yet doubt has now vanished, for no one else could know about the bed.

> "But now, since you have already described the distinct features
> of our bed, which no other mortal has seen—
> only you and I and one lone servant,
> Actoris, whom my father gave to me when I came here,
> who guards the doors of our well-built bed-chamber—
> you've convinced my heart, tough as it is." (23.225–230)

With these words, Penelope and Odysseus raise a cry of lament, as Odysseus holds his clever wife in his arms.

This is Homer at his best—and it doesn't get any better than Homer at his best! The poet has introduced the marriage bed of Penelope and Odysseus as the token by which Penelope recognizes that this indeed is her husband, returned after nearly twenty years—just as for Eurycleia, Odysseus' scar proved without a doubt that the stranger was her master.

But the bed is more than a token of recognition—it also proves Penelope's fidelity. If no one else knows about the bed being rooted to the earth, then she has had no lovers in her husband's absence. This issue was first raised in book 1, when Athena asked whether Telemachus was truly the son of Odysseus (well, he would be, if Penelope was faithful), but the youth's reply left it open: "No man truly knows his father." Repeatedly throughout the epic, Penelope is implicitly and explicitly compared with Clytemnestra (and Helen; see 23.218–224)—without any resolution. Has Penelope been faithful or not? This recognition scene not only demonstrates to Penelope that Odysseus has now returned, but also shows us—and Odysseus—that his wife has been true to him. Thus the bed takes on the symbolic meaning of a happy and faithful marriage—an emblem for "happily ever after" (see Scodel in "Further Reading").

But Homer is not quite done. As Odysseus holds Penelope in his arms, Homer introduces a simile.

> As when land joyfully appears to swimmers
> whose well-built ship Poseidon shattered
> on the sea, driven by wind and heavy waves.
> Only a few escape the gray sea, swimming
> toward land. Much brine is caked on their skin,
> and joyfully they step onto land, fleeing disaster.
> So then did her husband joyfully appear to her looking at him,
> and she never let go of his neck with her white arms. (23.233–241)

This simile comes close to recapitulating Odysseus' adventures: a shipwreck sent by Poseidon, swimming for his life, sea salt clogging his pores, finally emerging gratefully onto dry land. Yet when Homer begins the simile, it's not clear whether Odysseus or Penelope is the subject of the comparison—they're simply left in an embrace. Only as the simile concludes do we realize that it is *Penelope* who looks at her husband with the same joy that a shipwrecked survivor experiences upon reaching dry land. The point is that Penelope—who never journeyed by sea or battled a Cyclops or suffered Poseidon's wrath–has undergone adventures and endured suffering equal to that of her husband. She, too, is like a shipwrecked survivor—she, too, is as heroic as Odysseus. These two belong together! (See Cohen, H. Foley, and Winkler in "Further Reading.")

In one sense, the reunion of Odysseus and Penelope is simply that: a husband and wife separated for twenty years are brought back together. But in another sense, Homer suggests a kind of "remarriage" for Odysseus and Penelope in these late books in the epic. The rules for the contest of the bow stipulated that whoever strings the bow and shoots through the axes wins Penelope as his bride. Odysseus is the only one to succeed: he gets to "marry" Penelope. Also notice that the other times Penelope comes downstairs to address the suitors, she always leans against the doorpost, but never comes into the banquet hall (1.333, 18.96, 21.64, for example). When Penelope comes downstairs in book 23, she crosses the threshold (23.88). The significance? We must imagine that when Penelope married Odysseus twenty-some years earlier, she came to his house and one of the rites of passage that marked her as Odysseus' bride was her entering the house and "crossing the threshold" as they went up to bed—a ritual still familiar to us today. With the fake wedding dance and song thrown in, Homer has us thinking of this reunion as Odysseus once more winning Penelope as his wife.

JOURNEYS PAST AND YET TO COME (23.247–372)

Odysseus doesn't hide the truth from his wife: his wandering is not over. Upon prodding, Odysseus recounts the "underworld" prophecy of Teiresias. Odysseus must journey yet again. When he finds a people who use no salt in their food and think that a ship oar is a winnowing fan, Odysseus is to plant the oar and make a sacrifice to Poseidon, the god of the sea. We already knew this, but the significance here is that—even with the suitors dead—Odysseus' trials are not finished. He still needs to make peace on the human level with the people of Ithaca (especially the suitors' families) and, on the divine level, Odysseus must make amends to Poseidon for blinding his son Polyphemus.

Penelope interprets the prophecy optimistically, for at least it promises a fine old age awaiting Odysseus as his people around him thrive. The servant Eurynome leads them to bed with a torch (just as she did when they were first married?). But they don't just make love or sleep—they talk! Penelope tells the story of her struggles against the suitors and the many indignities she endured. Then Odysseus retells his adventures: the Cyclops, Circe, the "underworld," and finally how his men recklessly ate the cattle of Helius, the Sun god, on the island of Thrinacia (23.310–341—all of this was recounted for the Phaeacians in books 9–12).

One thing Homer doesn't tell us is how honest Odysseus is regarding his relations with Circe and Calypso. In this third-person synopsis, Odysseus tells of Circe's trickery and Calypso's desire to make him her immortal husband—there's no mention of Nausicaa and perhaps nothing of his sexual relations with the two goddesses. Homer has left it vague. Odysseus' gifts as a storyteller, however, are never in doubt. Penelope, who has been called Odysseus' (and Homer's) ideal audience, listens with delight and never gets sleepy.

On the next morning, the last day of this epic, Odysseus plans to visit his father. He also insists that Penelope say nothing and see no one, for word of the suitors' deaths will have gotten around. Although she will be highly praised in the next book, this is the final scene with Penelope. We have one more recognition scene in store, plus a confrontation with the surviving members of the suitors' families.

There's always a problem of knowing how to end a wonderful story like this. Homer has been second-guessed for over two thousand years. It was remarked in antiquity that the reunion of Penelope and Odysseus was the "goal" or "completion" of the *Odyssey*. This has led some modern readers to believe that the very end of book 23 and all of book 24 were not part of Homer's original work, but rather were added by a later "editor" or perhaps a hack poet. It's true that the poet has led his audience to focus on the defeat of the suitors and the reunion of Odysseus and Penelope as the great climax of the epic. And as far as Odysseus' later years are concerned, Teiresias' prophecy certainly offers some closure to achieving peace with the gods and a fixed—if ambiguous—ending to Odysseus' life. The *Iliad* also ends before the death of Achilles and the sack of Troy, but there, too, foreshadowing has clearly indicated what would transpire.

But book 23 does not complete the *Odyssey*. Odysseus has not yet established himself as king of Ithaca, nor has he seen Laertes, his father, about whom we have heard quite a bit. In fact, I have argued that one way of reading the final third of the epic is to think of Homer employing recognition scenes to construct Odysseus' identity. He is the father of Telemachus, the lord and master of Eurycleia, Eumaeus, and Philoetius, the rival of the suitors, and the husband of Penelope. An essential part of Odysseus, however—especially according to the Ancient Greek conception of self—is that Odysseus is the son of Laertes. Remember that this is how he describes himself when he reveals his identity to the Phaeacians: "I am Odysseus, son of Laertes" (9.19). We must distinguish between the climactic scenes of books 22 and 23 and the fuller sense of closure offered in book 24. Let's not stop before it's over.

BOOK TWENTY-FOUR

Homer still has a surprise or two in store for us. While we might anticipate Odysseus' reunion with Laertes, his father, there is no reason to expect a second scene in the House of Hades with Agamemnon and Achilles. In this episode, Homer uses the technique of characterization-by-comparison to reinforce our appreciation for the uniqueness of Odysseus and Penelope. In addition, we have been led to expect that any sort of resolution by the gods will come years later with Odysseus' missionary work for Poseidon. Yet the entire work closes with a divine intervention, bestowing a verdict of finality upon Odysseus' actions and Homer's story.

Book 24 may be divided into three sections: the Suitors in Hades; Dear Old Dad; and War or Peace?

THE SUITORS IN HADES (24.1–204)

The book opens with the god Hermes leading the spirits of the dead suitors to the house of Hades, lord of the dead. These spirits are once more described in eerie terms: they flutter and squeak like bats clustered on a cave wall. Soon they reach an asphodel meadow at the ends of the earth, near the White Rock and the gates of the Sun. It has been pointed out that asphodel—in spite of its romantic aura from later poetry—grows on poor, desolate ground, so the scene is not all that inviting. Once more the spirits of Greek heroes from Troy appear, chief among them Achilles and Agamemnon (whom we encountered in book 11).

These two were bitter antagonists in the *Iliad*, yet here they praise one another. Achilles speaks of Zeus' love for Agamemnon, while—at greater length—Agamemnon recollects the glorious funeral of Achilles, who died before Troy was sacked: seventeen days of mourning, the nine Muses sang the dirge, the urn containing Achilles' and Patroclus' bones was set prominently on a mound overlooking the Hellespont, visible to ships sailing by. Agamemnon concludes:

> "And so, although you died, your name did not perish, but always
> your brilliant glory will live among all men, Achilles." (24.93–94)

According to the logic of the *Iliad* (which this episode evokes), all humans die, but a select few will achieve undying fame, enshrined in song. Achilles has achieved this much.

As the horde of suitors' spirits approach, Agamemnon recognizes the spirit of Amphimedon and asks how such a large company of men perished: Shipwreck? Defending a city? Amphimedon reveals that they lost their lives courting Penelope, Odysseus' wife, and selectively recounts the story of books 1–23. Notice Amphimedon's emphases, for this is what Homer offers as a remembrance of Odysseus' and Penelope's success. Penelope tricked the suitors with the nightly unweaving at the loom and Odysseus, disguised as an old beggar, prevented the suitors from recognizing who he was. Agamemnon envies the lucky life of Odysseus, a man with a virtuous wife, and praises Penelope:

> "How fine was the mind of blameless Penelope,
> the daughter of Icarius. How well she remembered Odysseus,
> her wedded husband. Her glory—won by excellence—
> will never die, and the immortal gods will craft a delightful song
> about constant Penelope for those on earth." (24.194–198)

At this point, Agamemnon reviles his own wife, Clytemnestra, who killed her husband and brought a reputation for evil upon women everywhere.

To be sure, this episode has a retrospective feel to it—what else would the dead discuss other than their past lives? But both explicitly and implicitly, the more powerful lesson Homer offers is the contrast between these figures and Odysseus and Penelope. Let's take Achilles first. He was the mightiest fighter among the Greeks, he was honored like a god while he lived and at his funeral, and his fame is never-ending. Yet he *is* dead, he never made it home to see *his* father, Peleus. Homer's three themes—identity, homecoming, and hospitality—are still alive and well: it may have taken Odysseus ten years, but he made it home! Unlike Achilles, Odysseus has a successful—albeit belated—homecoming. A second and subtler point is that when Agamemnon refers to Odysseus, he calls him "city-sacker" (24.119). Indeed, it was Odysseus' (and Athena's) plan of the wooden horse that brought the war to an end—not Achilles' martial valor. Once again, Odysseus benefits from the comparison. The contrast between Penelope and

Clytemnestra is more explicit. After Amphimedon's tale, Agamemnon speaks first of Penelope's constancy and her immortal reputation, then of the faithlessness of his own wife, Clytemnestra, who treacherously betrayed him.

We should also note that Penelope and Odysseus are once more linked by their shared skill of trickery: Penelope's loom and Odysseus' disguise. (In fact, Amphimedon attributes a bit more to Penelope than she deserves, for he remarks that she "planned out our deaths"—this, in fact, was Odysseus' plan inspired by Athena.) The important point is that Homer has used a scene that once more contrasts Odysseus with Achilles and Agamemnon (and Penelope with Clytemnestra) to remind us why Odysseus and his faithful wife succeeded—they outsmarted everyone. In terms of Homer's dominant themes, it was Odysseus' skill of concealing his identity that was essential to success. Circe is tricky, the suitors conspire against Telemachus, but they are no match for the deviousness of Odysseus and Penelope.

DEAR OLD DAD (24.205–412)

The scene shifts back to Ithaca, as Odysseus visits his father, Laertes. The old man is working in his garden, dressed in dirty, patched clothes, with protective leggings, gloves, and a goatskin skullcap. He hardly looks like the grand patriarch. Although Odysseus weeps, he decides to "test" Laertes rather than immediately reveal himself. Odysseus praises Laertes' skill in gardening and tree care, but comments that the orchard is in better shape than Laertes himself: Laertes would look like an aristocrat if only he'd wash, eat, and sleep on a soft bed. At this point, Odysseus launches his final tale of deception, claiming to be an old guest-friend of Odysseus. The bond of hospitality links this traveler (so Odysseus claims) with Odysseus, lord of Ithaca—would this happen to be the island of Ithaca? Here is the third theme besides homecoming and identity, namely, hospitality. In a sense, the relevance of hospitality diminishes with the death of the suitors—the worst of all possible guests—but Homer actually employs this theme in the fictive story Odysseus tells his father.

Laertes weeps over the crimes of the suitors who (he believes) are still running the house, but he proves his mental quickness (like father, like son). He asks how many years ago Odysseus was a guest and then seeks to learn this traveler's name, parents, and city. Also, where is the ship that brought him? Odysseus makes up a fake home, name, father, and grandfather, but this leads to mourning by Laertes, who rolls in the dust. Odysseus abandons all pretense and kisses his father:

> "That son of yours is here—I am the one, father, whom you seek!
> I've returned to my fatherland in the twentieth year,
> so lament no more and cease your tearful wailing." (24.321–323)

I know what you're thinking. If this were any other family, the father would throw his arms around his son and welcome him back. But this is no ordinary family. Like Penelope and Odysseus, Laertes first tests the claims of this traveler who *says* he is Odysseus. "If you are my son," the old man insists, "give me a clear sign!" (24.328).

You know the drill. Odysseus could talk about the bed he built (it meant a lot to Penelope); he does in fact point to his scar; but what clinches his argument is a childhood memory of being in the orchard with his father. As a lad, Odysseus asked his father about all the trees and Laertes would enumerate his gifts to his son: thirteen pear trees, ten apple, forty fig, and fifty vines. By this clear sign, Laertes recognizes that this must be his son and resists no more. He embraces Odysseus and proclaims that the gods still exist on broad Olympus if the suitors are now dead. Odysseus leads his father to a meal, prepared by Telemachus and the servants. Laertes even bathes, puts on clean clothes, and recalls his glorious days in battles past.

This is the last recognition scene in the epic. Certainly it is not motivated by the plot—there is no danger if Laertes learns it's Odysseus. In part, Homer replays Odysseus' fondness for trickery; in part, Laertes proves his own mental acuity. As the final scene in the series, this recognition scene also demonstrates one more facet of Odysseus' identity: he is the son of Laertes. And once more the poet has used a token of recognition that is pregnant with meaning. The bed identified Odysseus, but also symbolized Penelope's fidelity to her husband. Here, too, the orchard not only proves to Laertes that this is his son, but also represents the inheritance that father has left son. Long after Laertes is dead, Odysseus will reap the benefits of this legacy. Once more we glimpse an aspect of Odysseus that is universally shared by anyone with an aging parent. There are moments when Homer highlights the heroic qualities of Odysseus, but now he underscores the link we all have with our parents—and the parents' wish to leave something of value to their children.

WAR OR PEACE? (24.413–548)

Although Laertes is joyful that the suitors are dead, his immediate worry is that the families of the suitors will attack. Word of the suitors' death now reaches town; the suitors' families mourn and bury their sons and cousins; and there's a meeting in town to decide how to respond. The first speaker is Eupeithes, Antinous' father, who denounces Odysseus' "great crime." First, the King of Ithaca took many men and ships to Troy and lost them all—not the most effective leadership. Second, upon his return, he killed the best of the young men from Ithaca and the surrounding islands. Eupeithes urges that they catch Odysseus before he flees, for they will be disgraced if they don't avenge the suitors' deaths. This sounds like an archaic form of justice—vengeance by the family—yet on the human plane, this is one way of resolving disputes: clan versus clan.

Supported by the singer Phemius, the herald Medon speaks next, insisting that Odysseus acted in accordance with the will of the gods: "I saw with my own eyes an immortal god, who stood close by Odysseus and looked just like Mentor!" (24.445–446). The seer Halitherses, who had cameo appearances in books

2 and 17, supports Medon's claim that Odysseus acted justly. He doesn't invoke the gods, but blames the townspeople who failed to restrain the recklessness of the suitors.

It's an interesting debate. We haven't obsessed about it, but the fact is that Odysseus failed to bring back any of the men he led to Troy. Both divine and human justice are introduced to defend him, but more than half of the crowd follows Eupeithes to battle Odysseus. Homer neatly links the two charges against Odysseus by a significant idea that first appeared in the seventh line of the epic. Although Odysseus strived to save his men's lives and their homecoming, "they perished by their own recklessness. Fools! who ate the cattle of Hyperion's son, Helius" (1.7–9). Similarly, Halitherses claims that the suitors "committed a great crime by their evil recklessness, wasting Odysseus' household and dishonoring the wife of a great man" (24.458–460). Once more we are back to Zeus' big question in book 1: When mortals suffer, is it their own fault or that of the gods? We should distinguish human justice from divine justice: Medon and Halitherses each introduce one type of evidence to exonerate Odysseus. Yet Homer also weighs in, for—with Halitherses' speech—the poet recalls the mistake Odysseus' men made: they were fools to eat the cattle of the sun, when they had been specifically warned against it. In the same way, the suitors should have known better than to abuse the hospitality of Odysseus's house, assuming he would never return. Telemachus and others denounced them, but the suitors didn't listen.

This is the argument in defense of Odysseus. Is it fully convincing? Is Odysseus blameless in the sight of mortals and gods? Homer induces us to take Odysseus' side once more, by immediately moving to a conversation between Zeus and Athena on the divine plane. Such dialogues are common in the *Iliad*, but in the *Odyssey* Homer hasn't had gods chatting to one another since book 13. When Athena asks Zeus what he has in mind, Zeus counters: "This was *your* plan. . . . Do as you wish" (24.479–481). But Zeus then lays out an idea for bringing an authoritative end to the conflict in Ithaca.

> "Since godlike Odysseus avenged the suitors,
> let both sides swear solemn oaths: let Odysseus rule always,
> and let us make the children and relatives of the suitors
> forget the slaughter. Let them be friends with one another
> as before, and let there be prosperity and peace." (24.482–486)

This is the best Zeus can do. Many men lost their lives—that can't be changed. The only way to ensure peace is for the gods to ratify Odysseus' reign and cause everyone to forget those deaths. Within Odysseus' household, husband and wife will live happily ever after; so also in Odysseus' kingdom, there will be peace and a time of prosperity—but only if this feud is nipped in the bud.

Odysseus arms, supported by his son, his herdmen, and six sons of Dolius, a servant of Laertes. The two old men, Laertes and Dolius, are pressed into service as well. When Odysseus challenges Telemachus not to shame his family in battle and Telemachus promises to be brave, Laertes is overjoyed.

> "What a day this is! Dear gods, how I rejoice!
> My son and grandson rival one another in valor!" (24.514–515)

All three generations march forth. Athena inspires Laertes with divine strength and the old man brings Eupeithes down with a spear. Odysseus and Telemachus then fall upon the front ranks of their opponents, but Athena cries out that all should cease fighting. Eupeithes' troops fall to the ground, but Odysseus is ready to leap forward like an eagle, when Zeus sends a smoking thunderbolt. Athena calls on Odysseus to stop fighting and administers oaths of friendship as the epic comes to a close.

In finishing this mighty work, we should reflect on a few key topics. Regarding the gods, we recall that Athena was the one to put everything in motion by calling upon Zeus in book 1 and volunteering to visit Telemachus. At the end it is Athena who once more orchestrates a plausible resolution to the difficult problem of vengeance and murder. For those familiar with Greek tragedy, the use of a divinity to bring about a solution goes by the name of *deus ex machina*—literally, "god from a crane." In several fifth-century tragedies, when it appears there is no solution to life's intractable problems, a god or goddess appears and imposes a resolution. In the Athenian theater, they used a crane (*machina* derives from the Greek word) to raise the actor playing that divinity up over the mortals below to utter appropriate remarks for the play's end. This literary device is only a small part of Homer's legacy to later literature.

In considering divine and mortal justice, we might distinguish between different types of right and wrong, transgression and punishment. The *Odyssey* contains a primitive sort of justice—that of retribution and vengeance—which Poseidon wreaks upon Odysseus for the blinding of his son, Polyphemus, and which Odysseus brings upon the suitors for insulting his honor and his wife. Zeus and Athena may represent a somewhat more developed type of justice in which guest and host honor one another and all bow before the will of the gods. The suitors (and Odysseus' men in their own way) flout the wishes of the gods. Throughout the epic, Odysseus does his best to follow the gods' wishes. In this final scene Odysseus proves to be a heroic warrior, but he is still dutiful to the gods and abides by Athena's decree (see Segal in "Further Reading").

It is instructive to contrast Odysseus in this final scene with our first picture of him on Calypso's island back in book 5. Then Odysseus was helpless and weeping, as he gazed out to sea, yearning for Ithaca. He was pitiful. Since the moment of Hermes' arrival, however, Odysseus has demonstrated many talents and much endurance. He builds and sails a ship, speaks persuasively, competes in the Phaeacian games, sings a spellbinding story, conceals his identity when he must, and plots revenge upon the suitors. Here at the end of the epic, Homer's final portrait is that of a great warrior, yet submissive to the Olympian gods.

But if the question is: who is this man?—Homer also offers another sort of answer. In addition to his many skills and achievements, Odysseus' identity is defined by his relationship with others: with father, son, and wife; with the people of his household and his kingdom; and with the gods and goddesses, especially Athena, who watches over him and has a clear affinity with this hero. Most striking is their shared propensity for deception and disguise. In this final scene, Athena appears in disguise once again: she looks like Mentor, one of Odysseus' Ithacan friends. It's hard not to appreciate the way in which Homer has raised a very profound issue. Not only who are you, but who is that other person? As the song comes to an end, the members of Homer's audience must have looked around and wondered: Are there any gods in disguise here? Are there any heroes, looking like beggars? When we first see someone, how confident can we be that we know who that person is? The answer is never easy—and it certainly won't be simple. There are many sides to Odysseus and it has taken Homer a long, long poem to show us the many facets of this one man.

APPENDIX 1

WHO'S WHO? CHARACTER INDEX WITH PRONUNCIATION

This character index includes the major characters and indicates their first significant appearance in the *Odyssey*.

I also offer a pronunciation guide. Keep the following in mind. First, Greek names are mostly phonetic, so there are few silent letters (Arete is three syllables, not two). Second, there are several ways of transliterating (spelling letter by letter) Greek names into our own alphabet. Some translations will spell Nausicaa as Nausikaa, and her father as Alkinoos rather than Alcinous. Ajax was Aias in Greek and Achilles was Akhilleus. I'll include what are traditionally the most frequent English spellings and pronunciations.

Don't be intimidated by all the names that begin with "A." Check out the charts for Recognition Scenes in books 13–24 (p. 8), Odysseus' Flashback Adventures in books 9–12 (pp. 9–10), and Odysseus' and Agamemnon's families (p. 40).

ACHAEANS (uh-kee′-uns): one of Homer's three names for the Greeks; he also calls them Argives and Danaans.

ACHILLES (uh-kill′-ees): great Greek warrior at Troy; speaks with Odysseus in the Land of the Dead (11.467).

AEGISTHUS (uh-jis′-thus): lover of Agamemnon's wife, Clytemnestra; kills Agamemnon (never appears; first mentioned at 1.35).

AEOLUS (ee′-oh-lus): king who controls the winds (10.1).

AGAMEMNON (ag-uh-mem′-non): King of Mycenae, leader of the Greek expedition to Troy, killed by his wife's lover, Aegisthus, upon his return (11.387).

AJAX (also spelled Aias; ay'-jacks): Greek warrior who committed suicide; encounters Odysseus in the Land of the Dead (11.543).

ALCINOUS (al-sin'-oh-us): King of the Phaeacians, sends Odysseus home to Ithaca (6.50).

AMPHINOMUS (am-fin'-oh-mus): a pretty good suitor (16.351).

ANTICLEIA (an-ti-clay'-uh): Odysseus' mother, meets him in the Land of the Dead (11.84).

ANTINOUS: (an-tin'-oh-us): one of the two leaders of the suitors, rougher and less subtle than Eurymachus (1.383).

APHRODITE (a-froh-die'-tee): goddess of love and beauty, wife of Hephaestus (8.267).

APOLLO (uh-poll'-oh): god of archery, music, and medicine; brother of Artemis (8.336).

ARES (air'-ees): god of war, sleeps with Hephaestus' wife, Aphrodite (8.267).

ARETE (uh-ree'-tee): Queen of the Phaeacians, wife of Alcinous, beseeched by Odysseus for help (7.141).

ARGIVES (ar'-gives): one of Homer's three names for the Greeks; he also calls them Achaeans and Danaans.

ARTEMIS (ar'-tuh-miss): goddess of archery and the hunt; a virgin goddess; sister of Apollo and bringer of swift death (see the simile at 6.102).

ATHENA (uh-theen'-uh): goddess who helps Telemachus, Odysseus, and Penelope (1.44).

ATREUS (ay'-tree-yus): father of Agamemnon and Menelaus, who are called the "Atreidae" (uh-try'-die), or "sons of Atreus" (1.35).

CALYPSO (cuh-lip'-so): goddess who keeps Odysseus on her island for seven years (5.73).

CHARYBDIS (cuh-rib'-diss): whirlpool near Scylla (12.235).

CICONES (si-kohn'-ees): Thracian people living near Troy, attacked by Odysseus' crew after the sack of Troy (9.39).

CIRCE (sir'-see): goddess who changes Odysseus' men into pigs; becomes Odysseus' lover (10.135).

CLYTEMNESTRA (clie-tem-nes'-tra): Agamemnon's unfaithful wife, seduced by Aegisthus (never appears; referred to at 1.39; first named at 3.266).

DANAANS (da'-nah-uns): one of Homer's three names for the Greeks; he also calls them Achaeans and Argives.

DEMODOCUS (de-moh'-doh-cus): blind singer at the court of the Phaeacians (8.62).

EIDOTHEA (ay-duh-thay'-uh): daughter of sea god Proteus who helps Menelaus (4.365).

ELPENOR (el'-pe-nor): one of Odysseus' crew, falls off Circe's roof, meets Odysseus in the Land of the Dead (11.51; appears at 10.552).

EUMAEUS (you-may'-us): swineherd (pig farmer) faithful to Odysseus (14.33).

EUPEITHES (you-pay'-thees): Antinous' father, tries to avenge his son's death (24.422).

EURYCLEIA (yuh-ri-clay'-uh): servant faithful to Odysseus and his family (1.428).

EURYLOCHUS (yuh-ril'-oh-cus): one of Odysseus' crew who challenges his orders (10.205).

EURYMACHUS (yuh-rim'-ah-cus): one of two leaders of the suitors; more subtle than Antinous (1.399).

EURYNOME (yuh-rin'-noh-mee): servant faithful to Penelope (17.495).

HALITHERSES (hal-i-ther'-sees): Ithacan seer (2.157).

HELEN (hell'-en): wife of Menelaus, runs off to Troy with Paris (4.121).

HELIUS (hee'-lee-us): god of the Sun; Odysseus' men eat his cattle (12.374; see also 8.270).

HEPHAESTUS (heh-fie'-stus): god of metalworking and crafts, husband of Aphrodite (8.270).

HERACLES (her'-uh-clees): son of Zeus; his wraith appears in the Land of the Dead; called Hercules (her'-cue-lees) by the Romans and us (11.601).

HERMES (her'-mees): messenger god, helps Odysseus, leads suitors to Land of the Dead (5.43).

INO (eye'-noh): mortal who became a sea nymph called Leucothea (5.333).

LAERTES (lay-er'-tees): Odysseus' father, who lives out in the countryside (24.226).

LAESTYGONIANS (les-tri-gohn'-nee-ans): giants who eat Odysseus' men and destroy their ships (10.82).

LEODES (lee-oh'-dees): prophet and suitor of Penelope (21.144).

LEUCOTHEA (luke-uh-thee'-uh): sea nymph, also called Ino, who helps Odysseus (5.333).

LOTUS-EATERS (loh'-tus): offer lotus to Odysseus' men (9.83).

MENELAUS (men-uh-lay'-us): King of Sparta, husband of Helen, brother of Agamemnon, receives Telemachus as a guest (4.24).

MENTES (men'-tees): one of Athena's as disguises as a mortal (1.105).

MENTOR (men'-tor): friend of Odysseus and Telemachus (2.224).

NAUSICAA (now'-si-cah): daughter of Phaeacian king and queen (Alcinous and Arete); helps Odysseus after his shipwreck (6.15).

NESTOR (nes'-tor): King of Pylos, host to Telemachus (3.32).

ODYSSEUS (oh-dis'-see-us): King of Ithaca, husband of Penelope, father of Telemachus, son of Laertes; called "Ulysses" by the Romans and many later writers (5.151).

ORESTES (oh-res'-tees): Agamemnon and Clytemnestra's son; avenges his father's murder (never appears; first mentioned at 1.30).

PENELOPE (pe-nel'-oh-pee): Odysseus' wife, Telemachus' mother, Queen of Ithaca (1.328).

PHEMIUS (fee'-mee-us): singer in the household of Odysseus in Ithaca (1.154).

PHILOETIUS (fi-lee'-shus): neatherd (cow herder) faithful to Odysseus (20.185).

PISISTRATUS (pie-sis'-tra-tus): one of Nestor's sons, accompanies Telemachus from Pylos to Sparta (3.36).

POLYPHEMUS (po-luh-fee'-mus): Cyclops who eats six of Odysseus' men (9.233).

POSEIDON (puh-sie'-dun): god of the sea, father of Polyphemus, angry at Odysseus (5.282).

PROTEUS (pro'-tee-us): sea god who reveals much to Menelaus (4.450).

SCYLLA (sill'-uh): dog-like monster with six heads (12.235).

SIRENS (sie'-rens): singing goddesses who lure sailors toward their shores (12.181).

SISYPHUS (sis'-uh-fuss): criminal punished in the Land of the Dead, rolls stone up-hill (11.593).

TANTALUS (tan'-tuh-luss): criminal punished in the Land of the Dead, eternally thirsty and hungry (11.582).

TEIRESIAS (tie-ree'-see-us): seer Odysseus meets in the Land of the Dead (11.90).

TELEMACHUS (teh-lem'-ah-cus): Odysseus' and Penelope's son; travels to Pylos and Sparta (1.113).

TITYOS (ti'-tee-yuss): criminal punished in the Land of the Dead; two birds eat his in-testines (11.576).

ZEUS (zuse'): sky god who rules over Olympian gods, father of Athena, brother of Po-seidon (1.28).

APPENDIX 2

ODYSSEUS AND THE *ODYSSEY* AFTER HOMER: THE EUROPEAN AND AMERICAN TRADITION

> I said, "Omeros*,"
>
> and *O* was the conch-shell's invocation, *mer* was
> both mother and sea in our Antillean patois,
> *os*, a grey bone, and the white surf as it crashes
>
> and spreads its sibilant collar on a lace shore.
> —Derek Walcott, *Omeros* 2.3 (*Modern Greek pronunciation of "Homer")

Certainly the most quotations in European and American literature come from the Bible and Shakespeare (and recently Bob Dylan), yet the figure of Odysseus and the themes of the *Odyssey* may be even more pervasive. Books have been written on the influence of Homer's *Odyssey* over the past 2,700 years and I have no intention of beginning another book at this stage. This brief section seeks merely to suggest some of the many later appearances of Odysseus and adaptations that owe much to the *Odyssey* as fashioned by Homer.

It will be valuable to distinguish the following: the figure of Odysseus himself in literature and other arts; the term "Odyssey"; and later situations, characters, and themes that to a greater or lesser degree derive from Homer's *Odyssey*.

First, let's consider the figure of Odysseus (called "Ulysses" by the Romans and many later writers). The most frequented stops along the European literary tradition include his appearance in Greek tragedy, Roman poetry, a great cameo in Dante's *Inferno*, Shakespeare's *Troilus and Cressida*, Tennyson's "Ulysses," Joyce's *Ulysses*, Kazantzakis' *Odyssey: A Modern Sequel*, and, most recently,

Derek Walcott's stage version of the *Odyssey* (1992). A wonderful book by Stanford, *The Ulysses Theme*, traces the various roles Odysseus plays until the 1950s—almost all of which find their seeds in Homer's epics. Odysseus becomes a stage villain in Greek tragedy: an amoral coward in Sophocles' *Philoctetes* and an evil demagogue in Euripides' *Iphigenia in Aulis*. Later he plays politician and rhetorician, wanderer, and—in every sense—hero.

I find Dante's portrayal of Odysseus especially intriguing. Like Odysseus and Aeneas before him, Dante himself journeys through the underworld. In Dante's vision of the afterlife (supplemented by the seven mountains of Purgatory and ten circles of Paradise), Hell has nine circles, each appropriate to a particular sin. Ulysses (as Dante calls him) and his comrade from the *Iliad* Diomedes are kept together within a flame, condemned to the eighth circle of Hell for being deceitful counselors. The soul of Ulysses explains to Dante that after he left Circe's island, he didn't return to Ithaca, but searched further. Yet when Ulysses describes his motivations, it sounds in many ways like Dante's own goals.

> "Neither my fondness for my son nor pity
> for my old father nor the love I owed
> Penelope, which would have gladdened her,
>   was able to defeat in me the longing
> I had to gain experience of the world
> and of the vices and the worth of men." (Dante. *Inferno*. 26.94–99. Mandelbaum's translation)

As he encounters those in Heaven and Hell, Dante, too, seeks to "gain experience . . . of the vices and the worth of men." Ulysses then recounts how he inspired his men to follow him beyond the Pillars of Hercules (the Straits of Gibraltar):

> "'Brothers,' I said, 'o you, who having crossed
> a hundred thousand dangers, reach the west,
> to this brief waking-time that still is left
>   unto your sense, you must not deny
> experience of that which lies beyond
> the sun, and of the world that is unpeopled.
>   Consider well the seed that gave you birth:
> you were not made to live your lives as brutes,
> but to be followers of worth and knowledge.'" (26.112–120)

Ulysses has become a seeker who would venture beyond the allowed limits on God's world—again not wholly unlike Dante the pilgrim, who travels to Heaven and Hell.

In Tennyson's "Ulysses," the nineteenth-century incarnation of Ulysses comments on his role in great affairs and his consequent fame:

> I am become a name.
> For always roaming with a hungry heart

Much have I seen and known; cities of men
And manners, climates, councils, governments,
Myself not least, but honour'd of them all;
And drunk delight of battle with my peers,
Far on the ringing plains of windy Troy.
I am a part of all that I have met.

After returning to Ithaca, Tennyson's Ulysses bequeaths his kingdom to Telemachus and goes wandering again. Tennyson highlights Ulysses' never-ending quest and his relentless endurance in an address to his crew.

Tho' much is taken, much abides; and tho'
We are not now that strength which in old days
Moved earth and heaven; that which we are, we are;
One equal temper of heroic hearts,
Made weak by time and fate, but strong in will
To strive, to seek, to find, and not to yield.

In Joyce's *Ulysses*, Odysseus is transformed into Leopold Bloom (with an *unfaithful* wife, Molly) who wanders around Dublin on June 16, 1904. He meets twentieth-century versions of the Sirens, Polyphemus, Circe, et al. Derek Walcott's Odysseus is a wanderer of the sea—Mediterranean or Caribbean, it matters little. While Proteus is one of the minor figures from Homer's *Odyssey*, clearly Odysseus' string of roles demonstrates his own protean character.

Outside literature, Odysseus is no less pervasive. He often appears as the subject of painting, sculpture, music, and film. In the early seventeenth century, Monteverdi put Odysseus on the operatic stage in *Il Ritorno d'Ulisse* ("The Return of Ulysses"). Gabriel Fauré's opera *Pénélope* (1913) was recently performed in Edinburgh. For a quick look at the appearance of Odysseus in art, music, and culture more generally, a great place to start—with very good plates—is Rubens and Taplin's *An Odyssey Round Odysseus: The Man and His Story Traced through Time and Place* (a book based on a BBC radio series).

Second, we should not ignore the importance of the term "Odyssey." As a title for Homer's epic, this word simply means the story of Odysseus, just as the "Iliad" is the story of Ilium (the city also known as Troy). Yet the term has come to capture a journey of adventure and daring. Arthur C. Clarke's *2001: A Space Odyssey* (book and movie) demonstrates the power of Odysseus' legacy. To transcend the earthly realm—and perhaps our humanity—is to recall the strivings of Odysseus. Indeed in April 2001, a 1,500-pound spacecraft named "2001 Mars Odyssey" was launched to orbit Mars for two years hunting for signs of water. It received its name not only from A.C. Clarke's book and movie, but also evokes Odysseus as a figure who wandered for many years, met countless misfortunes, yet finally made it safely home—an acknowledgment of the various misfortunes affecting the Mars missions in 1999. Use of the term is ubiquitous. For example, Bill Wyman, bass player for the Rolling Stones, has recently written a book about the blues called *Blues Odyssey: A Journey to Music's Heart and Soul*.

Beyond the figure of Odysseus himself and the name "Odyssey," the fun part comes with all the less direct adaptations of Odysseus and the themes and situations of Homer's *Odyssey*. That's right—wandering heroes, sons seeking fathers (or father-figures), underworld journeys, shipwrecks, recognition scenes, and happy reunions of husbands and wives. Let's talk about all the rip-offs!

It's not going too far to find echoes of Odysseus in wandering heroes who encounter adventure and romance in exotic locales: these figures range from Sinbad the Sailor and the Flying Dutchman to James Bond and Indiana Jones. For all their dangerous encounters and nearly fatal mistakes, they always make it back safely in the end.

The figure of the "orphaned son" is also pervasive. Suspecting that Odysseus is dead, Telemachus has been raised without a father and must make his own way in the world. This has become almost a cliché in books and film, whether we think of Stephen Daedalus in Joyce's *Ulysses*—the Telemachus character to Bloom's Ulysses—or Harry Potter's need for a father-figure such as Dumbledore.

Homer's stories within stories—his brilliant execution of having one character tell another a story—set the standard for millennia to come (in book 4, Homer tells the story of Menelaus telling a story to Telemachus of Proteus telling a story to Menelaus). In Vergil's *Aeneid* books 2 and 3, Aeneas recounts his adventures to the Queen Dido—a deliberate echo of books 9–12 of the *Odyssey*. Later famous examples of such tales-within-tales include Boccaccio's *Decameron* and Chaucer's *Canterbury Tales*.

Many stories were told of visits to the Land of the Dead—so-called "underworld journeys"—in Greek and Near Eastern mythology. Homer's tale was not the first. But Homeric influence makes its mark on the myth of Er at the end of Plato's *Republic*, Aeneas' journey in Vergil's *Aeneid* (book 6), and indirectly Dante's entire *Divine Comedy* and T.S. Eliot's *Wasteland*. Odysseus is not the only hero to make this journey, but Homer's depiction of conversation, tears, transgression, and punishment provides the model later versions have built upon.

I am particularly captivated by the idea of the shipwrecked Odysseus, landing naked and desperate on Calypso's and Nausicaa's shores. I'm convinced that directly or indirectly Shakespeare's *The Tempest*, Defoe's *Robinson Crusoe*, Tom Hanks in *Cast Away*, and even TV shows such as *Gilligan's Island* and *Survivor* owe much to that image of Odysseus emerging from the sea onto an unknown island. (There's a children's book series by Gordon Korman called *Island*. Book One is entitled "Shipwreck.") A playwright from Martinique, Aimé Césaire, in his 1968 update of Shakespeare's *Tempest* (called *A Tempest*) explicitly links *The Tempest* with Odysseus. Upon sighting Miranda, Césaire's shipwrecked Ferdinand remarks: "Seeing the young lady, more beautiful than any wood-nymph, I might have been Ulysses on Nausicaa's isle."

Perhaps the two quintessential situations from Homer's *Odyssey* are homecoming from war and those marvelous recognition scenes. Again I will be highly selective. In every war (real or fictional), there are missing in action. Parents, wives, and children have no idea whether the warrior has been captured, killed, or someday may return. Shay explores this dilemma for Vietnam veterans who

Illustration 8. *The Homecoming.* Stanley Bleifeld. A sailor embraces his wife and child upon returning home. This life-size statue appears in several locales, including the U.S. Navy Memorial Heritage Center in Washington, D.C.; Norfolk, Virginia; and San Diego, California. By permission of the artist.

have returned and attempted to reintegrate themselves into their families and communities in his book *Odysseus in America*—(this follows Shay's brilliant *Achilles in Vietnam*, which juxtaposes Homer's *Iliad* with veterans' experiences on the battlefield in Vietnam). A statue entitled *Homecoming* was erected in Norfolk, Virginia, (in 2000) to honor the sailors who died in the USS *Cole* in Yemen.

Shay's work and the Norfolk statue commemorate real life, but the homecoming hero is also a frequent figure in literature and movies. Frazier's *Cold Mountain: A Novel* (1997) recounts the desperate experiences of a confederate soldier who decides to walk home to his beloved and home in the Blue Ridge Mountains after the battle of Petersburg during the American Civil War. The Coen brothers' movie, *O Brother, Where Art Thou?* (2000) takes a lighter approach. In this movie, set in the American South during the Depression, we find Ulysses Everett McGill (played by George Clooney) escaping from jail and seeking to be reunited with his wife, Penny. The theme song, "Man of Constant Sorrow," brilliantly captures the adversities faced by Odysseus. (Of the various movie versions modeled directly on Homer's *Odyssey*, *Ulysses* (1955) starring Kirk Douglas is probably the best.)

The idea of homecoming after many years away is linked to the motif of recognition—and a tremendous problem: How does the wife know it's really him after so many years? A French movie based on a real incident from the sixteenth century, *The Return of Martin Guerre* (1982), exploits this Homeric crux in fine fashion, as a wife must test the true identity of her supposed husband (this was adapted to the American Civil War in *Sommersby* (1993), starring Richard Gere and Jodie Foster). The whole question of recognition scenes has been explored and parodied from the time of classical Greek tragedy and comedy (Oedipus seeks his own identity). I must mention the encounter between the Bruce Willis adult character and his "inner child" (an eight-year-old) in the movie *The Kid* (2000). Given the unusual circumstance, only a convincing sign could persuade the adult that he's actually looking at himself as a child. How can you prove it? While there's no scar on the knee from a boar hunt, the birthmark on the shoulder is no less persuasive (certainly the most hilarious version of the husband in disguise returning to his wife is found in the 1970s British comedy series *The Fall and Rise of Reginald Perrin*).

A friend once told me that the first time she read the *Odyssey*, she felt as though she already knew the story. Many have a similar experience, in part because, even without reading Homer, it's impossible to live in our world and not encounter later derivations of this rich, complex, and accessible tale.

APPENDIX 3

ACTIVITIES, CLASSROOM PROJECTS, AND MORE

> A plot-structure does not possess unity by virtue of centering on an individual.
> . . . As in other respects, Homer is exceptional by the fineness of his insight into
> this point. . . . Although composing an *Odyssey*, he did not include everything that
> happened to the hero. . . . Instead he constructed the *Odyssey* around a single ac-
> tion of the kind I mean, and likewise with the *Iliad*.
>
> —Aristotle, *The Poetics*

The brilliance of the *Odyssey* offers countless opportunities for teachers to engage students. These activities include storytelling, written work, group work,
reading aloud, acting out scenes, and travel. The possibilities are endless and I
will suggest just a few of the many paths to follow.

STORYTELLING

I might begin by saying that young children love the story of Odysseus (and
many other Greek myths). Retelling the stories of Polyphemus eating Odysseus'
men (and the "no-man" trick) and Circe changing the crew into pigs delights
first-, second-, and third-grade students. A follow-up would be to ask these children to illustrate one of the stories.

WRITTEN ASSIGNMENTS

For high school and college students, there are virtually no limits. For written assignments (prepared outside of class) a good place to begin is to demonstrate the difference between summary and analysis.

- After reading the first four books, the teacher might ask students to write a summary of WHAT HAPPENS in those books on a single sheet of paper.
- For the next class, ask the students to ANALYZE a simile or speech (or character or scene). That is, as opposed to simple recapitulation in the first assignment, analysis involves examining how a simile or speech unfolds, why the poet introduces a simile or speech at that point in the narrative, and how the simile or speech connects to the surrounding narrative. Great examples of similes from the first half of the *Odyssey* include Nausicaa compared to Artemis (6.102–109), the weeping Odysseus compared to a woman who's lost her husband in battle (8.523–531), and the "technological" similes describing the blinding of the Cyclops (9.382–396).
- Analysis can also be done in class by having students work in groups: first they discuss their simile or speech and then present their ideas to the class as a whole.

CLASS JUDICIARY

In my analysis of book 1, I stressed the importance of Zeus' pronouncement that mortals suffer due to their own mistakes—it's not the gods' fault, Zeus claims (1.32–34). Yet the story of the *Odyssey* is not so simple: the question of human suffering and divine involvement is explored in a complex set of situations.

- On the question of gods and justice, teachers may ask students to list five events and describe the cause of each one. For example, when Odysseus' men eat the cattle of the Sun, whose fault is that—the men's or the gods'? Are there extenuating circumstances? Why does Odysseus lose six men to Polyphemus? Is he wholly to blame? Does he deserve credit for rescuing the rest of his men?
- It's possible to set up a sort of tribunal or class judiciary with prosecutors, defenders, and judges. The case could be the death of the suitors. Was their slaughter justified? What could be said on their behalf? In what ways, was Odysseus justified in his deception and attack?

ARTISTIC RESPONSES

Certainly beyond these more conventional activities, the artistic options are many. Students might have an option of:

- illustrating scenes from the *Odyssey* (a comparable task for the *Iliad* is to ask students to draw the shield of Achilles based on 18.478–609),
- acting out episodes, or
- setting part of the epic to music.

In terms of creative writing, a challenge many students like is to update certain scenes:

- Write a series of "underworld" interviews set in 2003—whom might Odysseus meet and question? Are there modern figures who are analogous to the Greek warriors or the notorious criminals?

- At a minimum I highly recommend allotting part of at least one class to have students read aloud sections of the epic (or perhaps play part of Ian McKellen's narration on audiocassette). Don't let it drop there though. Ask the students: How does listening to an epic differ from reading one silently? In what ways is the imagination stimulated aurally? Obviously the pace differs—it takes approximately four times as long to hear as to read Homer. What's the effect?

DISCUSSION: HOMER AND HOLLYWOOD

Every few years a movie appears that adapts themes or situations from the *Odyssey*. Recently *O Brother, Where Art Thou?* deliberately echoes Homer's work in many ways, yet the scene is set in the southern United States during the depression, Odysseus (Ulysses) is an escaped convict, the Sirens appear on a river, and so on.

- After reading the *Odyssey* and seeing the movie, teachers might ask for obvious similarities between the two works—in what ways is *O Brother . . .* linked to the *Odyssey*? Once these connections are established, it's time to explore significant differences, especially the ways in which each work reflects its own historical period (archaic Greece, twentieth-century United States—I've found Kurosawa's *The Seven Samurai* works wonderfully juxtaposed with Homer's *Iliad*).

- Students often delight in being asked to cast an *Odyssey* movie. Who would you cast in the role of Odysseus? Circe? Athene? Telemachus? Poseidon? The tradition continues.

DISCUSSION: HOMER AND LITERATURE

In a literature course, once you begin, it's hard to stop finding links between Homer and later writers. For such comparison-and-contrast discussions, it's possible to stick to ancient Greek literature.

- Compare how Aeschylus in his *Oresteia* and Homer in the *Odyssey* treat the story of Agamemnon's homecoming (note how Aeschylus deliberately emphasizes Clytemnestra's justification for murdering her husband by highlighting the sacrifice of Iphigenia, who is never mentioned in the *Odyssey*).

- Odysseus' trip to the "underworld" is the prototype for Er in Plato's *Republic*, Aeneas in Vergil's *Aeneid*, Orpheus in Ovid's *Metamorphoses*, and Dante himself in the *Inferno*. Why does each figure journey to the Land of the Dead? How is the "underworld" described? Is there an organizing principle (are there punishments and rewards)? How does each story reflect its own historical context?

It's also valuable to bring Homer up to date. Derek Walcott, who won the Nobel Prize in Literature in 1992, wrote a stage version of the *Odyssey*.

- After studying Homer, why not read a few scenes aloud from Walcott's script (the Cyclops scene is wonderful) and then discuss what's changed. In such discussions, students confront the issue of Homer's influence on the course of the Western tradition.

TRAVEL AT HOME AND ABROAD

- It's wonderful to be able to travel to Greece, Turkey, and Italy in order to visit the sites of Ithaca, Troy, Mycenae, Sparta, and Pylos. This, however, is often overly ambitious, expensive, and impractical.
- It is fruitful to visit local museums that may house ancient Greek vases (with painted mythological scenes) and sculpture and painting from the time of the Renaissance and later that illustrate Odysseus' adventures and the various figures from Greek mythology, especially the gods and goddesses.
- If there is interest in the historical aspects of the Trojan War, one possibility would be to visit a local archaeological site to see what excavating the past consists of.
- Even sitting at a computer terminal can lead students in so many directions. A great place to begin exploring ancient Greece is the Perseus Web site at *www.perseus.tufts.edu* (see also "Homer On-Line").

APPENDIX 4

FURTHER READING

The following list is certainly not meant to be comprehensive; it merely offers some ideas to begin with. Almost all of these works have been mentioned with reference to a comparison, idea, or later tradition.

The Aeneid of Virgil. Tr. Allen Mandelbaum. New York: Bantam Books, 1971.

Apollonius Rhodios. *The Argonautica: The Story of Jason and the Quest for the Golden Fleece*. Tr. Peter Green. Berkeley: University of California Press, 1997.

Arnold, Matthew. "On Translating Homer." In *Essays: Literary and Critical*. London: J.M. Dent & Sons, Ltd., 1911.

Beissinger, Margaret, Jane Tylus, and Susanne Wofford, eds. *Epic Traditions in the Contemporary World: The Poetics of Community*. Berkeley: University of California Press, 1999.

Boccaccio. *The Decameron*. Tr. G.H. McWilliam. New York: Penguin, 1986.

Budgen, Frank. *James Joyce and the Making of Ulysses*. New York: Harrison Smith & Robert Haas, 1934.

Calvino, Italo. *Why Read the Classics?* Tr. Martin McLaughlin. New York: Pantheon Books, 1999.

Césaire, Aimé. *A Tempest*. Tr. Richard Miller. New York: Ubu Repertory Theatre Productions, 1992.

Chaucer, Geoffrey. *Canterbury Tales*. London: Edward Arnold, 1980.

Clarke, Arthur C. *2001: A Space Odyssey*. New York: New American Library, 1993.

Clarke, Howard W. *Homer's Readers: A Historical Introduction to the Iliad and the Odyssey*. Newark, NJ: University of Delaware Press, 1981.

Cohen, Beth. *The Distaff Side: Representing the Female in Homer's Odyssey*. Oxford: Oxford University Press, 1995.

A Commentary on Homer's Odyssey. Vol. I: Books I–VIII, A. Heubeck, S. West, J.B. Hainsworth. Vol. II: Books IX–XVI, A. Heubeck, A. Hoekstra. Vol. III: Books XVII–XXIV, J. Russo, M. Fernàndez-Galiano, A. Heubeck. Oxford: Oxford University Press, 1988–1992.

Cromer, Alan. *Uncommon Sense: The Heretical Nature of Science*. Oxford: Oxford University Press, 1993.

Dante. *The Inferno*. Tr. Allen Mandelbaum. New York: Bantam, 1980.

Defoe, Daniel. *Robinson Crusoe*. Cutchogue, NY: Buchaneer Books, 1986.

Dodds, E.R. *The Greeks and the Irrational*. Boston: Beacon Press, 1957.

Euripides. *The Trojan Women*. Tr. Shirley A. Barlow. Warminster, England: Aris & Phillips, Ltd., 1986.

Felson-Rubin, Nancy. *Regarding Penelope: From Character to Poetics*. Princeton: Princeton University Press, 1994.

Foley, Helen. "'Reverse Similes' and Sex Roles in the Odyssey." *Arethusa* 11 (1978): 7–26.

Foley, John Miles. *Immanent Art. From Structure to Meaning in Traditional Oral Epic*. Bloomington: Indiana University Press, 1991.

Frazier, Charles. *Cold Mountain: A Novel*. New York: Vintage Books, 1997.

Havelock, Eric A. *The Literate Revolution in Greece and Its Cultural Consequences*. Princeton: Princeton University Press, 1982.

———. *Preface to Plato*. Cambridge, MA: Harvard University Press, 1963.

Hesiod. *Theogony. Works and Days. Shield*. Tr. Apostolos N. Athanassakis. Baltimore: Johns Hopkins University Press, 1986.

Homer. *The Iliad*. Tr. Robert Fagles. New York: Penguin, 1990.

———. *The Iliad*. Tr. Robert Fagles. Abridged. Audiocassette, narrated by Derek Jacobi. Woodbury, MN: HighBridge Company, 1992.

———. *The Odyssey*. Tr. Robert Fagles. New York: Penguin, 1996.

———. *The Odyssey*. Tr. Robert Fagles. Audiocassette, narrated by Ian McKellen. New York: Penguin Audiobooks, 1996.

Hooper, Richard W. *Representative Chapters in Ancient History: An Introduction to the West's Classical Experience*. 2 vols. Lanham, MD: University Press of America, 2000.

Janko, Richard. "The Homeric Poems as Oral Dictated Texts." *Classical Quarterly* 48 (1998): 1–13.

Joyce, James. *Ulysses*. New York: Vintage, 1961.

Kazantzakis, Nikos. *The Odyssey: A Modern Sequel*. Tr. Kimon Friar. New York: Simon & Schuster, 1958.

Korman, Gordon. *Island. Book One: Shipwreck*. New York: Scholastic Books, Inc., 2001.

Lord, Albert Bates. *The Singer of Tales*. 2nd ed. Ed. Stephen Mitchell and Gregory Nagy. With audio- and videocassette. Cambridge, MA: Harvard University Press, 2000.

Malkin, Irad. *The Returns of Odysseus: Colonization and Ethnicity*. Berkeley: University of California Press, 1998.

Merrill, Rodney. *The Odyssey of Homer*. Ann Arbor: University of Michigan Press, 2002.

Morford, Mark P.O., and Robert J. Lenardon. *Classical Mythology*. 3rd ed. New York: Longman, 1985.

Morrison, James V. "Shipwreck Encounters: Odyssean Wanderings, *The Tempest*, and The Post-Colonial World." *Classical and Modern Literature* 20 (2000): 59–90.

Nagy, Gregory. *Poetry as Performance: Homer and Beyond*. Cambridge, UK: Cambridge University Press, 1996.

Newton, Rick M. "The Rebirth of Odysseus." *Greek, Roman, and Byzantine Studies* 25 (1984): 5–20.

The Odyssey of Homer. Ed. and comm. by William Bedell Stanford. London: St. Martin's Press, 1961.

Ong, Walter J. *Orality and Literacy: The Technologizing of the Word*. London: Methuen, 1982.

The Oresteia by Aeschylus. Tr. David Grene and Wendy Doniger O'Flaherty. Chicago: University of Chicago Press, 1989.

Ovid. *Metamorphoses*. Tr. Allen Mandelbaum. New York: Harcourt Brace & Company, 1993.

Parry, Milman. *The Making of Homeric Verse: The Collected Papers of Milman Parry*. Ed. Adam Parry. New York: Oxford University Press, 1987.

Plato. *Republic*. Tr. G.M.A. Grube; rev. C.D.C. Reeve. Indianapolis: Hackett Publishing Company, Inc., 1992.

The Poetics of Aristotle. Tr. Stephen Halliwell. Chapel Hill: University of North Carolina Press, 1987.

Pratt, Louise. "*Odyssey* 19.535–50: On the Interpretation of Dreams and Signs in Homer." *Classical Philology* 89 (1994): 148–153.

Raaflaub, Kurt A. "Homer, The Trojan War, and History." *Classical World* 91 (1998): 386–403.

Rose, Gilbert P. "Odysseus' Barking Heart." *Transactions of the American Philological Association* 109 (1979): 215–230.

Rubens, Beaty, and Oliver Taplin. *An Odyssey Round Odysseus: The Man and His Story Traced through Time and Place*. London: BBC Books, 1989.

Schein, Seth L. ed. *Reading the Odyssey: Selected Interpretive Essays*. Princeton: Princeton University Press, 1996.

Scodel, Ruth. "Homeric Signs and Flashbulb Memory." In *Epea and Grammata: Oral and Written Communication in Ancient Greece*. ed. Ian Worthington and John Miles Foley. Leiden: Brill, 2002. 99–117.

Segal, Charles. "Divine Justice: Poseidon, Cyclops, and Helios." In *Singers, Heroes, and Gods in the Odyssey*. Ithaca: Cornell University Press, 1994.

Shakespeare, William. *The History of Troilus and Cressida*. New York: Penguin, 2000.

———. *The Tempest*. New York: Bantam, 1988.

Shay, Jonathan. *Achilles in Vietnam: Combat Trauma and the Undoing of Character*. New York: Atheneum, 1994.

———. *Odysseus in America: Combat Trauma and the Trials of Homecoming*. New York: Scribner, 2002.

Snodgrass, Anthony. *Homer and the Artists: Text and Picture in Early Greek Art*. Cambridge, UK: Cambridge University Press, 1998.

Sophocles. *Ajax*. Tr. Richard Pevear. New York: Oxford University Press, 1999.

———. *Electra, Antigone, Philoctetes*. Tr. Kenneth McLeish. Cambridge, UK: Cambridge University Press, 1979.

Stanford, William Bedell. *The Ulysses Theme: A Study in the Adaptability of a Traditional Hero*. Dallas: Spring Productions, 1992.

Taplin, Oliver. "Reading Differences: The *Odyssey* and Juxtaposition." *Ramus* 17 (1988): 1–31.

Tennyson, Alfred. "Ulysses." In *The Poems of Tennyson*. Vol. I. Ed. Christopher Ricks. Berkeley: University of California Press, 1987.

Thomas, Carol G. "The Homeric Epics: Strata or Spectrum?" *Colby Quarterly* 29 (1993): 273–282.

Vermeule, Emily. *Aspects of Death in Early Greek Art and Poetry*. Berkeley: University of California Press, 1979.

Walcott, Derek. *The Odyssey: A Stage Version*. New York: Farrar, Straus & Giroux, 1993.

———. *Omeros*. New York: Farrar, Straus & Giroux, 1990.

Williams, Bernard. *Shame and Necessity*. Berkeley: University of California Press, 1993.

Winkler, John J. "Penelope's Cunning and Homer's." In *The Constraints of Desire: The Anthropology of Sex and Gender in Ancient Greece*. New York: Routledge, 1990, 29–161 (notes 232–233).

Wyman, Bill, with Richard Havers. *Bill Wyman's Blues Odyssey: A Journey to Music's Heart and Soul*. New York: DK Publishing, Inc., 2001.

APPENDIX 5

THE *ODYSSEY* AND ODYSSEAN THEMES AT THE MOVIES

As mentioned in Appendix 2, "Odysseus and the *Odyssey* after Homer: The European and American Tradition," movies are a part of the tradition that adapts themes or situations from the *Odyssey*. And as suggested in Appendix 3, "Activites, Classroom Projects, and More," classes that study Homer's *Odyssey* may benefit from comparing and contrasting the original with various Hollywood versions and adaptations. The following list is extremely selective and merely offers a place to start.

The Kid (2000). Directed by Jon Turteltaub. Written by Audrey Wells. Starring Bruce Willis and Spencer Breslin. The adult character (Bruce Willis) meets his "inner child" (an eight-year-old played by Spencer Breslin). But how can the adult be convinced that he is actually looking at himself as a child? You'd better have a pretty convincing token of recognition. There's no scar on the knee from a boar hunt, but it's a nice recognition scene.

O Brother, Where Art Thou? (2000). Directed by Joel Coen. Written by Ethan Coen and Joel Coen. Starring George Clooney as Ulysses Everett McGill, with John Turturro, Tim Blake Nelson, John Goodman, Holly Hunter, and others. Deliberately echoes Homer's work in many ways, yet the action is set in the American South during the Depression, Odysseus (Ulysses) is an escaped convict, and so on. Tremendous soundtrack with the "Odyssean" song, "A Man of Constant Sorrow."

The Return of Martin Guerre (1982). Directed by Daniel Vigne. Written by Jean-Claude Carriere and Daniel Vigne. Starring Gérard Depardieu and Nathalie Baye. Based on actual events in sixteenth-century France. Explores the ideas of homecoming and recognition: how does the wife know it's really her husband after many years' absence? Includes a climactic trial scene that seeks to unearth the truth. In French with subtitles.

Sommersby (1993). Directed by Jon Amiel. Written by Sarah Kernochan. Starring Richard Gere and Jodie Foster. An American remake of *The Return of Martin Guerre* (see above) set at the end of the American Civil War.

Ulysses (1955). Directed by Mario Camerini and Joseph Strick. Seven screenwriters worked to adapt Homer to the screen. Starring Kirk Douglas, Luana Mangano, Anthony Quinn, and Silvana Mangano. Still the best of the movie versions that follow Homer—more or less.

APPENDIX 6

HOMER ON-LINE

The Ancient Greek World at *http://www.museum.upenn.edu/Greek_World/Intro.html*. The University of Pennsylvania's Museum of Archaeology and Anthropology presents information about life in ancient Greece.

Ancient World Mapping Center (at University of North Carolina, Chapel Hill) at *http://www.unc.edu/awmc*.

Classical Myth: The Ancient Sources at *http://web.uvic.ca/grs/bowman/myth*. This Web site contains general information about Greek gods as well as historical timelines (many images).

Diotima at *http://www.stoa.org/diotima*. This Web site is dedicated to information regarding women in the ancient world.

The Homeric Odyssey and the Cultivation of Justice at *eon.law.harvard.edu/homer*. An on-line lecture and discussion series (now concluded) organized and led by Professor Gregory Nagy, Chair of the Department of Classics at Harvard University.

The Internet Classics Archive (including texts of Homer, Hesiod, and tragedy) at *http://classics.mit.edu/index.html*. Many stories from antiquity.

Metis at *http://www.stoa.org/metis*. Gives a sense of what's left of Troy, Sparta, Mycenae as well as other ancient Greek archaeological Web sites.

The Metropolitan Museum of Art: Greek and Roman Art at *http://www. metmuseum.org/collections/department.asp?dep=13*. The Metropolitan Museum or Art houses a fine collection of Greek and Roman art.

The National Archaeological Museum of Athens at *http://www.culture. gr/2/21/214/21405m/e21405m1.html*. Gateway to the National Archaeological Museum of Athens' collections and temporary exhibitions, as well as links to other resources on ancient Greek culture.

The Perseus Project at *http://www.perseus.tufts.edu*. A digital library for, among other subjects, Ancient Greek civilizations. Over 30,000 images are available on this Web site.

INDEX

About The Author

JAMES MORRISON is Associate Professor of Classical Studies and NEH Professor of the Humanities at Centre College in Danville, Kentucky. He is author of *Homeric Misdirection: False Predictions in the Iliad* and numerous articles on classical literature, mythology, and history.